This book examines the role of syntax in theories of sentence comprehension, and argues for a distinct processing component which is devoted to the recovery of syntactic structure and which utilizes the contrasting types of information found within a Government-Binding grammar.

Paul Gorrell contrasts the primary relations (dominance and precedence) and secondary relations (case assignment, theta-role assignment, etc.) in a phrase-structure tree, and shows how this computational distinction of information types is reflected in the internal structure of the parser, which consists of two subcomponents: a structure builder (responsible for creating nodes in a tree and positing primary relations between them), and a structure interpreter (responsible for analyzing the tree in terms of secondary relations). This model can also predict garden-path phenomena in the processing of verb-final clauses.

CAMBRIDGE STUDIES IN LINGUISTICS

General editors: J. BRESNAN, B. COMRIE, W. DRESSLER,
R. HUDDLESTON, R. LASS, D. LIGHTFOOT, J. LYONS,
P. H. MATTHEWS, R. POSNER, S. ROMAINE, N. V. SMITH,
N. VINCENT

Syntax and parsing

In this series

55 REGINA BLASS: *Relevance relations in discourse: a study with special reference to Sissala*
56 ANDREW CHESTERMAN: *On definiteness: a study with special reference to English and Finnish*
57 ALESSANDRA GIORGI and GIUSEPPE LONGOBARDI: *The syntax of noun phrases: configuration, and parameters and empty categories*
58 MONIK CHARETTE: *Conditions on phonological government*
59 M. H. KLAIMAN: *Grammatical voice*
60 SARAH M. B. FAGAN: *The syntax and semantics of middle constructions: a study with special reference to German*
61 ANJUM P. SALEEMI: *Universal Grammar and language learnability*
62 STEPHEN R. ANDERSON: *A-morphous morphology*
63 LESLEY STIRLING: *Switch reference and discourse representation*
64 HENK J. VERKUYL: *A theory of aspectuality: the interaction between temporal and atemporal structure*
65 EVE V. CLARK: *The lexicon in acquisition*
66 ANTHONY R. WARNER: *English auxiliaries: structure and history*
67 P. MATTHEWS: *Grammatical theory in the United States from Bloomfield to Chomsky*
68 LJILJANA PROGOVAC: *Negative and positive polarity: a binding approach*
69 R. M. W. DIXON: *Ergativity*
70 YAN HUANG: *The syntax and pragmatics of anaphora*
71 KNUD LAMBRECHT: *Information structure and sentence form: topic, focus, and the mental representations of discourse references*
72 LUIGI BURZIO: *Principles of English stress*
73 JOHN A. HAWKINS: *A performance theory of order and constituency*
74 ALICE C. HARRIS and LYLE CAMPBELL: *Historical syntac in cross-linguistic perspective*
75 LILIANE HAEGEMAN: *The syntax of negation*
76 PAUL GORRELL: *Syntax and parsing*

Supplementary volumes

MICHEAL O SIADHAIL: *Modern Irish: grammatical structure and dialectal variation*
ANNICK DE HOUWER: *The acquisition of two languages from birth: a case study*
LILIANE HAEGEMAN: *Theory and description in generative syntax: a case study in West Flemish*
A. E. BACKHOUSE: *The lexical field of taste: a semantic study of Japanese taste terms*
NIKOLAUS RITT: *Quantity adjustment: vowel lengthening and shortening in early Middle English*

Earlier issues not listed are also available

SYNTAX AND PARSING

PAUL GORRELL

University of Potsdam

CAMBRIDGE
UNIVERSITY PRESS

Published by the Press Syndicate of the University of Cambridge
The Pitt Building, Trumpington Street, Cambridge, CB2 1RP
40 West 20th Street, New York, NY 10011-4211, USA
10 Stamford Road, Oakleigh, Melbourne 3166, Australia

First published 1995

Printed in Great Britain at the University Press, Cambridge

A catalogue record for this book is available from the British Library

Library of Congress cataloging in publication data

Gorrell, Paul.
Syntax and parsing / Paul Gorrell.
  p. cm. – (Cambridge studies in linguistics; 76)
"This work has been supported by a grant from the National Science
Foundation (BNS-9021254)."
Includes bibliographical references and index.
ISBN 0 521 45282 1 (hardback)
1. Grammar, Comparative and general – Syntax. 2. Grammar, Comparative
and general – Parsing. 3. Government-binding theory (Linguistics) I. Title.
II. Series.
P291.G667   1995
415–dc20   94-20375   CIP

ISBN 0 521 45282 1 hardback

UP

This book is dedicated to the memory of
Anne Mercedes Gorrell 1924–1992

Contents

Acknowledgments   *page* xi

1.   **Introduction**   1

2.   **Properties of the grammar**   9
2.0 Grammatical assumptions: Government-Binding theory   9
2.1 Phrase-structure trees   11
2.2 The generation of trees   17
2.3 Submodules of syntax   20
2.4 Derivational GB   25
2.5 Representational GB   30
2.6 Summary   41

3.   **Analyses of previous work**   43
3.0 Structural ambiguity   43
3.1 Late Closure, Minimal Attachment, and reanalysis   47
3.2 Ranked Parallelism   57
3.3 Determinism and description theory   64
3.4 Minimal commitment theory   71
3.5 Generalized Theta Attachment and reanalysis   76
3.6 Parallel processing and constraints on processing load   84

4.   **Properties of the parser**   94
4.0 Introduction   94
4.1 Node creation and attachment   99
4.2 Experimental studies of structural ambiguity   120
4.3 Lexical information   125
4.4 Empty categories   130
4.5 Head-final clauses   138
4.6 Summary   147

x   *Contents*

5.   **Modularity and Structural Determinism**   *page* **149**

6.   **Conclusion**   163

     References   167

     Index   178

Acknowledgments

One of the good problems in life is to have too many people to thank. Over the course of the last few years I have had the opportunity to present portions of the material covered here to audiences at the University of Massachusetts, MIT, Princeton University, the University of Arizona, the University of Connecticut, University of Geneva, Johns Hopkins University, the Penn Linguistics Circle at the University of Pennsylvania, NELS 21 at the University of Quebec in Montreal, the Sixth CUNY Sentence Processing Conference held at the University of Massachusetts, and the International Symposium on Japanese Syntactic Processing held at Duke University. I am grateful to these audiences for helpful comments and challenging questions.

I would also like to thank Peggy Antonisse, Tor Aschan, Josef Bayer, Bob Berwick, Julie Boland, Matt Crocker, Janet Fodor, Lyn Frazier, Ted Gibson, Atsu Inoue, Carol Mason, Reiko Mazuka, Paola Merlo, Don Mitchell, Keiko Muromatsu, Mineharu Nakayama, Weijia Ni, Janet Nicol, Martin Pickering, Susan Powers, Brad Pritchett, John Trueswell, Juan Uriagereka, Eric Wehrli, and especially Sungki Suh, for discussions along the way.

Over the course of the last year Janet Fodor, Ken Forster, Merrill Garrett, Mark Steedman and David Swinney have been particularly supportive. I very much appreciate their presence in my chosen field. Cecile McKee deserves special thanks for being virtually everywhere.

This work has been supported by a grant from the National Science Foundation (BNS-9021254). I am grateful for this support.

I would also like to thank both Betty Pollin and the Library of Congress for providing wonderful places to write. Nikky Twyman deserves special thanks for all her work on the manuscript.

Lynn Brown and Ian Brown-Gorrell have earned (at least) a year's worth of evenings and weekends. It will be a pleasure to pay my debt. My gratitude to Lynn goes beyond words, but Ian I must thank for staying healthy and for, more often than not, sleeping through the night.

1   *Introduction*

There should be clear linkages between linguistic descriptions and
cognitive/perceptual requirements.

William Marslen-Wilson

Since the mid-1970s specific proposals for the form of syntactic knowledge
have had difficulty finding their way into theories of language comprehension. This is not to say that syntax does not play a role in such
theories, but it is usually limited to a reference to a fairly imprecise phrase
structure. Much of the work that is of interest to syntacticians provokes (at
best) scant interest from those working in experimental psycholinguistics.
To a certain extent this is justified; investigations into syntactic knowledge
and into sentence processing are related, but clearly distinct, research
programs.

It is a central thesis of this book that recent work within Government-
Binding (GB) theory (Chomsky 1981, and subsequent work) raises
questions about the nature of syntactic knowledge that have long
concerned researchers into syntactic processing (parsing). Consider the
term *minimal*. Since the important work of Frazier and Fodor (1978),
which introduced the concept of *Minimal Attachment* to the psycholinguistics literature, the concept of minimal structure building has played
a significant role in studies of properties of the parser.[1] More recently,
work in syntactic theory has become concerned both with insuring minimal
structure generation (e.g. Speas 1990) and with establishing minimal
connections between related elements within a structure (e.g. Rizzi 1990).
As will become clear below, the form of the grammar within much current
work in GB requires principles of minimal structure generation in much
the same way that properties of the parser require a principle of minimal
structure computation.

---

[1] I will use the term *parser* to refer to the mechanism responsible for the computation of
syntactic structure in sentence comprehension. See Chapter 4 for further discussion.

1

But, clearly, it has not always been the case that syntactic theory seemed particularly suited to theories of sentence processing. This is most clearly seen in three influential works that were published in the mid-1970s. The first of these, Marslen-Wilson (1975), demonstrated convincingly that the computation of lexical, structural, semantic, and discourse representations for an input string must be fast and continuous. This demonstration of the incremental nature of structure building and structure interpretation appeared at odds with generative theories of syntactic processing that failed to address the important issue of the time course of use of syntactic knowledge in perception. Within psycholinguistics, and more recently, computational linguistics, incremental structure building is now a necessary component of any model of language comprehension.

The second important work of the mid-1970s was Kimball (1973). This work sought to explain certain parsing phenomena in terms of surface structure strategies. One influential aspect of this work was that it only referred to a single level of representation, surface structure. The proposed parsing principles were empirically adequate across a wide range of phenomena and yet did not refer to deep structure or the transformational mapping between levels. Of course, also influential was the concept of a "parsing strategy" that was essentially nonsyntactic. However, Kimball's strategies did refer to the nodes and branches of a phrase-structure tree.

The concept of a parsing strategy was familiar from the work of Bever (1970) and Fodor *et al.* (1974). This latter work, perhaps more than any other single publication, set the tone for future research in sentence processing. Consider the following three points concerning a model of syntactic processing which summarize the conclusions of Fodor *et al.* concerning models of syntactic processing.

(1a)   There exist no suggestions about how a generative grammar might be concretely employed as a sentence recognizer in a psychologically plausible model.

(1b)   Experimental investigations of the psychological reality of linguistic structural descriptions have, in general, proved quite successful. But experimental investigations of the psychological reality of grammatical rules, derivations, and operations – in particular, investigations of DTC[2] – have generally proved equivocal. This argues against the occurrence of grammatical derivations in the

---

[2] The derivational theory of complexity was the hypothesis that the perceptual complexity of a sentence was, in part, a function of the derivational complexity of the transformational mapping between deep structure and surface structure.

computations involved in sentence recognition and hence against a concrete employment of the grammar by the sentence recognizer.

(1c) On the other hand, there appear to be phenomena in sentence recognition which are not, in any direct way, predictable from the grammar and which presumably must be attributed to the character of the recognition device.

The general conclusion drawn from these specific points was that an adequate theory of sentence comprehension could be fashioned with only minimal reference to work in syntax. An added complication was the fact that the time between 1965 and 1980 was a period of rapid change in syntactic theory (Newmeyer 1980). It was difficult enough to keep up with proposed changes in the grammar without having the additional burden of trying to incorporate these changes into theories of comprehension that were themselves developing quite rapidly. Further, real progress was being made in parsing theory without any apparent need to refer to the particulars of syntactic theory.

The second point of Fodor *et al.* (1974) was particularly troublesome. That is, the derivational mapping between levels of representation (probably the most salient characteristic of transformational grammar in the 1970s) appeared to play no discernible role in sentence processing. The situation was quite paradoxical. On the one hand, the work of Chomsky (1965) and its descendants was a very elegant treatment of a broad range of syntactic phenomena. For most of the 1960s and 1970s there were no serious competitors to transformational generative grammar. It hardly seemed possible to formulate a coherent theory of syntactic knowledge without incorporating the main points of generative grammar. Yet theories of sentence processing simply could find no role for the more interesting aspects of syntactic theory.

Thus the attention of psycholinguists turned to the third point of Fodor *et al.*, namely the characteristics of the perceptual device. Although an *Aspects*-style notion of phrase structure was retained, there appeared to be little need to refer to the more intricate (and more interesting) properties of the grammar. In general the grammar was pushed to the side and the proper formulation of parsing strategies became the central topic of research. For example, the Sausage Machine model of Frazier and Fodor (1978) and Frazier (1978) discussed the properties of the parser in great detail, but discussed only the broad outlines of the form of the competence grammar.

The aim of this book is to give as much attention to the form of the grammar as to the form of the parser. Chapter 2 details a particular version of GB theory, the representational (i.e. monostratal) framework of Koster (1978, 1986). The last several years have seen the development of a number of representational grammatical frameworks, e.g. Gazdar *et al.* (1985) and Ades & Steedman (1982). But it is often not recognized that GB, even in its derivational versions (e.g. Chomsky 1986a, 1992), has incorporated many of the characteristics of representational theories. Consider the following proposal for treating A-chains (e.g. NP-movement) and A'-chains (e.g. Wh-movement).

(2)   [I]n the case of an A-chain the address of an antecedent can in principle be transmitted downward to the trace, whereas in the case of an argument A'-chain the address can be transmitted upward from the trace to the antecedent.

Out of context it would not be surprising to attribute this quote to a work within GPSG or some other representational framework. Actually it is from Manzini (1992), a work within the strongly derivational framework of standard GB. It will become clear in Chapter 2 that, although I will adopt Koster's representational GB and not specifically discuss other frameworks, the issues that arise in fashioning a parsing model that is responsive to the form of a particular grammar are, in fact, quite general.

For example, I will argue that an important distinction in GB is that between primary and secondary structural relations. Primary relations are the primitive relations in a phrase-structure tree, dominance and precedence. Secondary relations are those (e.g. government) that are defined in terms of the primary relations. But any theory of grammar must make such a distinction. Further, I will argue that such a distinction plays a central role in distinguishing the operations of the parser.

It is unfortunate that detailed discussion of a GB-based parsing model does not leave space for an analysis of parsing theory within frameworks such as categorial grammar (e.g. Pickering 1991). One reason this is unfortunate is that it may give the impression that the claim is being made that only GB (or the version assumed here) is compatible with the parsing phenomena discussed below. This claim is not being made and would be premature in any case. We are simply not at the point in theory development where it is possible to conclude that the parser demands the grammar include property X, but not property Y, where X and Y serve to distinguish competing syntactic models.

Despite the fact that I will only be discussing GB in any detail, the parsing model I will propose in Chapter 4 is not a "full" GB grammar in that I have not demonstrated how each aspect of the grammar is incorporated in a parsing model. For example, one aspect of the grammar that will not play a prominent role in the parsing theory to be developed below is the concept of locality. This may seem surprising as the influential work of Berwick and Weinberg (1984) focused on the role of locality in the grammar and the parser. Further, the proper definition of local relations, and the local nature of apparent long-distance relations, are important research topics in syntactic theory. But work in GB is currently calling into question the very basis of theories of locality. I will touch on this in Chapter 2 as this research is important for motivating the representational alternative to derivational GB. But the fact that there is no firm analysis of locality phenomena in GB makes it quite difficult to formulate specific hypotheses concerning the role of grammatically-defined concepts of locality in the parser.

The focus of the parsing model proposed in Chapter 4 is the incorporation of Minimal Attachment (MA) into a principle-based parser. Although a number of other grammatical and processing phenomena are examined in detail, the parser's preference for building the minimal structure justified by the input is the core of the proposed parsing model. I will argue that MA is best characterized as the incremental application of the principle of economy of representation (Chomsky 1991). This principle states that each element in a representation must be licensed, i.e. justified by some principle of grammar. I have renamed MA as the principle of *Simplicity* because I incorporate a number of properties not necessarily associated with MA. The first is that I assume the parser is constructing a phrase-structure tree (see Chapter 2 for discussion) rather than some other form of representation, e.g. a reduced phrase marker (Lasnik and Kupin 1977) or a set of structural relations (Barton and Berwick 1985). MA does not entail a particular form of representation. Also, MA was originally argued to follow from the temporal benefits of minimal (phrase-structure) rule accessing and structure building. In a principle-based grammar this explanation is unavailable and a more parsimonious account in terms of economy of representation is adopted.

A working hypothesis is that the properties of the parsing model proposed in Chapter 4 are universal. This follows the proposal of Inoue (1991) who argues that the parser is an invariant cognitive mechanism with distinct processing phenomena arising from language-particular ways (e.g.

word-order variation) in which relevant information becomes available to the parser. Given that English is the only language that has been studied in any depth from a parsing perspective, it is clear that claims concerning universality can only be taken as initial hypotheses to be tested as more languages are studied. But syntactic theory provides us with a universal vocabulary for discussing syntactic processing, and the discussion in Chapter 4 regarding the processing of Japanese and German verb-final clauses yields some initial support for the cross-linguistic relevance of the proposed parsing model.

In Chapter 5 the important issue of the role of semantic and discourse factors in syntactic processing is discussed. In recent years there have been a number of convincing demonstrations of the rapid availability of non-syntactic factors to affect the parse. An important question is, given the role of these factors in incremental structure building, is there still a need to retain structure-based parsing principles? Although I will adopt a serial version of weak interaction, I will also argue that there is still justification for including a principle such as Simplicity in a processing model.

A general outline of the book is as follows. In Chapter 2 I discuss the important aspects of GB. I begin by describing the basic properties of phrase-structure trees. In particular I discuss the distinction between primary and secondary relations in GB theory. This distinction, as stated, will play a crucial role in the parsing theory to be developed in Chapter 4. The last two sections of Chapter 2 contrast derivational and representational versions of GB. As Fodor *et al.* (1974) and J. D. Fodor (1983) point out, there appears to be little motivation for incorporating derivational properties of grammar in a parsing model. This in itself should not be sufficient motivation for abandoning derivational accounts of syntactic knowledge. But given that there are well-motivated representational counterparts with comparable empirical coverage, the perspective of parsing theory clearly favors the monostratal approach.

In Chapter 3 I discuss a number of parsing models which share important properties with the model I develop in Chapter 4. I depart in important ways from these models but my intellectual debt to these theories is clear. One property shared by all the models I discuss is that they assume a monostratal grammar. This is almost always unstated, i.e. only one level of representation is referred to (s-structure). The other syntactic levels are simply ignored. In part this is justified by trace theory which encodes the d-structure position of elements in the s-structure representation (see Chapter 2 for details). But, despite the fact that many of the parsing models outlined in Chapter 3 adopt a transformational grammar, the complete absence of any effect of the derivational mapping between levels has never been addressed in the psycholinguistic literature.[3] The discussion of the grammar in Chapter 2 and the parser in Chapter 4 makes this unstated monostratal assumption explicit. It remains the responsibility of parsing models which assume a derivational grammar to justify this assumption (see Wu 1993 for one recent proposal from a computational perspective). Carlson and Tanenhaus (1982) note that the de-emphasis on transformations in monostratal theories and GB allows for a grammatically-principled focus on s- (or, surface-) structure phenomena. It should be noted that the characterization of Move alpha in standard GB does not represent a reduction of the derivational mapping between levels. Recent proposals within the minimalist program of Chomsky (1992) should make this clear. The mapping between levels in GB (even pre-minimalist GB) is the product of numerous applications of Move alpha. The description of the transformation is reduced (i.e. simply Move alpha) but the derivation itself is quite similar in complexity to an *Aspects* derivation.

An important issue that affects both the characterization of the grammar and the characterization of the parser is modularity. The present study looks at both aspects of this issue: modularity in terms of syntactic knowledge (i.e. distinct from semantic and pragmatic knowledge) and modularity in terms of a specialized psychological mechanism. But, as Chomsky (1975) has observed, the "thesis of the independence of grammar ... does not imply what is in fact false, that the interpretation of sentences by hearers is independent of questions of fact and belief. What is implied is that the contribution of grammar to sentence interpretation is very different in kind from the contribution of fact or belief."

Of course there is no pre-theoretic division of information types and how we construe the distinction between, for example, syntactic and semantic information will have important implications for theories of language comprehension. Consider a sentence such as (3), given in Chomsky (1955) as an example of the cognitive distinction of form and meaning.

(3)   Colorless green ideas sleep furiously

In the grammar of Chomsky (1955), (3) was syntactically well-formed but semantically anomalous. But within the framework of Chomsky (1965), (3) is syntactically ill-formed. This is because in the *Aspects* framework, lexical

---

[3] But see Bresnan (1978) for a grammatical perspective and Berwick and Weinberg (1984) for a GB-based computational view.

insertion was constrained by selectional restrictions incorporating information, such as animacy, that the earlier framework had treated as nonsyntactic.

However, subsequent work by McCawley (1971) and Jackendoff (1972) argued that the approach of Chomsky (1965) introduced serious problems and redundancies into the theory of grammar. Consider a sentence such as (4).

(4)   John is crazy and thinks that rocks talk

The particular implications we draw for parsing theory from work investigating the processing of sentences such as (4) is dependent, to a large extent, on the representational assumptions we have concerning the syntactic wellformedness of the embedded clause.

Consider also a sentence such as (5), also from Chomsky (1955).

(5)   The detective brought the man who was accused of having stolen the automobile in

Chomsky (1955), among other things, was attempting to motivate a number of transformational operations which could alter basic properties of phrase markers. One of these transformations was particle movement which operated to derive (6a) from (6b).

(6a)   The detective brought the man in
(6b)   The detective brought in the man

But Chomsky (1955) noted that "in general the separability of the preposition is determined by the complexity of the object NP."[4] He further remarked that this need to refer to the internal characteristics of the NP "may indicate a limitation of the whole approach." The problem for Chomsky was that the structural description of a transformation such as particle movement only made reference to the fact that there was a NP in a particular configuration. Therefore the acceptability of the output of the transformation should not be affected by the internal structure of the NP. Of course the awkwardness of (5) is now considered to be due to properties of the parser and not properties of the grammar. But this characterization presupposes numerous assumptions concerning the nature of syntactic knowledge and sentence processing. In the next chapter I detail the grammatical assumptions which underlie the design of the parser discussed in Chapter 4.

---

[4] See Antonisse (1990) and Milsark (1983) for discussion of the distinction between length and structure effects originally noted by Chomsky (1955).

2 *Properties of the grammar*

Dick Feynman told me about his "sum over histories" version of quantum mechanics. "The electron does anything it likes," he said. "It goes in any direction at any speed, forward or backward in time, however it likes, and then you add up the amplitudes and it gives you the wave function." I said to him, "You're crazy." But he wasn't.

Freeman Dyson

2.0   Grammatical assumptions: Government-Binding theory

In order to properly investigate the nature of the relation between syntax and perception, it is necessary to begin with a discussion of the syntactic framework being assumed. I will outline two aspects of syntactic phenomena as they are treated within the GB framework: the generation of structure and the relations which exist between elements in a syntactic representation. The particular type of structure I will consider is a phrase-structure tree.[1] Structural relations involving discontinuous dependencies will first be discussed from the derivational perspective of standard GB (Chomsky 1981). I will then turn to the representational approach of Koster (1986). As noted in Chapter 1, it is this representational form of GB which I will assume in subsequent discussion of the parser's properties (Chapter 4).

As noted above, there are many aspects of syntactic theory in general, and GB in particular, which I will gloss over or ignore. The intent of this chapter is to describe the form of syntactic knowledge in sufficient detail so that we can, in a meaningful way, address the issue of the manner in which syntactic knowledge is put to use in the perceptual process. I will ignore, therefore, some aspects of recent work which have become salient in the recent GB literature (e.g. the nature of adjunction, the internal structure of IP) and I will give a prominent role to aspects of syntax (e.g. concepts such

---

[1] This is not a necessary assumption. See, for example, Lasnik and Kupin (1977) for an alternative view, and McCawley (1982) and Higginbotham (1985) for discussion.

as *dominance* and *precedence*) which receive comparatively little attention in current work in syntax.[2]

Work in generative grammar has two primary goals: on the one hand it seeks a precise characterization of syntactic knowledge prior to experience (Universal Grammar, or UG), while on the other, it also seeks to describe, in a detailed manner, the mature state of an individual who has acquired a particular grammar. GB is often described as a theory of principles and parameters.[3] Principles of grammar are assumed to be invariant, whereas parameters are specifications of permissible variation (see the discussion of [60] below). It is often the case that the manner in which parameters are formulated will preclude a range of logical possibilities, thereby restricting the hypotheses that are entertained in the acquisition process. For example, consider a parameter which states that, for a particular grammar, verbs either precede or follow their objects. If the parameter is formulated with respect to the category *verb*, then the acquisition device will not attempt to test the hypothesis that individual verbs may vary as to the position of their objects. The parameter, then, amounts to the claim that UG precludes (or, marks) grammars in which the lexical information for individual verbs includes a specification for object position.

Imagine a different parameter; one that states that, within a particular language, all verbs either have or do not have syntactic objects. The claim represented by such a parameter can be falsified by motivating the existence of grammars in which individual verbs vary as to the necessity of syntactic objects. Thus it is clear that the formulation of a parameter represents a number of interesting theoretical claims about the nature of UG, the form of particular grammars, and the process of acquisition. The goal of this approach is that, given parameters of this type, the acquisition device will be able to specify the value of such a parameter on the basis of quite simple input (see Gibson and Wexler 1993 for discussion).

Although there is still much work to be done in formulating a precise theory of the nature of parameters, the rationale for such an approach is clear: particular grammars do not vary in random ways and they are readily acquired on the basis of impoverished data. Therefore an optimal theory will seek to characterize UG in such a way as to account for the variation that does (and does not) occur, and in such a way that the

---

[2] An exception to this is Kayne (1993).

[3] Chomsky (1991) refers to "Government-Binding" as a "misleading" term, preferring "principles and parameter" theory. I will use "government-binding" (GB) to refer to work closely tied to the framework of Chomsky (1981).

acquisition of particular syntactic knowledge can be accomplished on the basis of the available linguistic input.

GB is a modular theory. That is, the principles and parameters of the theory are aspects of particular submodules (e.g. case theory, theta theory). Certain relations (e.g. *government*) are referred to in the formulation of operations within a number of modules. The intent of a modular approach to syntactic phenomena is to account for the diversity and complexity of particular grammars, not by recourse to a diverse and complex rule system, but in terms of modules whose internal principles are comparatively simple. In Section 2.3 I discuss the different submodules of the grammar. In Sections 2.4 and 2.5 I focus on the properties of derivational and representational approaches to "movement" phenomena within GB. But first I outline a theory of phrase structure, in particular the wellformedness conditions on phrase-structure trees and the manner in which trees are generated. These are important aspects of the grammar from a processing perspective. I will argue in Chapter 4 that there is a distinct, tree-building, component within the syntactic processor. They are also important from a grammatical perspective as the postulation of structural relations requires a set of primitive relations which are used in defining additional, secondary, relations. By assuming that syntactic representations are trees, we can posit *dominance* and *precedence* as the primary structural relations.

2.1   Phrase-structure trees

A phrase-structure tree is a structural representation for a sentence which encodes the following information (Partee *et al.* 1993):

(1a)   The hierarchical grouping of the parts of the sentence into constituents.

(1b)   The left-to-right order of the constituents.

(1c)   The grammatical type of the constituents.

A tree is composed of *nodes* representing grammatical categories, and *branches* which connect the nodes. Like many other grammatical approaches, GB defines hierarchical relations between nodes in terms of the predicate *dominance*. Dominance is defined as in (2).

(2)   For two nodes x and y, x dominates y iff the connection between x and y is composed exclusively of descending branches.[4]

---

[4] As Paola Merlo (personal communication) points out, the reference to *descending* branches presupposes a particular orientation of the tree. She suggests that dominance can be defined as in (i).

I will indicate "x dominates y" by writing: d (x, y). If there are no intervening nodes, then x *immediately dominates* y. Left-to-right order is defined in terms of *precedence*. I will write "x precedes y" as p (x, y). In addition to the intuitive notion of the precedence relation ("x precedes y if x is to the left of y"), it is common to require that two nodes be in a precedence relation iff they are not in a dominance relation. Partee *et al.* state this requirement as an Exclusivity Condition on well-formed trees. One version of this condition is given in (3).

(3)   In any well-formed tree, either p (x, y) or p (y, x) is true iff neither d (x, y) nor d (y, x) is true.

As Partee *et al.* note, it is usually assumed that every node dominates itself. Thus, if x = y, then d (x, y) is true and p (x, y) is false. The intent of the Exclusivity Condition is to restrict the class of permissible trees. Consider (4), and the trees in (5).

(4)

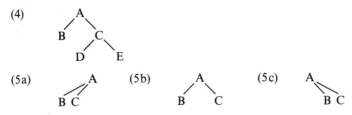

(5a)   (5b)   (5c)

In (4) the node A dominates all other nodes in the tree. Thus A is not in a precedence relation with any other node. In (4) the node B precedes C and all the nodes that C dominates, i.e. D and E. We will see below that other relations between nodes will be defined, in part, by reference to dominance and precedence.

Turning to (5) the Exclusivity Condition entails that trees (5a), (5b), and (5c) are equivalent. That is, because node A dominates nodes B and C, there cannot be a precedence relation between A and B or between A and C. Thus, linguistic theory cannot define, for example, some relation R such that R holds iff a node both precedes and dominates another node.

Partee *et al.* discuss another condition, the Nontangling Condition, which we will assume to be a property of phrase-structure trees. The Nontangling Condition is given in (6).

(i)   Let t be a tree rooted in r, and x and y two nodes in t. Then x dominates y iff x lies on the path that connects y to r.

I do not know of any empirical implications of the choice between (i) and the definition in the text. The conceptual issues involved are not germane to the issues addressed here.

(6)   In any well-formed tree, if p (x, y), then all nodes dominated by x
        precede all nodes dominated by y.

The Nontangling Condition rules out trees in which either (i) a node is
immediately dominated by more than one node, or (ii) where branches
cross.[5] Thus neither (7a) nor (7b) is a well-formed tree.

(7a)   (7b)

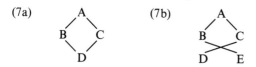

The tree (7a) is ill-formed because D is dominated by both B and C. If p (B,
C) then all nodes dominated by B must precede all nodes dominated by C.
Therefore, for (7a) to be a well-formed tree would require that p (D, D) be
true. But if, as we assumed above, a node dominates itself, i.e. d (D, D),
then the Exclusivity Condition requires that p (D, D) be false. Tree (7b) is
ill-formed because if p (B, C), d (B, E), and d (C, D) are true, then (by the
Nontangling Condition in [6]), p (E, D) must be true. But p (E, D) is true
just in case the branches do not cross.
    It is important to note that the dominance and precedence relations
among nonterminals cannot be determined from properties of the terminal
string (either in isolation or in conjunction with general wellformedness
conditions). Consider a terminal string *abc* and the trees in (8).

(8a)   (8b)

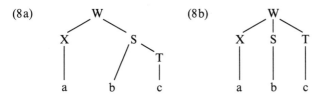

In both (8a) and (8b) the terminal *b* precedes the terminal *c*. But this does
not determine the relations between the nonterminals *S* and *T*. In (8a) a
dominance relation exists whereas in (8b) *S* and *T* are in a precedence
relation. Note also that appeal to the Nontangling Condition can only
determine the specific precedence relation among nonterminals *if it is
known that the nonterminals are in a precedence relation*. In general,
wellformedness conditions can only serve to restrict the possibilities to the

---

[5] See Solan and Roeper (1978) for an experimental investigation of children's use of
constraints such as (6). Also, see Huck and Ojeda (1987) for a discussion of the necessity
of conditions such as (6).

class of well-formed trees. We will see in Chapter 4 that the type of structural ambiguity illustrated in (8) is to be found as well in natural language.

A further condition on the form of trees refers to the labelling of the nodes. X-bar theory (Chomsky 1970, 1986a) states that each lexical category "projects" dominating nodes. For example, the major lexical categories are Noun (N), Verb (V), Adjective (A), and Preposition (P). A lexical category projects dominating nodes as in (9), where X° refers to the lexical category, the *head* of the phrase.[6] The node X' (the single bar level) immediately dominates the head and is immediately dominated by the XP node (the maximal projection).

(9)

The asterisk (*) indicates that the X' level may be recursive (or absent). Thiersch (1985) points out that the nodes which appear to play a crucial role in GB are the maximal projection and the lexical node (see also Frazier 1990). For example, as discussed in Section 2.3 below, an X° may be a governor and an XP may be a barrier to government. Thus the X' node plays a limited role in establishing grammatical relations. Further, in formalisms such as Lasnik and Kupin (1977), nonbranching domination cannot be specified. Therefore, unless otherwise licensed (see below), I will assume that the projection of a lexical category only includes an X' if such a node branches. In addition, an X° may have a sister node, a maximal projection called a *complement* of X. An X' may have a sister node, a maximal projection called a *specifier* of X. Thus, we may have the tree (10), with YP the complement of X° and ZP the specifier of X'.

---

[6] Higginbotham (1985) points out that the lexical node redundantly specifies information contained in the terminal element. For example, *see* is specified as a verb, and the terminal element would be composed of, among other types of information, *see*, [+V, −N] . Therefore, removing the redundancy would yield (i) as the structure for a VP headed by *see*.

(i)

I will continue to follow common practice and indicate the lexical node as distinct from the terminal element as there do not appear to be any implications for parsing theory.

(10)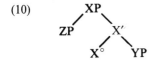

Speas (1990) notes that the recursive nature of projection (e.g. the intermediate X′ node) requires some form of constraint on structure generation. Although it is possible to state the restriction as a rule or template, Speas formulates a constraint (given in [11]) which follows from general principles of economy of representation (Chomsky 1991).

(11)   No vacuous projection

A projection is vacuous if it is not required by a principle of grammar. Thus superfluous projection is disallowed. In general, branching nodes will be licensed (i.e. required by a principle of grammar) as generating positions for specifiers, arguments, and adjuncts. But nonbranching intermediate nodes will not be licensed unless required by some specific property of the grammar.[7] Given this, we can list the properties of X-bar theory in (12) (cf. Speas 1990).

(12a)   There are three bar levels: XP, X′, X°.[8]
(12b)   Every X° projects to an XP.
(12c)   Every XP is a projection of an X°

We do not need to specifically state that every X′ must be licensed (or that each projection must be licensed) as this follows from the general Principle of Full Interpretation (PFI) which, as Chomsky (1991) states, "holds that an element can appear in a representation only if it is properly 'licensed.'" This principle can be stated as in (13).[9]

(13)   PFI: No vacuous structure

One aspect of syntactic structure that is not determined by the properties of the grammar discussed above is the position of adjuncts such as adverbs

---

[7] Note that this constraint is distinct from the reduced phrase marker's inability to define nonbranching domination (Lasnik and Kupin 1977).

[8] Note that Speas (1990) specifically argues against the use of bar levels. I will continue to use X′ to identify intermediate projections as the issues motivating Speas' approach do not bear on the parsing issues to be discussed below.

[9] As noted in Chapter 1, the representational version of GB I will assume obviates the need to discuss principles involved in the economy of derivations. See Chomsky (1991, 1992) for a discussion of the global nature of the derivational approach.

and non-argument phrases. Following Speas (1990) and other work, I will assume that only complements can appear in the position held by YP in (10). That is, adjuncts cannot be sister to a lexical head. Given this, the position of an adjunct phrase (WP) is as indicated in (14).

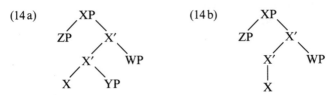

(14 a) XP / ZP \ X′ / X′ \ WP / X \ YP

(14 b) XP / ZP \ X′ / X′ \ WP | X

A nonbranching intermediate node (e.g. the lower X′ in [14b]) is licensed if it provides an adjunct position. For example, if X in (14b) is an intransitive verb, then a nonbranching V′ would be licensed to allow adjuncts to be attached into the tree without creating an unlicensed complement position.

Following Chomsky (1970), we take the labels N, V, A, and P to represent the features $[\pm N]$, $[\pm V]$, as given in (15).

(15)   NOUN: $[+N, -V]$
        VERB: $[-N, +V]$
        ADJECTIVE: $[+N, +V]$
        PREPOSITION: $[-N, -V]$

In addition to the lexical categories, the nonlexical categories of complementizer (C) and inflection (I) are assumed to follow (12). CP is the maximal projection of C and is the highest node of a clause (cf. S-bar). The maximal projection of I, IP, is comparable to the traditional S node. Thus the subject position is SPEC of IP (specifier of the inflectional phrase). Abney (1987) proposes that the category determiner (D) also projects to a maximal projection and takes NP as a complement.[10] Although this proposal will not be motivated here, in Chapter 4 I will discuss one potential implication of the DP hypothesis for parsing theory.

The precedence relations between nodes are determined by other modules of the grammar (see the discussion of case theory and theta theory in Section 2.3). The presence or absence of complements is assumed to follow from lexical specifications of heads (e.g. subcategorization information). I will assume that C subcategorizes for an IP.

We can now look at a phrase-structure tree for a clause. Note that we have not yet motivated precedence relations, nor the properties of specific

---

[10] See Grimshaw (1991) for an interesting discussion of the role of DP and other functional projections in syntactic theory.

complements. Here, and below, I will omit details of the inflectional phrase (IP) and the determiner phrase (DP) entirely.

(16)

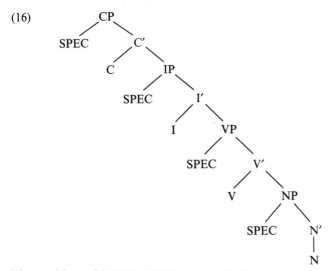

The position of [SPEC, VP] has recently become more prominent in the syntactic literature due to its role in the *Internal Subject Hypothesis* (ISH). According to this hypothesis (Koopman and Sportiche 1985; Sportiche 1988; Kuroda 1988; Huang 1993), the subject of a clause is initially generated internal to the VP. It is unclear whether the subject occupies the specifier position or is part of an adjoined structure. In subsequent discussion of the ISH I will simply assume the subject is in [SPEC, VP] as the details of the proposal will not be relevant to parsing theory. As with other details of phrase-structure trees (e.g. IP, DP), I will only indicate the VP specifier position when it is relevant to the point at hand.[11]

2.2   The generation of trees

In traditional work in generative-transformational grammar (e.g. Chomsky 1965), an initial phrase-structure tree in a derivation was the product of what was called the "base component." The base component consisted of phrase-structure rules and syntactically relevant lexical information. Consider the rules in (17) and the subcategorization information in (18), adapted from Baltin (1989).

---

[11] In Chapter 4 I note that the ISH is potentially relevant to the processing of reduced-relative ambiguities such as (i).

(i)   The horse raced past the barn fell

(17a)   VP → V
(17b)   VP → V NP
(17c)   VP → V NP S′
(17d)   VP → V S′
(17e)   VP → V NP NP
(17f)   VP → V NP PP
(17g)   VP → V PP

(18a)   *elapse*, V, [__ 0]
(18b)   *buy*, V, [__ NP]
(18c)   *tell*, V, [__ NP S′]
(18d)   *say*, V, [__ S′]
(18e)   *give*, V, [__ NP NP]
(18f)   *put*, V, [__ NP PP]
(18g)   *talk*, V, [__ PP]

A phrase-structure rule represents various types of information, as listed in (19).

(19a)   the syntactic category of the phrasal head
(19b)   the syntactic category of projections
(19c)   permissible complements
(19d)   the syntactic category of the complements
(19e)   immediate dominance relations
(19f)   precedence relations

Many researchers have noted (e.g. Heny 1979; see Lasnik and Uriagereka 1988 for discussion), that the information in (19) is redundantly specified in the lexicon. Moreover, the generalization that each XP of a lexical category must contain an X of that category cannot be captured.[12] GB (see Stowell 1981; Chomsky 1981) has sought to eliminate this redundancy by eliminating phrase-structure rules.[13] But rules such as (17) do indicate the precedence relations between elements in a structure. If phrase-structure rules are eliminated, precedence relations must be indicated in another component of the grammar.

One possibility is simply to state that UG specifies that grammars may vary in the precedence relation between heads and complements. That is, where YP is a complement of X, either (20a) or (20b) will be true for a

---

[12] See Lyons (1968).
[13] Note that the redundancy could not, in general, be eliminated by removing the information from lexical entries. But see Gazdar *et al.* (1985) for another approach.

particular grammar. This has often been referred to as the head-initial/head-final parameter.[14]

(20a)   p (X, YP)
(20b)   p (YP, X)

Thus, for English, (20a) is true. This is reflected in the various rules in (17). Given (20a) as a general statement, we do not need to repeat this information in the lexical entries of the verbs (or heads) of a particular language.

The grammar outlined here accounts for the information in (21) in the following way.

(21)   *TYPE OF INFORMATION*   *HOW IT IS REPRESENTED*
     a. category of head   lexical information
     b. category of projections   X-bar theory
     c. permissible complements   lexical information
     d. category of complements   lexical information
     e. dominance relations   X-bar theory[15]
     f. precedence relations   head parameter[16]

Let us now consider the phrase-structure tree for the English clause *that Ian hit the ball*. The tree is given in (22).

---

[14] See Koopman (1983) and Travis (1984) for an analysis of this parameter in terms of the directionality of case and theta-role assignment.

[15] I will return to the issue of dominance relations in terms of the concept of *government*.

[16] The head parameter does not address the question of the order of specifiers relative to the X'. I will put this issue aside, simply assuming that specifiers precede X'.

(22)

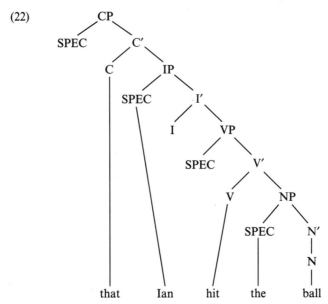

that   Ian   hit   the   ball

If the permissible complements of a head are listed as lexical information, then the complement of a complementizer such as *that* (the maximal projection IP) must be listed in the lexical entry for *that*, as in (23).[17]

(23)   *that*, C, [__ IP]

As we will see in Section 2.4, in addition to the generation of an initial phrase-structure tree, derivational GB includes transformational operations which alter properties of the initial tree. In the next section I discuss properties of the submodules of syntax.

2.3   Submodules of syntax

In addition to X-bar theory, discussed above, Government-Binding theory distinguishes a number of submodules, listed in (24) (see Chomsky 1982):

(24a)   case theory
(24b)   theta theory
(24c)   bounding theory

[17] One possible problem for this approach is that an I node always selects a VP complement. Thus to list this as lexical information would fail to capture the generalization. This may be part of a more general problem. For example, there are close correlations between the semantics of verbs and the types of complements they allow. See Chomsky (1986b) for an approach to this problem along lines originally suggested by Grimshaw (1981) and Pesetsky (1982). I will continue to refer to subcategorization information, ignoring the possibility that this may follow from semantic properties of lexical items.

(24d)   binding theory
(24e)   control theory

A core concept relevant to each of these subsystems is *government*. The intuition is that lexical heads, such as verbs, govern their complements. Consider the tree in (25):

(25)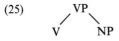

Here we can say that the verb governs the NP. But a purely structural definition, such as sisterhood, would also define the NP as governing the V. In order to keep to the intuition that government is a property of lexical heads, we can make this a part of our definition of government: heads are governors. But we also want to impose a locality restriction on government. That is, we do not want a head to govern the complements of other heads. One way of restricting government is to say that a head governs all XPs within its maximal projection. But consider the trees in (26) and (27).

(26)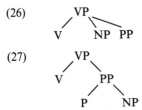

(27)

In (26) the verb governs both the NP complement and the PP. But in (27) the NP is within another maximal projection, the PP. Yet, it is still the case that the NP is within the VP. In order to restrict government of the NP to the P in (27), government is defined such that maximal projections block the government relation from holding, or, in the terminology of Chomsky (1986a), they are *barriers* to government. Thus, the verb governs the PP, but the PP prevents the verb from governing the NP. A definition of government sufficient for our purposes is given in (28) (see Aoun and Sportiche 1983; Chomsky 1986a).

(28)   x governs y iff
    (i)   x is a governor
    (ii)   either p (x, y) or p (y, x) is true[18]
    (iii) for each XP, d (XP, x) iff d (XP, y)

---

[18] This clause is often stated in terms of domination, e.g. x does not dominate y. But this would permit x to govern y in cases where y dominates x. I'm aware of no such cases, so the stronger prohibition, referring to precedence, seems preferable. Of course this depends upon the correctness of the Exclusivity Condition.

Note that *government* is defined in terms of the primary relations *dominance* and *precedence*. I will refer to structural relations that are so defined as *secondary* relations.[19] It is also commonly assumed that, if an XP is governed, all the bar levels of this projection are governed. Given this, the verb governs not only the PP in (27) but also the P. The intuition is that if a maximal projection is governed, then all projections are governed. This can be instantiated in various ways, for example by feature sharing. We will return to this aspect of government in the discussion of Pritchett (1992) in Chapter 4.

Within GB, grammatical features are assigned under government.[20] The two core features which will concern us are *case* and *theta roles*. The principles of grammar which refer to these features are the Case Filter (29) and the Theta Criterion (30).

(29)   *Case Filter*: A lexical NP must have (abstract) case.

(30)   *Theta Criterion*: Each argument is uniquely assigned a theta role; each theta role is uniquely assigned to an argument.

Consider the sentences in (31), from Lasnik and Uriagereka (1988).

(31a)   It is likely that Ian is here
(31b)   * It is likely Ian to be here

GB accounts for the unacceptability of (31b) as due to a Case Filter violation. The NP *Ian* is not in a position where it can receive case. It cannot receive case from *likely* as *likely* is not a case assigner. Nor can it receive case within the embedded infinitival clause, as nominative case is only assigned in finite clauses (cf. * *I want he to win*).

However, there are structures in which infinitival clauses contain lexical subjects, in apparent violation of the Case Filter, as shown in (32).

(32a)   I believe him to be here
(32b)   I believe Ian to be here

---

[19] Note that, although terms such as *subject* and *object* could be readily defined with GB, despite the fact that they are commonly used as shorthand to refer to structural positions, these grammatical relations are not part of GB theory. See Williams (1984) for a discussion of grammatical relations in Lexical-Functional Grammar (Kaplan and Bresnan 1982).

[20] Note that, given the definition of government above, the concept of *immediate dominance* plays no role in GB. That is, structural relations requiring government will either hold or fail to hold depending on the presence or absence of intervening barriers. Of course it is possible to define concepts such as 2-dominance (where a node dominates another node and there are two intervening, dominating, nodes) or 0-dominance (where there are no intervening, dominating, nodes) but there is no motivation for doing so. I return to this issue in Chapter 4.

Although the sentences in (32) are somewhat more awkward than their tensed counterparts (cf. *I believe that he is here*), they are clearly more acceptable than sentences such as (31b). Sentences such as those in (32) are referred to in GB as "exceptional case-marking" structures. This is due to the fact that, in apparent violation of the government requirement on case assignment, the verb *believe* assigns accusative case to the subject of the infinitive. I am not aware of any elegant treatments of this phenomenon within GB. Common to most analyses is a process of "S-bar (CP) deletion" or, perhaps more simply, a failure to initially generate a CP in these (lexically determined) contexts. Lasnik and Uriagereka (1988) remark that "evidently an S boundary does not count as too much intervening structure for the purposes of government."

Thus, case theory consists of the two components in (33):

(33a)   case assignment requires government
(33b)   the Case Filter (29)

Similar remarks hold for theta theory, as is clear from (34):

(34a)   theta-role assignment requires government
(34b)   the Theta Criterion (30)

The *Theta Criterion* insures that syntactic structures respect lexical properties, most notably the argument structure of lexical items. Note that the theta criterion does not refer to specific thematic role *labels* (e.g. *agent*, *theme*), but rather requires only that arguments be assigned theta roles (or be in theta positions).

Bounding theory constrains the operation of Move alpha, in particular, instances of Wh-movement.[21] In subsequent discussion we will be most concerned with the principle of Subjacency (Chomsky 1973, 1986b), to be discussed below in Section 2.4.

Within GB, the features $[\pm a]$, $[\pm p]$ are used to define a typology of NP types. Binding theory is concerned with the structural conditions determining the distributional possibilities of these different types of NPs. Consider the list in (35). The binding conditions are given in (36).[22]

---

[21] Move alpha, the transformational mapping between syntactic levels of representation, is a maximally general mapping which allows any constituent to be moved to any position. Constraints on overgeneration are usually thought to apply at the output levels, i.e. s-structure and LF. I will discuss Move alpha in more detail in Sections 2.4 and 2.5.

[22] The binding conditions in the text are adapted from Chomsky (1981). There has been much recent work in this area (e.g. Chomsky 1986b; Manzini 1992). I will briefly touch on this in Section 2.5.

(35a)   anaphors: [+a, −p] e.g. *themselves, each other*
(35b)   pronouns: [−a, +p] e.g. *he, her*
(35c)   names: [−a, −p] e.g. *Ian*
(35d)   PRO: [+a, +p]

(36a)   A [+a] NP must be bound in its governing category.[23]
(36b)   A [+p] NP must not be bound in its governing category.
(36c)   A [−a, −p] NP must not be bound.

The binding conditions account for the distributional possibilities illustrated in (37).

(37a)   Ian$_1$ likes himself$_1$
(37b)   * Ian$_1$ likes him$_1$
(37c)   Ian$_1$ thinks he$_1$ is intelligent
(37d)   * Ian$_1$ thinks Ian$_1$ is intelligent
(37e)   * Ian$_1$ thinks himself$_1$ is intelligent
(37f)   Ian$_1$ considers himself$_1$ to be intelligent
(37g)   * Ian$_1$ considers him$_1$ to be intelligent
(37h)   Ian$_1$ tried PRO$_1$ to solve the puzzle
(37i)   Ian$_1$ persuaded a friend$_2$ PRO$_2$ to solve the puzzle

The ungrammaticality of (37b) is due to the fact that the pronoun is bound in its governing category. In (37d) it is due to the fact that the second occurrence of the name is bound. In (37e) it is due to the fact that the anaphor is not bound in its governing category. Note that (37f) is grammatical as the governing category is the matrix clause due to the fact that the verb *consider* governs (and case marks) the anaphor. This explanation extends to (37g), where an ungrammaticality results when a pronoun replaces the anaphor.

As Lasnik and Uriagereka (1988) discuss, the binding theory can restrict the occurrence of PRO to ungoverned contexts (where it has no governing

---

[23] I assume the following definitions:

(i)   An NP is *bound* if it is coindexed with a c-commanding NP.
(ii)   x c-commands y iff
    (i) either p (x, y) or p (x, y) is true
    (ii) for each XP, if d (XP, x) then d (XP, y)
(iii)   The *governing category* for x is the minimal NP or IP containing x and a governor of x.

Note that, formally, the definitions of government (28) and c-command (cf. Aoun & Sportiche 1983) are quite similar. Government is more local, requiring that domination by any XP be mutual. As Sells (1985) notes, "government is roughly a case of mutual c-command."

category and is subject to neither (36a) nor (36b), but it cannot determine the choice of antecedent. This is the domain of control theory (Manzini 1983).

Although the preceding discussion has only sketched the properties of the various submodules of GB, it is sufficient for subsequent discussion involving the issues of levels of representation within GB, as well as for providing background for the parsing model to be detailed in Chapter 4.

2.4   Derivational GB

Although, as mentioned in Chapter 1, I will be adopting a representational version of GB (Koster 1978; 1986), it will be useful to initially discuss the three syntactic levels of representation (d-structure, s-structure, LF) traditionally assumed (Chomsky 1981, 1986b), as shown in (38).

(38)   d-structure
                            |
        PF ———— s-structure
                            |
                           LF

The level of d-structure satisfies the requirements of both X-bar theory and the theta criterion. Thus there can be no adjunction structures at d-structure as these structures violate the X-bar requirement that every XP be a projection of an X°.[24] The theta criterion is satisfied in that each argument is in a theta position. Thus d-structure represents the interaction of lexical information and X-bar theory. At d-structure arguments are in theta positions, i.e. positions to which theta roles may be assigned. For example, consider the sentences in (39).

(39a)   Ian sees a toy
(39b)   A toy is seen by Ian
(39c)   Which toy does Ian see

In English, verbs assign theta roles to their right. Thus the NP *the toy* must be preceded by the verb at d-structure. This is reflected in the word order

---

[24] There are two forms of movement, *substitution* and *adjunction*. Substitution moves a phrase into a position generated at d-structure. Thus, substitution is a structure-preserving operation. Adjunction, on the other hand, creates a position to which a phrase is moved. Specifically, a node is copied and the copy is placed in the structure immediately dominating the original node. A moved phrase may then be attached (to the left or right) under the created node, as (i) illustrates. Here y is adjoined to x.

(i)

in (39a). But this word order is not observed in (39b) and (39c). But in the d-structures of these sentences, the NPs must be in theta positions, as in (40).

(40a) $[[_{NP}$ Ian $]$ $[_{IP}$ see a toy]]
(40b) $[[_{NP}$ $]$ $[_{IP}$ BE-EN see a toy by Ian]]
(40c) $[_{CP}$ $[_{SPEC}$ $]$ $[_{IP}$ Ian see which toy]]

Of course, for (40b) and (40c) it is not the case that the d-structure position of these NPs is also their position in the surface string. The relationship between d-structure and s-structure (which "feeds" PF and yields a phonetic realization of the sentence) is mediated by the transformational component, i.e. by Move alpha.[25]

The word order observed in (39b) results from the movement of the object into the vacant subject position (an instance of NP movement). The position of the Wh-phrase in (39c) shows the output of Wh-movement, i.e. the movement of a Wh-phrase to the specifier of CP, [SPEC, CP]. Note that each of these types of movement is "structure preserving" in the sense of Emonds (1970). Both NP-movement and Wh-movement prepose phrases into base-generated positions.

The position of the arguments in (40b) and (40c) satisfies the Theta Criterion (30) and it is at this level of d-structure that the generalization holds that verbal complements (in English) follow the verb. The Case Filter (29), however, must apply at s-structure (and not at d-structure) as examples such as (41a), from Lasnik and Uriagereka (1988), demonstrate.

(41a)   Ian is likely to be here
(41b)   ___ is likely Ian to be here

The d-structure position of the NP is subject position within the embedded infinitival (41b), where it receives a theta role. It moves to its s-structure position where it receives case and satisfies the Case Filter.

The GB analysis of constraints on Wh-movement has its roots in the proposal of Chomsky (1973), where it is argued that each application of Wh-movement is subject to Subjacency (42). Apparent "unbounded" movement is argued to involve successive instances of COMP-to-COMP movement. Consider the sentences in (43).

---

[25] Note that the change from a list of specific transformations to the general rule of Move alpha does not necessarily decrease the derivational "distance" between d-structure and s-structure (Chomsky 1988). That is, a GB derivation involving Move alpha may contain no fewer applications of this single, more general, rule, than of its more specific predecessors in the standard theory.

(42)   An application of Move alpha can cross at most one bounding node, where (in English) the bounding nodes are NP and IP.

(43a)   Ian knows what Steve said Judy saw
(43b)   * Ian knows what Steve said who saw

In (43a) the Wh-phrase is able to "escape" its d-structure clause (and obey Subjacency) by first moving to the most embedded COMP, i.e. [SPEC, CP], and then to the next higher COMP. In (43b) this possibility is precluded by the presence of *who* in the embedded COMP.[26]

In addition to being constrained by Subjacency, movement operations also have the property of leaving behind a *trace* (t). It is not necessary to stipulate this as it follows from the *Projection Principle*. The Projection Principle states that lexical properties must be respected at each syntactic level, i.e. at d-structure, s-structure and LF. Thus if a verb requires an object, this object must, in some sense, be present throughout the derivation. If an object is preposed by Move alpha, a trace must remain to satisfy the Projection Principle. Consider the structures in (44).

(44a)   I know that Ian saw an animal
(44b)   I know which animal$_1$ Ian saw t$_1$
(44c)   This animal$_1$ was seen t$_1$ by Ian

In (44b) the d-structure object *which animal* has been moved to [SPEC, CP]. But the Projection Principle requires that the theta position occupied at d-structure still contain an element to receive the theta role assigned by *have*. In the s-structure in (44b), it is the Wh-trace which receives the theta role and, via the coindexation link, transmits the theta role to the Wh-phrase. Similar remarks hold for NP-movement, as shown in (44c). Here the movement of the object to subject position leaves behind an NP-trace.

Much of the interest in trace theory comes from its interaction with binding theory. In addition to the analysis of PRO as [+a, +p], Wh-trace bears the features [−a, −p] and NP-trace is [+a, −p]. That is, a Wh-trace bears the same features as a name, and an NP-trace is treated as an anaphor. The sentences in (45) illustrate the effect of treating traces as NPs subject to the binding conditions.

(45a)   * He$_1$ said that Steve$_2$ likes Ian$_1$
(45b)   * Who$_1$ did he$_1$ say Steve$_2$ likes t$_1$
(45c)   Who$_1$ did Judy$_3$ say Steve$_2$ likes t$_1$

---

[26] This oversimplifies greatly. Other restrictions, such as the Strict Cycle Condition, are also required.

(45d)   * Ian$_1$ believes himself$_1$ is intelligent
(45e)   * Ian$_1$ was believed t$_1$ to be intelligent

In (45a) the name *Ian* is illicitly bound by the matrix subject *he*. In (45b) the Wh-trace is similarly bound and the ungrammaticality of the sentence indicates that this binding is also illicit and supports not only the validity of positing a trace of Wh-movement but also the analysis of the trace as a name-like element. The grammaticality of (45c) demonstrates that the movement of the Wh-phrase to the matrix COMP is well-formed, thus isolating the binding of the trace by the subject *he* as the source of the ungrammaticality. In (45d) we see, as previously discussed, that an anaphor must be bound in its governing category. This also appears to be the case for the trace of NP-movement in (45e).

In addition to the transformational mapping between d-structure and s-structure, GB also posits a transformational analysis of the derivation of LF from s-structure. The most well-known example of this mapping is the application of *Quantifier Raising* (QR), originally proposed in May (1977). The effect of QR is to prepose phrases containing quantifiers to a position indicating their scope domain. For example, in the analysis of May (1977), the s-structure (46a) would map into either LF (46b) or (46c). Structurally, QR is an operation that adjoins a QP to IP. Note that QR leaves a trace, as required by the Projection Principle.

(46a)   Every child likes some toy
(46b)   [every child$_1$ [some toy$_2$ [t$_1$ likes t$_2$
(46c)   [some toy$_2$ [every child$_1$ [t$_1$ likes t$_2$

Thus, the LF (46b) would map into a semantic representation in which the universal quantifier had wide scope whereas (46c) would yield a wide scope interpretation for the existential quantifier. Thus, May (1977) argued that LF is an unambiguous representation of relative quantifier scope.[27] It is also argued that QR is an instance of Move alpha and that locality conditions on its application (e.g. Subjacency [42]) are able to explain certain scope restrictions, e.g. a QP's scope domain tends to be clause bound.[28] For example, May argued that if QR is adjunction to IP (= S) and (i) IP is a bounding node, and (ii) adjunction creates a second, dominating, IP, then further movement must necessarily cross more than one bounding node (at least the two Ss of the adjunction structure).

[27] May (1985) argues that the LF representation of sentences such as (46a) is, in fact, ambiguous. I will discuss this point in the next section.
[28] I discuss this issue further in Section 2.5.2.

Huang (1982) argued that the mapping to LF could also be used to explain certain facts concerning Wh-constructions in Mandarin, a language lacking overt Wh-movement. Consider the sentences in (47) and (48).

(47a)   Zhangsan xiang-zhidao [ta muqin kanjian shei
        Zhangsan wonder   his mother see   who
        "Zhangsan wondered who his mother saw"
(47b)   Zhangsan xiangxin [ta muqin kanjian shei
        Zhangsan believe   his mother see who
        "Who does Zhangsan believe his mother saw"
(47c)   Zhangsan zhidao [ta muqin kanjian shei
        Zhangsan know   his mother see who
        (i) "Who does Zhangsan know his mother saw"
        (ii) "Zhangsan knows who his mother saw"

(48a)   Ian wondered who his mother saw
(48b)   * Who did Ian wonder his mother saw
(48c)   * Ian believes who his mother saw
(48d)   Who does Ian believe his mother saw
(48e)   Ian knows who his mother saw
(48f)   Who does Ian know his mother saw

As the sentences in (48) illustrate, *wonder* requires an embedded question, *believe* does not permit one, and *know* may occur with or without one. The explanation for this is often given in terms of the selectional properties of the individual verbs, e.g. *wonder* (obligatorily) selects for a [+ WH] COMP. Further, Wh-movement is accounted for by the requirement that a [+WH] COMP dominate a Wh-phrase. This requirement is sometimes called the *Wh-criterion* (see May 1985).[29]

Huang (1982) argued that the Wh-criterion is universal, applying at s-structure in English and at LF in languages such as Mandarin. Thus the interpretation of the sentences in (47) can only be as indicated in the gloss, i.e. with *xiang-zhidao* (wonder) taking an embedded question, *xiangxin* (believe) forcing a matrix question, and *zhidao* (know) allowing either reading. Thus, despite the structural differences at s-structure, the interpretive possibilities in the Mandarin and English examples are identical. May (1985) argues that "Huang's observations provide ... a very

---

[29] The Wh-criterion also requires that (at LF) every Wh-phrase must be dominated by a [+WH] COMP. I will discuss this issue in Section 2.5.2.

strong prima facie case for the existence of LF-movements and hence for the level of LF itself."

I will return to this issue in Section 2.5 where it will be argued, following Koster (1986), that it is possible to give an empirically adequate account of these observations within a representational framework.

2.5   Representational GB

The purpose of this section is to demonstrate that there is a viable alternative to the derivational approach to GB that is familiar from Chomsky's work. As stated in Chapter 1, the motivation stems from the fact that, since the mid-1970s, parsing theory has either implicitly or explicitly adopted a monostratal approach to syntactic phenomena. This is not an accident, but rather the result of the complete inapplicability of derivational syntax to issues in language comprehension. I will return to this issue in Section 2.5.1. Here, the goal is simply to outline a representational framework for investigating the principles and parameters governing syntactic competence. Note that, for present purposes, it is not necessary to demonstrate an empirical or conceptual superiority for a representational approach, but merely to show that the two approaches are comparable with respect to the normal criteria of theory evaluation. It is the additional, parsing-theoretic, considerations which will serve to tip the scales. I will discuss this in more detail in Section 2.6. Here, I will first take up the d-structure/s-structure mapping before turning to issues involving LF.

2.5.1   *Eliminating d-structure*

In the second chapter of *Lectures on Government and Binding* (1981), Chomsky states that "An obvious alternative to the theory outlined so far would be to suppose that base rules generate s-structures directly ... ". It is this alternative which has been the focus of Koster's (1978, 1986) work on locality in grammar.[30] The emphasis on locality is due to the fact that, prior to the Minimalist approach of Chomsky (1992),[31] the specific locality constraint on movement (Subjacency [42]) was argued to be the distinguishing characteristic of dependencies created by the mapping from d-structure to s-structure. That is, there is no conceptual advantage

---

[30] In this section I will refer to Koster (1986) simply as "Koster." References to other works will be specifically indicated.

[31] Where it is argued that the nature of the derivation must be considered.

(within syntactic theory) in reformulating the d-structure/s-structure mapping as part of the s-structure representation so long as Subjacency cannot be subsumed under other, independently-motivated, s-structure properties.

Despite the focus on locality, Koster's argument for a representational, i.e. monostratal, GB also examines the nature of Move alpha and the mapping from s-structure to LF. The main point of Koster's argument is that there are no properties which uniquely hold of movement or its traces, and therefore there is no reason to distinguish dependencies arising from movement from those which are base-generated. For example, consider the sentences in (49):

(49a)   Which book$_1$ won't you read t$_1$

(49b)   That book$_1$, I won't read it$_1$

In (49a) there is a Wh-trace which transmits its theta role to its antecedent phrase *which book*. Similarly, in (49b) *it* transmits its theta role to its antecedent phrase *that book*. As Koster notes, it is generally accepted in the GB literature that the dependency (or chain) in (49b) is not the result of Move alpha. Given this, Koster argues that whatever mechanisms we posit for the base generation of (49b) will also be sufficient for generating (49a). That is, d-structure can be dispensed with in favor of directly generating chains, whether or not they have been traditionally analyzed as arising from movement.

But in order for this representational approach to be more than a notational variant of the movement analysis, it must be demonstrated that there are not two types of s-structure chains, one constrained by Subjacency and one subject to distinct locality conditions. That is, what is required is a *unified* theory of locality. Koster's discussion of this issue focuses on Wh-movement because Subjacency is superfluous with respect to NP-movement, i.e. NP-trace, analyzed as an anaphor, is subject to the stricter binding condition governing the distribution of [+a] NPs. Koster begins by listing the apparent differences between bounding and binding theory (50).

(50a)   Bounding theory constrains derivations whereas binding theory constrains representations.

(50b)   Bounding theory refers to two domain nodes (e.g. NP *and* IP) whereas binding theory refers to one (i.e. NP *or* IP, cf. the definition of governing category).

(50c)   Unlike bounding, binding (through the definition of governing category) may refer to factors such as tense or subject.

The difference given in (50a) is the most easily addressed. Given trace theory, as noted in Chomsky (1973) and argued in Freidin (1978), there is nothing to prevent a reformulation of Subjacency as a condition on representations. Koster (1978) argues that the difference in (50b) is more apparent than real, i.e. that a one-node condition (referring to the minimal XP and certain additional factors) is sufficient. He further argued that the opacity factors referred to in (50c) are relevant for all types of dependencies, not only for those which are base-generated.

This attempt toward unification of binding and bounding, although conceptually well-motivated, faces a number of empirical problems. For example, the move to a one-node condition appears problematic as it rules out simple Wh-constructions such as (51). This is because Koster's one-node condition refers to the minimal XP containing a governor for the Wh-trace.

(51)   Which book does Ian like?

In (51) the Wh-phrase has been extracted from (at least) a VP. Thus the VP is the minimal XP containing the trace and its governor. But, clearly, the preposed Wh-phrase is outside the VP. As Koster notes, "For some unexplained reason, it appears that the value of [XP] is usually not VP, but S′." Of course, given the structure assumed above, this problem extends to IP. Another problem which Koster (1978) faced was that long-distance anaphora was such a comparatively unexplored phenomenon that unbounded Wh-movement appeared to exhibit properties clearly distinct from those found in cases of anaphoric binding.

Despite these types of empirical problems, the conceptual advantages of unifying the theories of bounding and binding are clear. The motivation, of course, need not be the elimination of the d-structure/s-structure mapping. It may simply be the elimination of redundancy. For example, Chomsky (1986a) investigated "the possibility of a unified approach" to the theories of government and bounding while still maintaining that the specific constraint on movement (Subjacency [42]) could not be reduced to binding.[32] But Chomsky (1986a) notes, "A natural speculation would be

---

[32] Chomsky's (1986a) investigation of the relationship of *government* to bounding is similar to Koster's concern with the relationship of *binding* to bounding because government, as in the definition of governing category, is a central concept in binding theory.

that the same categories are barriers" to both government and movement, although stressing throughout that government is "more local" than movement. That is, unlike earlier approaches, the primitives of bounding and binding theory are the same (government, barriers) but the definition of locality domains, although now composed entirely of this common vocabulary, remain distinct.

But note that the relation of government, as well as the binding conditions, are representational concepts. That is they hold or fail to hold of a given structure, not of a given derivation or operation. Thus any unification of the concepts of government and binding (or, bounding and binding) facilitates the reinterpretation of derivational phenomena in representational terms.

Further, the binding conditions must hold at s-structure, as (52) indicates.

(52a) ___ seems to each other [the women to be intelligent
(52b) the women seem to each other [t to be intelligent

In the d-structure (52a), the anaphor *each other* is not bound as it fails to be c-commanded by an antecedent. However, in the s-structure (52b) the NP *the women* is in a c-commanding position and serves as the binding antecedent for the reflexive, satisfying condition (36a). However, if this condition held at d-structure, such sentences would be incorrectly excluded. As Burzio (1986) points out, observations such as these indicate that s-structure configurations are necessary for interpretive processes.[33] Further, they are sufficient as they preserve, via trace theory, the d-structure configurations relevant for interpretation.

Thus, a unified approach to binding and bounding based on government not only enhances the representational view, but it also forces the particular representation at which government and other relations hold to be s-structure, not d-structure. Note that this is the case even if there is not a complete unification of locality theory. But it is also true that, even though Chomsky (1986a) views movement as less local than binding, within the *Barriers* framework movement has become more local than in previous accounts. For example, the derivation of (51) must include two movements: an initial adjunction to VP and a subsequent movement to [SPEC, CP]. The initial movement is motivated as a solution to the

---

[33] Recall the discussion of (41) which demonstrated that the Case Filter (29) must apply at s-structure, not d-structure.

problem Koster noted concerning VP. Why is it possible to extract from a VP, but not an NP?[34] In earlier approaches this followed from the stipulation that VP was not a bounding node. The *Barriers* approach maintains that it is a bounding node (now reformulated as a barrier to government), but that adjunction is an operation that may create an "escape hatch." Consider the adjunction structure in (53).

(53)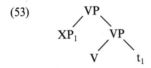

I'll refer to the highest VP in (53) as the *created* VP (as it was created by the operation of adjunction) and the lower VP as the *original* VP. Each VP node is said to be a "segment" of the VP projection. If a maximal phrase is a barrier to government, it might be thought that government of the trace by the XP in (53) would be blocked by the original VP. But Chomsky (1986a), following the work of May (1985), redefines government so that the original VP is not a barrier to government. More formally, the VP is not a barrier for government by the XP as one segment of the VP dominates the XP. Thus XP governs t in (53).

This accounts for the extractability from VP. But exactly the same issue surfaces with respect to IP. Here it is merely stipulated that IP is not a barrier. Thus, the *Barriers* s-structure for (51) is (54).

(54)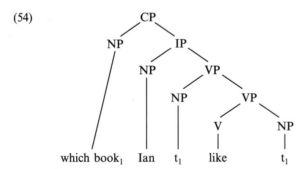

The trace in object position is (antecedent) governed by the intermediate trace. In turn, this intermediate trace is governed by the Wh-phrase as (i)

---

[34] It is interesting to note that a similar question arises within binding theory, as (i) demonstrates.

(i)   Ian$_1$ [$_{VP}$ likes himself$_1$]

IP is not a barrier, and (ii) the created VP is not a barrier as the intermediate trace is not dominated by all VP segments.

Thus part of Chomsky's approach to a unified theory of locality is to construe movement as more local than in previous work. In one sense, this research strategy has its roots in Chomsky (1973) where (apparent) unbounded movement is analyzed as a series of local movements, resulting in a chain of intermediate traces relating a Wh-phrase to its d-structure position. When combined with trace theory, this yields an analysis of unbounded movement as a chain of intermediate empty categories (locally) connecting the surface position of an antecedent to the position in which it is assigned a theta role.

Thus the derivational approach of Chomsky (1986a) pursues an agenda that is quite similar to the representational theory of Koster. In each case, the goal is to unify the primitive concepts of the theories of bounding and binding, with Koster pursuing the additional goal of unifying the locality domain. Given this similarity, it is worth exploring the role of government in the two theories and the particular role that adjunction plays in Chomsky (1986a).

Each theory begins with the "core" concept of government: mutual domination by all and only the same XPs. Thus the simplest dependency is between two elements in a government relationship. Apparent violations of this strong locality condition are treated as a chain of government relations. One instance of this is (54), where the traces in the chain (*which book*$_1$, t$_i$, t$_i$) are each governed. The problem which adjunction solves is the exceptional status of VP as a non-barrier to government. Compare this to the *Domains and Dynasties* approach of Koster, where the core domain is the minimal XP containing a dependent element and its governor. Larger domains, *dynasties* in Koster's terminology, are created by "a chain of successive governors." As Koster's approach does not have recourse to movement operations such as adjunction, he must simply stipulate that VP does not count as a minimal XP.[35] Given this it is interesting to note that much of the discussion in Chomsky (1986a) concerns the peculiar status of VP and IP with respect to adjunction and barrierhood.

An important aspect of Koster's argument is to show that the formal distinctions between bounding and binding in derivational GB are

---

[35] The Internal Subject Hypothesis is a potential solution to the problematic status of VP in a unified locality theory. That is, a Wh-trace or anaphor within the VP can be bound by the VP-internal trace of the raised subject. See Huang (1993) for a discussion of binding and the ISH. Of course, the exceptional status of IP within Koster's approach remains.

motivated, to a large degree, by certain idiosyncratic properties of English. For example, Koster argues that, in Dutch, the similarities between bounding and binding phenomena are more salient than any observed differences. As noted above, Koster claims that the basic locality domain is the minimal XP containing a dependent element and its governor. But this domain may be "extended" in a small number of well-defined ways, as indicated in (55).

(55a) $\ldots [_b \ldots (\ ) \ldots _g \ldots _d \ldots] \ldots$

(55b) $\ldots [_b \ldots (_o) \ldots _g \ldots _d \ldots] \ldots$

(55c)   if $\ldots [_b \ldots (_o) \ldots _g \ldots _d \ldots] \ldots$

          then $\ldots [_{b'} \ldots _{g'} \ldots [_b \ldots (_o) \ldots _g \ldots _d \ldots] \ldots$

In (55a), the basic locality domain, d stands for a dependent element (e.g. trace or an anaphor); g is the minimal governor for d; and b is the minimal XP containing d and g. The reference to (o) in (55b) indicates an "opacity factor" such as *subject* or a tense element. The recursive definition in (55c) allows for an unlimited extension of a particular locality domain.

Within Koster's framework, (55a) is the locality domain for sub-categorization, theta assignment, and control. This basic domain is the "core" notion of government: mutual domination by all and only the same XPs. Koster also notes that certain dependent elements such as French reflexive *se* must be bound by the domain described in (55a), as the contrast in (56) shows.

(56a)   Il$_1$ se$_1$ lave
        He self washes
        "He washes himself"

(56b)   * Il$_1$ parle [$_{PP}$de   se$_1$]
        He talks   about self
        "He talks about himself"

In (56b) *se* is governed by the preposition *de* and thus the minimal relevant XP is the PP. But *se* is not bound within this domain and the sentence is ungrammatical.

Note that the grammaticality of (56a), *modulo* the Internal Subject Hypothesis, again demonstrates the problematic status of VP with respect to locality domains based on government. One way of addressing this problem is to extend the definition of domain, as in (55). This definition is familiar from cases in English for which the definition of governing category given above is inadequate. Sentences such as (57) have been taken as motivation for extending the notion of governing category to include factors such as *subject*.

(57)   Ian$_1$ drew [$_{NP}$ a picture of himself$_1$]

The grammaticality of (57), in which the anaphor fails to be bound in the NP (where it is governed by *picture*) requires a larger domain definition. Various refinements of this, e.g. reference to a *c-commanding* subject, are able to account for the grammaticality of sentences such as (58).

(58)   [Ian$_1$ thinks that [$_{CP}$ [$_{IP}$ [$_{NP}$ pictures of himself$_1$] amuse me]]]

Here *Ian* is the only c-commanding subject and the entire sentence is the relevant locality domain.

The recursive definition in (55c) is one of the more interesting aspects of Koster's approach. Its applicability is most clearly seen in the phenomenon of long-distance anaphora. Consider the following sentences in Mandarin, from Huang and Tang (1991).

(59a)   Zhangsan$_1$ shuo [Wangwu$_2$ zhidao [Lisi$_3$ chang piping   ziji$_1$
         Zhangsan say   Wangwu know   Lisi often criticize self
(59b)   * Zhangsan$_1$ shuo [wo$_2$ zhidao [Lisi$_3$ chang piping   ziji$_1$
         Zhangsan say   I   know   Lisi often criticize self

The reflexive *ziji* may take as its antecedent a subject that is outside its clause, as (59a) indicates. But there is an interesting restriction on this relationship. That is, all the intervening subjects must agree in certain features (e.g. person, number) with the antecedent. Thus long-distance binding of *ziji* is blocked in (59b) because the intervening subject *wo* is first person, unlike either *Zhangsan* or *Lisi*.

Huang and Tang (1991) argue for an analysis of this phenomenon in terms of a series of local relationships similar in spirit to Chomsky's original analysis of long-distance Wh-constructions as instances of successive-cyclic movement. Although Huang and Tang (1991) adopt an LF-movement analysis, Koster's proposal for extending domains in terms of successive governors (in Koster's terms, a *dynasty*) which share certain features is applicable to the Mandarin data. For example, via the mechanism of subject–verb agreement (which is independently required) it can be readily seen that the domain extension necessary for long-distance binding of *ziji* can refer to features such as person and number.

Thus the dynasty, or binding domain, for *ziji* will be able to extend through superordinate clauses so long as agreement features are shared. If this agreement fails then so does the domain extension. Similar remarks apply to Icelandic reflexives (Thrainsson 1976, Maling 1981, Anderson 1983) where the binding domain of the reflexive *sig* can be extended so long as the verbs of each embedded clause are in the subjunctive mood. Although it may appear as if this approach requires reference to a number of different grammatical concepts (agreement features, mood specification), it is important to note that all current approaches must refer to these (or similar) features whose nature appears specific to the particular types of dependencies. It is interesting that, in other grammatical frameworks (e.g. categorial grammar and GPSG), long-distance Wh-movement is accounted for in a similar fashion, i.e. by reference to the local recurrence of a specific feature. In fact, one of the interesting aspects of work within a representational framework is that "unbounded" phenomena must often be analyzed as stemming from the recursive nature of properties of grammar which operate within a local domain. This is the motivation for (55c) in Koster's representational approach to bounding and binding.[36]

Of course, what is important from the representational perspective is that there not be a specific locality domain for bounding, but rather that the domains defined by (55) serve as a "menu" of permissible variation from which various dependencies (or dependent elements) might choose. This is similar to the approach of Manzini and Wexler (1987) who, following work by Borer (1984), argue that differences in locality domains must be stated in terms of particular (dependent) lexical items. Consider Manzini and Wexler's (1987) *Lexical Parameterization Hypothesis*.

(60)   Values of a parameter are associated not with particular grammars but with particular lexical items.[37]

Thus some languages may have both short-distance and long-distance anaphors (e.g. *taziji* and *ziji* in Mandarin). This fact appears problematic for locality theories which determine that locality must be stated for types of categories (e.g. anaphors) within a particular language. Manzini and Wexler's (1987) subset hierarchy of governing categories is similar to Koster's domain extensions, as both exhibit a markedness effect and refer crucially to government. Although (60) was originally formulated to apply

---

[36] Cf. the (unified) locality principle of Manzini (1992), given in (i).

(i)   x is a dependent element iff there is an antecedent y for x, and a sequence (y, ... ,x) that satisfies government.

[37] Note that the term *lexical items* is not a reference to the surface form of words, as this would incorrectly distinguish, for example, *himself* and *herself*.

specifically to binding phenomena, Manzini (1992) builds on this approach in formulating a unified locality theory that is similar in many respects to Koster's framework.

Clearly, important issues remain undecided in the debates concerning locality domains and the viability of representational approaches to bounding phenomena. But, just as clearly, the fact that there is a lively debate is evidence that the representational view is empirically adequate across a wide range of phenomena. From the parsing perspective this is good news. One issue that remains to be addressed concerns how LF phenomena might be accounted for in a GB theory without LF.

2.5.2   *Eliminating LF*

Koster's argument for the elimination of LF is similar to the argument for eliminating d-structure and the d-structure/s-structure mapping (Move alpha). The argument focused on the demonstration that there were no properties which uniquely held of movement or its output. As is clear from the prior discussion of May (1977) and Huang (1982), there are two basic types of movement to be considered when discussing LF: Wh-movement and QR.

LF movement of Wh-phrases is motivated by the Wh-criterion (May 1985), given in (61).

(61a)   Every [+WH] COMP must dominate a Wh-phrase
(61b)   Every Wh-phrase must be dominated by a [+WH] COMP

In a language with overt Wh-movement, such as English, (61a) applies both at s-structure and at LF. In languages lacking overt wh-movement, e.g. Mandarin, (61a) only applies at LF. But the second part of the Wh-criterion cannot apply at s-structure, even in languages with overt movement, as (62) demonstrates.

(62)   Who saw what

Thus, (61b) applies only at LF in English and Mandarin (although it may apply at s-structure in languages such as Polish). Given this, the LF representation of (62) is (63).

(63)   [who$_1$ [what$_2$ [t$_1$ saw t$_2$]]]

Wh-movement, then, may apply either in the syntax (generating s-structure) or at LF. This is not surprising if the mapping to each level is mediated by Move alpha. But Huang (1982) argued that, contrary to May (1977), LF movement is not governed by Subjacency. Consider the contrast in (64):

(64a)   * which warning$_1$ did Ian leave [despite t$_1$]
(64b)   who left despite which warning

The ungrammaticality of (64a) shows that the bracketed phrase is an island, barring Wh-constructions in which the trace is bound outside this domain. But, under the LF-movement account, the grammaticality of (64b) must be due to the fact that the preposing of *which warning* is not subject to the same restriction which rules out (64a). Koster argues that this type of example, which is not uncommon, indicates an important formal dissimilarity between Wh-chains present at s-structure and their putative counterparts at LF. For Koster, this dissimilarity is to be captured by the fact that there is a dependency relation between two s-structure elements in (64a) whereas there exists only one element (with a specified scope domain) in (64b).[38]

The concept of a specified scope domain is central to Koster's account of quantifier phenomena which May (1977, 1985) analyzed in terms of QR. Following work by Haik (1984) and others, Koster adopts an indexing approach to specifying the domain of quantifiers. Consider the scope indexing rule of Haik (1984), one formulation of which is given in (65).

(65a)   If NP$_a$ is to be interpreted as within the scope of NP$_b$, then append $/=b$ to the index of NP$_a$, yielding NP$_{a/b}$.
(65 b)   Scope indexing applies freely when NPs belong to the same minimal S. Otherwise, an NP$_a$ is interpreted within the scope of NP$_b$ iff NP$_b$ c-commands NP$_a$ at s-structure.

As Haik (1984) observes, the scope indexing rule expresses the restrictions on scopal domains discussed by May (1977), i.e. "Logical form, then, does not have a different structure than s-structure; it is simply s-structure

---

[38] Koster presents an intricate argument for the scope of Wh-phrases in argument positions being determined by his unified locality domains. It would take the discussion too far afield to discuss it in detail. The basic point is that, following Baker (1970), Koster assumes a Q element in COMP which is linked to Wh-elements in argument positions. Nonpronominal elements must be linked locally whereas the domain for nominal or pronominal phrases may be extended in the familiar way. This distinction accounts for the argument/adjunct distinction observed in Huang (1982).

Distinctions between s-structure and LF Wh-phenomena are said to follow from differences in the nature of the dependent elements (traces at s-structure and lexical phrases at LF).

enriched with indices." Note that the first part of Haik's indexing rule (65b) correctly accounts for within-clause scopal ambiguities. Following May (1985), LF is no longer considered a level of representation in which scopal relations are necessarily disambiguated. The fact that the syntax does not bear sole responsibility for determining scopal relations may account, in part, for the difficulty of formulating structure-based approaches to the parsing of sentences containing multiple quantifiers (see Kurtzman and MacDonald 1990).

To conclude this section, it is clear that a derivational account of LF phenomena can be reformulated in a representational format without loss of empirical adequacy. Further, it can be plausibly argued that there is also the conceptual advantage inherent in eliminating two levels of representation, the distinct conditions which apply to them, and the mechanisms for mapping from one level to another. Of course it may prove to be the case that separate structural levels of representation are necessary components of syntactic theory. But if so, it will hardly gladden the hearts of researchers concerned with the interaction of syntax and perception.[39]

2.6   Summary

In this chapter I have outlined a specific theory of syntactic knowledge: a representational version of GB theory. I assume that primary structural relations (dominance and precedence) are represented in the form of a phrase-structure tree. These primary relations allow for the definition of secondary relations such as government, c-command, etc. which are important concepts for the assignment of additional structural relations such as theta-role and abstract case assignment. The grammar is "principle-based" in that the generation of structure is motivated by grammatical principles such as the Case Filter, the Theta Criterion, etc. But the grammar is also "structure-based" in that the move from rules to principles does not alter the fundamental importance of primary structural relations. Recall that government, clearly a crucial property of the grammar, is defined in terms of the primary relations of dominance and

---

[39] Note that adopting the Minimalist framework of Chomsky (1992), which eliminates s-structure, poses a serious problem for the s-structure parsers discussed in Chapter 3. That is, if d-structure and LF are the only syntactic levels of representation, how are structural variables to be isolated from thematic and scopal properties? In all the work considered below, this isolation was achieved by assuming the parser to be building an s-structure (and not a d-structure or LF). From a parsing perspective, Koster's approach becomes even more attractive in light of the Minimalist program.

precedence. Despite the focus on secondary relations in recent years, primary structural relations are no less fundamental than those in earlier grammatical frameworks.

In the parsing model to be detailed in the next chapter, I will show that this distinction between primary and secondary relations, although motivated independently within syntactic theory, has an important role to play in parsing as well. Similarly the principle of economy of representation ("No vacuous structure") will also be an important principle governing the parser's operations.

The representational view adopted here dispenses with the need to either address the issue of the computation of multiple levels of representation or put this important issue aside for future research. It should be noted that, although many of the theories to be discussed in the next chapter explicitly adopt a GB framework, two concepts which play no role in these theories are *d-structure* and *LF*.

3 *Analyses of previous work*

Be on the watch to take the best parts of many beautiful faces.

Leonardo da Vinci

3.0   Structural ambiguity

The parsing model to be described in detail in Chapter 4 addresses particular questions that have arisen from two related, but distinct, research programs investigating natural language processing. The first seeks to investigate hypotheses concerning human sentence comprehension within the context of experimental psycholinguistics; the second is concerned with the computational implications of such hypotheses. In recent years there has been a considerable amount of convergence concerning basic principles of language comprehension. For example, the important role of phrase structure in language processing has been convincingly demonstrated, and it is a rare processing model which does not make some reference to syntactic constituents and structural relations. There is a growing consensus that, given ambiguous input, the perceptual mechanism has an initial bias toward the reading consistent with the minimal structural representation.

Further, owing to the important work of Marslen-Wilson (1973, 1975) there is general agreement that models of syntactic processing must be responsive to the experimental demonstrations of the speed and efficiency of human language processing.

As this chapter will make clear, important, and interesting, differences remain, but real progress has been made since the mid-1970s. The purpose of this chapter is to outline some of the main avenues of research responsible for this progress. This will give a context for the parsing model described in Chapter 4. This model, as will become clear, incorporates significant aspects of the parsers described in the following sections.

But this chapter is not an exhaustive history of studies investigating the role of syntax in sentence comprehension. It focuses on particular studies which have influenced aspects of parsing theory within the framework of generative grammar. More specifically, it focuses on research with implications for a GB-based parsing model. Thus work which presupposes other grammatical frameworks (e.g. categorial grammar, GPSG, HPSG, LFG, etc.) is not discussed here. This is unfortunate for many reasons. For example, it may give the impression that a claim is being made that only GB is a valid grammar for a psychologically plausible theory of syntactic processing. This is not the case. The state of the art is such that any such claim would be premature. The inability of any one study of sentence processing to encompass all the major grammatical frameworks simply reflects the explosion of information in both syntactic theory and psycholinguistics.

Also, I will delay a discussion of the role of semantic and discourse information in syntactic processing until Chapter 5. The models to be discussed here (and in Chapter 4) all reflect the view that the parser's response to syntactic indeterminacy cannot be fully explained by reference to nonsyntactic factors. In Chapter 5 we will see that these factors do play an important role in ambiguity resolution. But a proper appreciation of this role, and its relation to structural variables, is impossible if the structural variables are not first clearly delineated. The discussion of the syntactic assumptions in the last chapter was the first step in this process. Analysis of current models of syntactic processing is also an important preliminary to the proposal to be made in Chapters 4 and 5.

A central concern of all these theories, and for many this is a defining characteristic, is the manner in which the parser responds to structural ambiguity. As discussed in Chapter 1, an input string (or substring) is defined as structurally ambiguous if it is compatible with more than one grammatical structure. A string is temporarily ambiguous if the ambiguity is resolved by subsequent lexical material within the sentence.

Following Fodor *et al.* (1974) we can begin by distinguishing two general types of processing models: (i) *parallel* models which construct multiple analyses, and (ii) *serial* models which construct a single analysis.[1] To illustrate how these models function, we need to refer to three distinct areas of an ambiguous string: the onset of the ambiguity, the ambiguous region, and the resolution of the ambiguity. Consider the string (1).

---

[1] See Garrett (1990) for a more complete discussion of these models.

(1)   Ian knows Thomas is a train

In (1) the onset of the ambiguity is the verb *know*. This is because *know* allows either a nominal or sentential complement.[2] The ambiguity is resolved by the presence of the verb *be*, which signals a sentential complement. The area between the onset of the ambiguity and its resolution is the ambiguous region of the sentence. In (1) it is the NP *Thomas*. It is important to note that these areas of the sentence are independent of the particular properties of the parsing model one assumes. For example, it may be that the parser initially fails to make use of the subcategorization information associated with the verb *know*, but this does not change the fact that the input is ambiguous.

At the onset of an ambiguity, a parallel model will construct multiple structures, abandoning particular structures as they become incompatible with subsequent input. For (1) a parallel parser would respond to the onset of the ambiguity by computing a nominal clause structure and a sentential clause structure, abandoning the nominal clause structure at the point of resolution. In contrast to this, a serial parser would respond to the onset of the ambiguity by computing only a single structure. If this structure is incompatible with subsequent material, some form of reanalysis is required. The initial structure computed by a serial parser must be determined by some property of the parser. Serial parsers differ as to the nature of this decision procedure (I return to this issue below). But serial parsers share the property that, once the decision as to which structure to pursue is made, the parse proceeds as if the input were unambiguous. This aspect of serial parsers will be important in determining the nature of reanalysis.

The processing of ambiguous input has received a great deal of attention in the psycholinguistic and computational literature, but, despite this, there is still no general agreement among researchers as to the precise nature of the parser's response to ambiguity. However, there is growing consensus that the processing difficulty of sentences such as (2a) and (2b) is strong evidence for the parser structuring input as it is received, i.e. *incrementally*.

---

[2] As will become clear below, this way of looking at the onset of an ambiguous string underdetermines the ambiguity of natural language. Consider the case where the first item of an input string is *John*. For example, this word may function as the subject of the sentence, as part of a conjunct that functions as the subject (*John and Mary*), as part of a conjunct modifying the subject (*John and Mary's house*), as a topicalized phrase (*John, I like*), or as a left-dislocated phrase (*John, I like him*).

(2a)   While Mary was mending the sock fell
(2b)   The horse raced fell

If the parser delayed the attachment of the NP *the sock* until the next word (*fell*) was processed, a garden-path effect could be avoided. Similar remarks hold for (2b). In addition, the work of Marslen-Wilson (1973) and Marslen-Wilson and Tyler (1980) has demonstrated the rapid processing of linguistic input. Thus it appears that the parser does not delay in structuring input, even when the input is ambiguous. A core issue that must be addressed by any parsing model is the conditions under which immediate structuring of ambiguous input leads to conscious processing difficulty and the conditions under which such structuring fails to produce such disruptions.

There are a number of issues which arise when one talks about "garden-path" phenomena. We will see that experimental studies (e.g. Frazier and Rayner 1982) are often designed to reveal processing difficulties that would not otherwise be evident. Other investigations (e.g. Marcus 1980) draw a distinction between structures which cause "conscious difficulty" and those that do not. This is just to say that the definition of the term *garden-path* is not independent of one's assumption concerning the nature of sentence comprehension. In this chapter I will adopt the distinction drawn by the theory being described, postponing a more thorough discussion until Chapter 4.

In terms of the parser's initial response to ambiguity, a parallel parser must address the issue of why alternative analyses are not always available at the point of resolution. Each type of parser must address the question of why certain ambiguities produce more severe disruptions than others. Again, I will return to these issues within the context of specific approaches to structural ambiguity in the following sections.

The work of Marcus *et al.* (1983) introduces a third type of parsing model, one in which the parser constructs a representation that is underspecified with respect to the grammatical formalism. For many ambiguities, this type of model is able to delay certain structural commitments until disambiguating information is processed, thus avoiding many potential misparses.

The work of Frazier (1978) and Frazier and Fodor (1978) argues for a serial, incremental, parser which reanalyzes computed structure when necessary. The design of the parser is motivated by the need to structure input quickly and efficiently, before it becomes a burden to short-term memory. Much of the work investigating the relation between syntactic structure and sentence comprehension undertaken since 1978 has been influenced by the seminal work of Frazier and Fodor. The next section outlines the basic design of the Sausage Machine model, as well as proposals for the nature of reanalysis in Frazier (1978) and Frazier and Rayner (1982).

3.1   Late Closure, Minimal Attachment and reanalysis

The work of Frazier (1978) and Frazier and Fodor (1978) elegantly unites the various parsing strategies of Bever (1970) and Kimball (1973) into two general principles of parsing, Late Closure (LC) and Minimal Attachment (MA).[3] Since 1978, these two principles have generated a considerable amount of research into the nature of human sentence processing. The papers by Frazier and Fodor outline a two-stage serial parsing model (the Sausage Machine) in which the initial structuring of lexical items into phrases is accomplished by a first-stage parser called the preliminary phrase packager (PPP). Subsequent structuring of those phrases into a complete phrase marker is the responsibility of the sentence structure supervisor (SSS). The PPP's initial decisions as to structural relations between nodes are determined by LC and MA. Also, the PPP has a limited "viewing window" of approximately 7 ± 2 words[4] which predicts that the length of the input string can affect processing decisions. The PPP may also use phrase or clause boundaries in determining what units to package for the SSS.

(3)   *Late Closure*: When possible, attach incoming material into the clause or phrase currently being parsed.

(4)   *Minimal Attachment*: Attach incoming material into the phrase marker being constructed using the fewest nodes consistent with the wellformedness rules of the grammar.

Note, in particular, that these parsing strategies are quite general. They refer to nodes and phrases, not particular types of nodes and phrases. This

---

[3] See Frazier (1978) and Garman (1990, Chapter 6) for a detailed discussion of the proposals of Bever and Kimball.

[4] As Frazier (1978) and Frazier and Fodor (1978) note, the proper unit for defining the capacity of the PPP may not be words, but may be best characterized in terms of syllables or morphemes. Also, the SSS may well have a "viewing window" of about 7 units, but here the units would not be words but the phrasal packages constructed by the PPP.

is in sharp contrast to the specific strategies discussed in Fodor *et al.* (1974) which referred to specific node labels such as V and NP. Together, these two parsing strategies predict that the parser will (initially) minimally attach incoming material into the current phrase. Thus, in (5), the preferred attachments of the post-verbal NPs will be as direct objects.

(5a)   While Mary was mending the sock ...

(5b)   Mary was mending the sock ...

(5c)   Ian knew the woman ...

In (5a) and (5b) the ambiguity is caused by the fact that *mend* may appear either with or without an object. Frazier (1978) argues that LC causes the parser to analyze the NP *the sock* in (5a) as the object of *mend* because the VP is the current phrase. The other grammatical attachments would necessitate attaching the NP as part of a new phrase or clause. MA does not apply here if it assumed that, at the point that *the sock* is processed, the main-clause node has been computed.[5] Without this assumption, MA would suffice to force the object attachment of the NP because it would be the minimal attachment site.

In (5b), despite the fact that a similar effect is evident, it is MA which causes the parser to analyze the post-verbal NP as the object of the verb. The other grammatical possibility would be a conjoined structure such as *Mary was mending, the sock was lying on the table, and the cat was fast asleep.*[6]

In (5c) the ambiguity is caused by the verb *know*, which permits either a nominal or sentential complement. Thus the post-verbal NP is either an object of the main clause or the subject of a (possible) subordinate clause. Here, it is MA which causes the parser to attach the NP *the woman* as the direct object of the verb, as it is the minimal attachment site.

Frazier (1978) also discusses the preferred attachment of prepositional phrases, such as *to Mary* in the sentences in (6).

---

[5] We return to this issue below. Many parsing models (including the Sausage Machine) permit the parser to compute structure prior to the appearance of the relevant lexical items if that structure is obligatory (i.e. predictable), given the grammatical requirements of the current input. Frazier and Fodor (1978) "permit both the PPP and the SSS to postulate obligatory nodes in the phrase marker as soon as they become predictable, even if their lexical realizations have not yet been received." For example, given a verb such as *put*, the parser may postulate structure consistent with its subcategorization frame as soon as the verb is processed.

[6] MA would play a similar role in (5a), precluding the conjoined reading within the preposed clause, as in (i).

(i)   While Mary was mending, the sock was lying on the table, and
        the cat was fast asleep, Fred left for work.

(6a)   Ian mailed the letter to Mary.
(6b)   Ian mailed the postcard the note the memo and the letter to Mary.

In contrast to the X-bar position of adjuncts described in Chapter 2, the structure Frazier (1978) assumes for a prepositional phrase modifying a NP is $[_{NP} [_{NP}] [_{PP}]]$, where the presence of the PP requires an additional NP node.[7] Frazier assumes that the structure for an adjunct PP attached to a VP, unlike NP attachment, does not require the computation of an additional node.[8] Given this, MA predicts that the preferred PP attachment for sentences such as (6a) and (6b) is VP attachment. But, Frazier argues, this is incorrect for (6b), where the preferred attachment is within the NP. At the point in (6b) when the PP is being processed, the PPP (due to its limited viewing window) no longer has access to the verb *mail*; the only accessible attachment site is the NP. Thus, MA applies to the PPP's attachment decisions only as a procedure for choosing between the available alternatives, where "available" means within the capacity of the PPP. This length effect is also argued to explain a number of attachment preferences similar to those in (7).

(7)   The detective brought the man who was accused of having stolen the automobile in

MA also accounts for the preferences evident in the sentences in (8).

(8a)   The horse raced past the barn fell.
(8b)   They told the girl that Ian liked the story.

For (8a), the parser will prefer the simple main clause analysis of the lexical material preceding *fell* because this involves postulating a simpler structure

---

[7] In Chapter 2 we argued for a different structure, one in accord with X-bar theory. Frazier (1990) argues that the structure $[_{NP} [_{NP}] [_{PP}]]$ must be a grammatical option which English allows, given sentences such as (i).

(i)   The girl and the boy in the park

This is clearly an empirical problem which must be addressed by the X-bar analysis as coordinate structures can be modified by relative clauses and reduced relatives as well, as (ii) and (iii) illustrate.

(ii)   The girl and the boy who met in the park
(iii)   The girl and the boy stung by the bee

Brad Pritchett (personal communication) points out that coordinate structures are the only structure potentially problematic for the X-bar analysis. He suggests that a possible solution might be offered by Goodall's (1987) parallel-structure approach to coordination. I return to a discussion of the issue of ambiguities with NP modification in Chapter 4.

[8] See Abney (1989), Frazier (1990), and Pritchett (1992) for discussion of this point.

than the alternative past participle reading. For (8b), as with (6a), the preferred attachment is to the VP and not the NP. This is because VP attachment of the clause *that Ian liked the story* does not require the computation of an additional node, as would NP attachment.

In addition to sentences such as (5a), LC accounts for the parsing preferences evident in (9).[9]

(9a)   Ian said Thomas left yesterday.

(9b)   Without her contributions would be inadequate.

LC predicts that the preferred attachment of the adverb *yesterday* in (9a) will be to the VP headed by *leave*. This is because that VP is the current phrase being processed. The application of LC to (9b) is less straight-forward. Assuming that the processor is making attachment decisions as each word is processed, the lexical ambiguity of *her* permits attachment either as a genitive modifier of a following noun, or as an accusative pronoun.

MA would appear to be applicable here, assuming (as was necessary to explain the non-applicability of MA in [5a]) that the parser precomputes obligatory structure. If the parser analyzed *her* as a modifier, then an NP node would be computed. But this node would not be necessary if the parser attached *her* as an accusative pronoun. Thus MA would favor this latter attachment. But intuition suggests that, contrary to the prediction of MA, this attachment is not preferred.

Frazier (1978) addresses this problem by arguing that MA and LC "may influence the lexical categorization of an item not only in cases where this allows the incoming lexical item to be optimally attached into the phrase marker ... but ALSO in examples like [9b] where categorization may be determined by the optimal attachment of the following word." Thus, for (9b), the optimal attachment of *contributions* would be within the current clause. Frazier suggests that the parser may delay the resolution of lexical ambiguities until further material is processed (see also Frazier and Rayner 1987b). Specifically, "the parser might analyze the word *her* as a constituent of a noun phrase, but not assign a lexical category to this word until after it has received the immediately following word *contributions*." At this point LC would determine the preferred analysis of the items in question as the alternatives require an equal number of nodes. What is not clear here is why MA would not be operative at the point at which *her* is

---

[9] This oversimplifies. See the discussion of LC and Right Association in Fodor and Frazier (1980) and Wanner (1980).

processed, i.e. to influence the lexical categorization of that item. Clearly, MA would predict an analysis of the pronoun as an accusative object of *without*. We will return to this structure in subsequent sections.

The motivation for the PPP processing input in accord with the strategies LC and MA is that (i) they allow the parser to structure material even at points where grammatical information is insufficient, and (ii) by attaching new input into existing phrases (rather than creating new phrases) the parser decreases the number of phrases ("packages") the SSS must structure into a complete phrase marker.

Frazier states that

> the Late Closure Strategy is not really a decision principle which the parser relies on when it is unsure about the correct attachment of incoming material; rather, late closure of phrases and clauses is the result of the fact that the first stage parser functions most efficiently by (minimally) attaching incoming material with material on its left which has already been analyzed. Hence, within the particular model of the parser which I have proposed, Late Closure is simply part of the characterization of the operation of the first-stage parser; it does not have to be stated as a specific strategy. (1978: 114)

But it is not clear in what way the principle of LC follows from the design of the parser. Assuming that LC contributes to efficient parsing does not change the fact that its effects must either follow from other properties of the parser or be specifically stated. But LC cannot follow from the two-stage design even if its operation would contribute to efficient parsing, nor does it follow from the PPP's limited viewing window. A larger viewing window would presumably contribute to more efficient processing by the PPP. But this is not an argument for this property. Frazier and Fodor (1978) state that "Efficient functioning of the system demands that each of the two stages should do as much of the work as it is able to within the limits on capacity at its level of analysis." But the question remains: If the late closure of phrases is a component of efficient parsing, what properties of the PPP cause it to be efficient in this way?

These remarks do not apply to MA. Frazier and Fodor (1978) state that it can be dispensed with as an independent strategy because the parser, due to the demands of time pressure, pursues the first structural analysis it computes. All else being equal, this will be the analysis which requires the accessing and application of the least number of grammatical rules and principles. We can see how the minimal attachment becomes the one pursued by the parser if we look at the grammar in (10) and the corresponding trees in (11a) and (11b).

(10)   A ----▸ B C
        B ----▸ a
        C ----▸ D E
        D ----▸ b
        E ----▸ c
        E ----▸ F G
        F ----▸ c
        G ----▸ d

(11a)

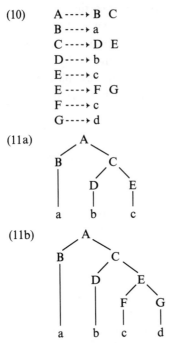

(11b)

When the parser processes the item "c," the parser will attempt to construct, in parallel, the two grammatical analyses of the string "abc." But the representation in (11a) requires the accessing of fewer rules (E → c) than the representation in (11b): E → F G; F → c. Thus, for (11b), the parser will initially assert that "E" directly dominates "c." If this initial analysis is proved incorrect by the appearance of "d," reanalysis is required.

MA has a number of advantages for parsing design. In a grammar with recursion, it solves the problem of overgeneration of structure for ambiguous input. Also, as Frazier and Fodor (1978) note, MA allows for a simplification of reanalysis procedures, because such procedures "will all consist of adding extra nodes to the phrase marker." We will return to the issue of minimal structure and forms of reanalysis within the context of the proposal of Marcus *et al.* (1983).

In general, the Sausage Machine model argues that the parser will initially structure ambiguous input as if it were unambiguous. This is because, with both ambiguous and unambiguous input, the parser pursues the first available analysis. If there is an ambiguity which is subsequently resolved in violation of MA and LC, then a reanalysis of the input is required. Frazier (1978) states that a reasonable hypothesis about reanalysis procedures would be that "processing complexity is not influenced simply by the NUMBER of nodes which must be revised, but also by the type of revision and its consequences for the semantic interpretation of the sentence." The motivation for this is the contrast between the processing of sentences such as those in (12), (13), and (14).

(12a)   We gave the man the grant proposal was written by last year a copy of this year's proposal.

(12b)   We gave the man the grant proposal we wrote because he had written a similar proposal last year.

(13a)   Sally found out the answer to the physics problem was in the book.

(13b)   Sally was relieved when she found out the answer to the physics problem.

(14a)   Because of the blizzard the guests left before the evening meal was finished.

(14b)   Because a blizzard had been forecast the guests left before the evening meal.

For each of these pairs, MA predicts that the (a) versions will be more difficult to process than the corresponding (b) forms. Intuition, and the results of Frazier's Experiment IV, confirm this prediction – with one exception. Frazier reports that there was no significant difference between sentences such as (14a) and (14b) in her experiment. What is of interest is the fact that (12a) is much more difficult than either (13a) or (14a). Frazier used a grammaticality judgment task; the results are given in (15). Reaction time is in milliseconds, with percent correct in parentheses.

(15)   [12a]   3150 (5 percent)
       [12b]   1359 (88 percent)

       [13a]   1647 (84 percent)
       [13b]   1224 (81 percent)

       [14a]   1237 (93 percent)
       [14b]   1187 (89 percent)

It is clear that the difference between (12a) and (12b) is greater than the difference between (13a) and (13b). As stated, there is no significant difference between (14a) and (14b).

Frazier (1978) suggests that "there are certain types of revisions which the parser might easily make during its first pass through the sentence, namely 'structure additions' (i.e. the insertion of additional nodes into the phrase marker that has already been constructed)." One possible reason for this stems from the fact that MA is argued to follow from the parser attempting to compute all possible analyses for ambiguous input, but pursuing only the first analysis computed. Frazier (1978) speculates that if this first syntactic analysis is compatible with other information available to the parser, then the computation of additional analyses is terminated. However, if the minimal structure yields an implausible or contextually inappropriate analysis, the parser could continue to compute alternative syntactic analyses until one was found to be consistent with available information.

Assuming this framework for reanalysis, Frazier (1978) argues that the parser would "postulate all and only as much structure as it had evidence for, i.e. when the minimal attachment analysis of the material was not suitable but some later analysis turned out to be, the parser would insert into the phrase marker whatever additional structure the later, more appropriate, analysis entailed." Frazier also notes that "structure addition" appears to be less costly than altering existing structure. This structure-addition hypothesis will play an important role in subsequent developments in parsing theory (see Marcus *et al.* 1983 and the theory to be developed in Chapter 4).

This approach to reanalysis departs from a strictly serial approach to parsing. That is, when processing ambiguous input, the parser is only serial if the minimal syntactic analysis fails to conflict with (or, perhaps, is confirmed by) nonsyntactic information available to the parser. However, it is not clear how this approach might apply to reanalysis initiated by the (subsequent) appearance of lexical or syntactic information incompatible with the initial analysis. In this situation the parser presumably has terminated its computation of alternative analyses and the "staggered parallel" approach would have been abandoned in favor of a serial analysis. Also, it is not clear whether certain types of reanalysis could be handled by the PPP, or whether reanalysis is solely the responsibility of the SSS.

Frazier (1978) does discuss a form of "intelligent" reanalysis (originally due to Winograd 1972) which would be the responsibility of the SSS. Frazier argues that the SSS could take advantage of its extended viewing window to perform intelligent reanalysis. That is, when confronted with problematic input, the parser would not merely search through the sentence in some general fashion for the source of the error, but that attempts at reanalysis would reflect the information ("clues") available to the SSS.

Frazier and Rayner (1982) further investigated the hypothesis that the parser intelligently performs reanalysis, as well as the hypothesis that initial structural decisions are in accord with LC and MA. Although designed to investigate theories of reanalysis as well as hypotheses concerning the parser's initial structural commitments, the results of these experiments have been most influential as evidence that the parser makes early structural commitments consistent with LC and MA. We will first briefly review the evidence for LC and MA before turning to a discussion of reanalysis.

Frazier and Rayner (1982) measured subjects' eye movements as they read sentences containing temporary ambiguities. This technique is a particularly useful tool for investigating on-line sentence processing as there is no need to interrupt the parsing of the input string for the presentation of a secondary task. Rather, a subject's fixation durations and eye movements are recorded as each sentence is read. Total reading time per letter for each sentence was also recorded. FR tested sentences such as those in (16) and (17). In addition FR tested sentences with longer ambiguous regions, e.g. *that stupid science fiction story* instead of *the story* in (16), and *the answer to the difficult physics problem* instead of *the answer* in (17).

(16a)   Though George kept on reading the story Susan bothered him.
(16b)   Though George kept on reading the story really bothered him.

(17a)   Sally was relieved when she found out the answer.
(17b)   Sally found out the answer was in the book.

For closure sentences such as (16), they reported that total reading time per letter was significantly slower for the early-closure sentences (62.5 milliseconds/letter) than for the late-closure sentences (52.5 milliseconds/letter). There was also a significant interaction between type of sentence (early v. late closure) and length of the ambiguous region (long v. short).

It is also important to note that the reading times did not differ between sentence types until the appearance of the disambiguating word, and that once this word was encountered, reading times were significantly slower for the early closure sentences. For the attachment sentences (e.g. [17]), Frazier and Rayner (1982) report a similar reading-time pattern.[10] Reading time per letter was significantly slower for the non-minimal attachment sentences (56 milliseconds/letter) than for the minimal attachment sentences (47 milliseconds/letter). Again there was a significant interaction between type of sentence and length of ambiguous region.

In contrast to the closure sentences, sentences such as (17a) do not include a lexical item which serves to resolve the ambiguity. In sentences of this type, it is the end of the sentence which serves as the point of disambiguation. Thus it is not possible, as with the closure sentences, to compare reading times when the disambiguating word appears. However, FR do report that, for the non-minimal attachment sentences (e.g. (14b)), reading times were significantly slower in the disambiguating region when compared with the region prior to disambiguation. For both sentence types, there was no difference in reading times between the initial portion of the sentence and the ambiguous region.

The pattern of eye movements is consistent with the view that, given ambiguous input, the parser initially makes a structural commitment it may later need to revise. The dominant form of regressive (leftward) eye movement was a regression from the disambiguating region to the ambiguous region. FR interpret this to "probably indicate that subjects have detected an error in their initial analysis of the sentence and have identified the source of the error."

Specifically, they argue that the pattern of regressions is inconsistent with a theory of reanalysis in which the parser either initiates reanalysis by returning to the beginning of the sentence and proceeding forward or by proceeding backward through the sentence entertaining alternatives at choice points. Instead FR argue that the results support a *selective reanalysis strategy* in which the parser "will use whatever information indicates that its initial analysis is inappropriate to attempt to diagnose the source of the error." In other words, properties of the trigger for reanalysis can be used to determine the source of the misanalysis.

Although the selective reanalysis hypothesis is more a framework for future research than an articulated theory of reanalysis, Frazier and Rayner note that it would help to explain why some misanalyses are easier

[10] The findings for the attachment sentences were somewhat less robust than the closure sentences. That is, for the closure sentences F_1 (subjects analysis), F_2 (items analysis), and min F' were all significant at the .05 level; for the attachment sentences, both F_1 and F_2 were significant at this level but min F' ($< .10$) was not.

to reanalyze than others. Consider the sentences in (18), where MA predicts an initial misparse of both strings.

(18a)   Ian knew the solution to the problem was complex

(18b)   The horse raced past the barn fell

For (18a), they argue that, when the VP *was complex* is processed, the fact that it requires a subject could aid the parser in reanalyzing the already computed NP *the solution to the problem* as that subject.[11] But for (18b) there would be no NP already computed that could serve as subject of *fell*. They conclude that sentences which present severe processing difficulties are those which garden-path both the initial structure-building component of the parser as well as its attempts at reanalysis.

3.2   Ranked parallelism

Frazier and Rayner's (1982) interpretation of their findings was challenged by Kurtzman (1985). He proposed a parallel processing model in which the parser could rank alternative syntactic analyses, which it had constructed in parallel, according to conceptual criteria. Using an acceptability judgment task timed to occur at the point of disambiguation, he found that, by manipulating the plausibility of a particular structural analysis of a sentence, performance could be affected in such a way that it was the more plausible (and not the Minimal Attachment or Late Closure) analysis which was preferred.

The logic of the argument is that plausibility could only affect the selection of a preferred analysis if there were multiple analyses from which to select.[12] Frazier and Rayner (1982) had argued that experimental evidence which demonstrated that the parser exhibited consistent structural preferences given ambiguous input argued for a serial parser which pursued initial analyses consistent with LC and MA. Kurtzman's view of a parser which computes multiple analyses but "prefers" one over the other can account for some of these asymmetries. This type of parallel parser is distinct from the pure parallel models discussed above and is not subject to the criticisms often levelled against these models. Kurtzman's claim is that processing asymmetries result, not from the parser pursuing

---

[11] It is also the case that the operation of reanalysis must resolve ambiguities, as (i) indicates. When *were* is processed an additional clause is unambiguously signalled. But an ambiguity remains: the correct structuring of the string *the men and the women*.

(i)   John knew the men and the women were strangers

[12] See also Lackner and Garrett (1973) for similar arguments using a dichotic-listening task.

a single preferred analysis, but from a parser that pursues analyses in parallel with the different alternatives ranked. Thus the eye-movement data which FR report for the nonminimal sentences could be interpreted as the computational cost associated with the parser being forced to adopt a less-preferred analysis (which would occur at the point of disambiguation).

Using an acceptability judgment task to test his hypothesis, Kurtzman presented subjects with ambiguous sentences in which the final word (which signalled the subject to make a judgment) resolved the ambiguity. He tested strings such as those in (19).

(19a)   The boy trained for a medical career
(19b)   His second wife will claim the inheritance

Minimal Attachment predicts that in (19a) the parser will have constructed a representation in which *trained* is analyzed as a past tense matrix verb. In (19b) MA predicts that *the inheritance* is attached as the direct object of the verb. Kurtzman argued that the parser may prefer these analyses but that alternative structures are computed in parallel and available to affect performance.

Kurtzman argues that the reason the parser appears to prefer the minimal attachment in (19a) is that there isn't a strong conceptual expectation for specific information about the referent of the main subject NP, but that there is a strong expectation for information about the state or action the subject of the sentence is engaged in. The matrix verb analysis of *trained* satisfies this strong expectation. Concerning sentences such as (19b), Kurtzman states that there is a conceptual preference for simple term referents rather than propositions to be involved in the activities expressed by main clause verbs. Hence an analysis of *the inheritance* as a direct object rather than as the subject of a proposition is preferred.

Kurtzman reasoned that a serial model would predict the results of an acceptability task for ambiguous materials to reflect a near-complete (if not complete) absence of the less-preferred analysis. This is because a serial parser will pursue a single analysis, with alternative structures able to influence performance only after reanalysis. Kurtzman did find that subjects' response times and accuracy reflected a preference for the minimal analysis, but also that subjects did not completely reject strings compatible only with the nonminimal analysis. Accuracy for these sentence types ranged from 33 percent for structures such as (19a) to 70 percent for structures such as (19b). In all cases the accuracy rates for the nonminimal structures (even in conditions that included a strong semantic or pragmatic bias) were significantly less than for sentences in which the resolution of the ambiguity was consistent with MA.

Kurtzman argued that the correct responses for the nonminimal structures reflected the availability of the nonminimal analysis. But it is also possible that the responses to these structures reflected cases in which reanalysis had occurred prior to the subject making a decision. Kurtzman implicitly assumed that the responses reflect the state of the parse prior to reanalysis. But without the inclusion of unambiguous materials to serve as a baseline, the validity of this assumption cannot be evaluated.

Gorrell (1987, 1989) tested the predictions of the ranked-parallel hypothesis by means of a lexical decision task that included both ambiguous stimuli and unambiguous controls. These experiments extended work by Wright and Garrett (1984), who conducted a series of experiments designed to investigate the effect of syntactic context on lexical decision. Several studies (e.g. Goodman *et al.* 1981; Lukatela *et al.* 1983) had demonstrated an effect on lexical decision times produced by syntactic context. Before turning to the experiments investigating ranked parallelism, it is necessary to first discuss the experiments conducted by Wright and Garrett.

Their first experiment was designed to test whether a reliable effect of syntactic structure could be obtained if a lexical decision target was presented at the offset of a sentential context. They used quadruples such as the one in (20), with the lexical decision target in capitals.

(20a)   If your bicycle is stolen, you must FORMULATE
(20b)   * If your bicycle is stolen, you must BATTERIES
(20c)   * For now, the happy family lives with FORMULATE
(20d)   For now, the happy family lives with BATTERIES

All targets were matched for frequency and were selected so that they were not semantically or pragmatically predictable.[13] In (20a) and (20b) the modal verb *must* requires a main verb for a grammatical completion of the string. This requirement is met in (20a). In (20c) and (20d) the preposition *with* requires an object. This requirement is met in (20d). Wright and Garrett found that noun and verb targets were recognized significantly

---

[13] See Carello *et al.* (1988) for a discussion of variable plausibility in Wright and Garrett's (1984) materials. Reese (1989) addressed this concern and found a response pattern consistent with Wright and Garrett's findings.

more quickly when they were grammatical continuations of the syntactic context than when they were not.[14]

On the basis of the results of additional experiments, they argued that the proper distinction was not between targets that represent grammatical continuations of the context and those that do not. Rather, decreased lexical decision times were produced only when the target belonged to a syntactic category required for a grammatical completion of the sentence. For example, in one experiment, they tested adjective targets in contexts where an adjective was required (e.g. [21a]) and in contexts where an adjective was grammatical, but optional (21b).

(21a)   The interesting clock seems very TOLERABLE
(21b)   Your visiting friend should enjoy TOLERABLE

WG found that adjectives in contexts requiring an adjective produced faster lexical decision times than contexts in which an adjective was optional. To account for these findings, Wright and Garrett proposed a *heads-of-phrases hypothesis* which stated that the parser, in some way, seeks the heads of predicted phrases. For example, if a verb or preposition requires a NP object, then that NP must have a noun head. The combination of subcategorization information and X-bar theory are sufficient information for the parser to predict the appearance of a head of a predicted phrase.

In (21a) *very* functions as a specifier of an AP, which requires an adjective head. But in (21b), there is no grammatical requirement for an adjective. The general finding of WG is that syntactic context produced faster lexical decision times only for targets belonging to syntactic categories predicted by the context, whereas targets belonging to categories either optional or ungrammatical, given the presented context, failed to produce such decreased times. In Gorrell (1987), this finding plays a crucial role in the argument that only the predictions of the ranked-parallel hypothesis are confirmed by the experimental results reported there. We return to this issue below.

Before describing the results in Gorrell (1987, 1989), it is necessary to first examine how syntactic context might exert an influence on reaction times for lexical decision targets (see Wright and Garrett 1984 for a more general discussion). If we view one operation of the parser as integrating

---

[14] Note that the grammar does not force the target in either (20a) or (20d) to be the next item in the surface string, as the italicized words in (i) and (ii) demonstrate.

(i)   You must *not* formulate ...
(ii)   The happy family lives with *a lot of* batteries

lexical items into a syntactic structure, we can interpret the WG results in the following way. If a syntactic category is required, given an existing structure, then the parser may confidently construct, in advance, structure appropriate to that item.

This was the proposal of Frazier and Fodor (1978). In terms of the Sausage Machine "both the PPP and the SSS postulate obligatory nodes in the phrase marker as soon as they become predictable, even if their lexical realizations have not yet been received." Gorrell (1987) referred to this as the *precomputation* of structure. This would ease the integration of the predicted item into the structure when it does appear, because the predicted structure would not have to be computed in response to the appearance of the item. Also, as Frazier and Fodor (1978) argued, if the predicted item failed to appear, the precomputed structure could serve to signal this ungrammaticality.

Precomputation of structure can account for WG's results in the following way: if lexical decision is delayed until the more reflexive operation of syntactic integration (of lexical items) is attempted, then we would expect faster recognition times when the cost of this operation was comparatively light. Such a situation would occur when the parser had precomputed much of the necessary structure for a predicted item. This situation could not arise if the item was an optional continuation of the string or was ungrammatical, given prior context.

Note that a string of words can only produce an effect on a following lexical decision target if the comprehension device has computed a representation for that string that is related to properties of the string affecting reaction times. Thus the WG results also reinforce the view that the parser is constructing a structural representation of a sentence on-line. The experiments reported in Gorrell (1987) were designed to investigate the operation of the parse when the context string is structurally ambiguous.

Consider the contrasting predictions of serial and parallel models. Given Wright and Garrett's (1984) results, a serial model predicts that lexical decision times will be decreased for targets belonging to categories predicted by the preferred reading of the ambiguity (e.g. the Minimal Attachment reading). But targets belonging to categories predicted by the nonpreferred reading should not produce faster times as the parser is not computing the relevant structure.

In contrast, a parallel parser will compute structures which will predict the appearance of items required by both the preferred and nonpreferred readings of the ambiguity. Thus, the parallel hypothesis predicts that decreased lexical decision times should be observed for targets belonging to categories required by the nonpreferred reading of an ambiguity. Gorrell (1987) tested ambiguities such as those in (22) and (23), where "^" indicates where the sentence was interrupted for presentation of the lexical decision target (see Gorrell 1987 for details).

(22a)   It's obvious that Holmes saved the son of the banker ^ right away
(22b)   It's obvious that Holmes suspected the son of the banker ^ (right away/was guilty)
(22c)   It's obvious that Holmes realized the son of the banker ^ was guilty

(23a)   The company was loaned money at low rates ^ to ensure high volume
(23b)   The company loaned money at low rates ^ (to ensure high volume/decided to begin expanding)
(23c)   The company they loaned money at low rates ^ decided to begin expanding

For each ambiguous (b) context, two unambiguous versions were constructed: an unambiguous minimal version (a) and an unambiguous nonminimal version (c). The inclusion of the unambiguous contexts allows for an examination of the parser's response to the ambiguities.

Again, given the results reported by Wright and Garrett (1984), a parallel parser, but not a serial parser, would predict decreased lexical decision times for targets required by the nonpreferred reading of the ambiguity. Preference is defined by Minimal Attachment for the ambiguities tested. Thus for both (22b) and (23b) a verb is predicted by the nonpreferred analysis of the string prior to the presentation of the target.[15]

The results for both the (a) and (c) versions of the context strings were consistent with Wright and Garrett's findings. Verb targets following the (c) contexts, which required such a category, were recognized significantly faster than verb targets following the (a) contexts, which disallowed such a category. For the ambiguous (b) contexts in both (22) and (23), verb targets produced reaction times significantly faster than the (a) contexts and not significantly different from the (c) contexts.

---

[15] Presentation was as follows: the context string appeared from left to right across a computer screen, with a new word appearing every 350 milliseconds (all words remained on the screen). To signal the appearance of the target, two asterisks appeared 350 milliseconds after the last word of the context. The target appeared 350 milliseconds after the asterisks.

This result is consistent with the parallel hypothesis and inconsistent with the serial hypothesis. The serial hypothesis predicts that the (a) and (b) contexts should pattern together because, prior to reanalysis, the parser will have computed similar structures for both the unambiguous minimal contexts and the ambiguous contexts. This is because such a parser will adopt the minimal analysis for ambiguous contexts.

However, this claim presupposes that lexical decision precedes reanalysis. It is important to examine the validity of this supposition.[16] Within the framework of a serial parsing model, we can list the possible relationships between lexical decision and syntactic integration, as in (24).

(24a)   Lexical decision precedes both syntactic integration and reanalysis.

(24b)   Lexical decision follows syntactic integration but precedes reanalysis.

(24c)   Lexical decision follows syntactic integration and reanalysis.

If lexical decision is prior to the parser's initial attempt to integrate the target into the existing structure (or if there is no attempt to integrate the target into the structure) then lexical decision must be independent of syntactic context. Thus we would expect to find no significant interaction between context and target. But this expectation is incompatible with these and WG's results.

If, however (as assumed above), lexical decision occurs after the initial attempt at syntactic integration, but before reanalysis, then the (a) and (b) contexts should pattern together, as stated. But the results disconfirm this prediction. But suppose that lexical decision follows reanalysis. This could explain why the reaction times for verbs in the ambiguous contexts were faster than the unambiguous minimal context. That is, verbs, as a predicted, grammatical, continuation of the reanalyzed structure, could be expected to produce faster times than verb targets following the (a) contexts.

But if lexical decision followed reanalysis, then we would expect, contrary to what was found, ambiguous contexts to produce slower times than the (c) contexts. This is because, for the ambiguous strings, the serial parser would first compute the minimal structure, then recognize its error through the appearance of the verb target, and then construct the alternate

---

[16] Below, I return to the role that the 700 msec delay between offset of the context and onset of the target may have played in these results.

structure. Thus if lexical decision follows reanalysis *and* reanalysis takes time, as Frazier (1978) and Frazier and Rayner (1982) argue, then this should be reflected in the lexical decision times following the ambiguous contexts (compared with unambiguous contexts).

Thus the lexical decision times for verb targets following the contexts in (22) and (23) appear to offer strong support for a parsing model in which multiple structures are computed in parallel when ambiguous input is analyzed. Such was the conclusion reached in Gorrell (1987, 1989).[17] But subsequent work has shown that the 700 millisecond interval between the offset of the context string and the onset of the target played a significant role in the results for the ambiguity shown in (23). If the interval is reduced to 100 milliseconds, the results for this ambiguity are consistent with a serial model. That is, verb targets after contexts such as (23b) produce reaction times significantly slower than verb targets after the (c) contexts and not significantly different from the (a) contexts. The results for the ambiguity in (22) were not affected by the reduction in the interval between context and target.[18]

Ranked parallelism can account for these more recent results by appealing, in some way, to a metric whereby certain alternative structures are ranked so low that they are abandoned before disambiguating material becomes available. But is unclear what the nature of such a metric would be. I return to this issue from a computational perspective in Section 3.6. In the next section I describe a computational approach that offers a general way of distinguishing ambiguities which produce garden-path effects from those that do not.

3.3   Determinism and description theory

Description theory (Marcus *et al.* 1983) is best understood within the context of the Marcus (1980) parser, a framework within which d-theory is embedded. The discussion of the Marcus parser will focus on the *Determinism Hypothesis* as it has become a core concept motivating much

---

[17] The proposal was actually quite similar to the Sausage Machine model. Recall that the SM attempted to build all structures compatible with an ambiguity, but only pursued the first structure computed. The ranked-parallel model presented in Gorrell (1987) argued that alternative structures were pursued (in a manner suggested by Frazier's [1978] structure-addition hypothesis), but that the MA structure was the preferred structure.

[18] I return to this issue in Section 4.2, where experimental results are considered in light of the proposed parsing model.

of the current research in natural language processing.[19] This hypothesis can be stated in (25), from Marcus (1980).

(25)   The syntax of any natural language can be parsed by a mechanism which operates "strictly deterministically" in that it does not simulate a nondeterministic machine.

A parse is strictly deterministic if all the structure created by the parser in the parse sequence is part of the final output. This means that the parser cannot *backtrack*, i.e. the parser cannot either prune nodes from the tree, remove feature specifications from nodes, or alter the attachment site for a node. Also, the parse cannot proceed in parallel, abandoning structure as it proves incompatible with subsequent input.

Although the initial motivation for the determinism hypothesis was computational efficiency (see Berwick and Weinberg 1984), the discussion here will focus on the strengths and weaknesses of such an approach with respect to questions concerning properties of the human sentence comprehension mechanism. Thus the main concern here will be with what Marcus (1980) called the "psychological" formulation of the hypothesis, given in (26).

(26)   All sentences which can be parsed without conscious difficulty can be parsed strictly deterministically.[20]

We can interpret this as the claim that the automatic, reflexive operations of the parser (J. A. Fodor 1983) are deterministic. If the correct resolution of an ambiguity cannot be accomplished within the constraints of determinism, then conscious problem-solving is required. The interest in the determinism hypothesis as a claim concerning human sentence processing is that it restricts the class of possible theories. If empirically adequate, a deterministic parser is potentially a simpler theory, i.e. one which lacks a reanalysis component.

The core problem for a deterministic parser, of course, is the persuasive ambiguity of natural language. We can think of a deterministic parser as a serial parser with no reanalysis capability. In fact, the attractiveness of the determinism hypothesis for theories of natural language comprehension is

---

[19] I will use the term *determinism* to indicate that the parse sequence is monotone increasing. Strictly speaking a device could be deterministic without obeying monotonicity if it has a unique instruction to delete information, given a particular current state of the device and a particular input symbol.   [20] Note that this is not a biconditional.

that it severely restricts the class of possible parsers. If a deterministic parser can be formulated in such a way that it can account for a wide range of perceptual phenomena, then it is to be preferred over a nondeterministic parser with comparable empirical coverage.

Although Berwick and Weinberg (1984) present specific computational arguments for determinism over a purely parallel nondeterministic approach in which reanalysis can proceed "at no apparent cost," it should be emphasized that there are no psycholinguistic models to which this argument is applicable. That is, there are no current proposals for pure parallelism in the psycholinguistic literature. In a subsequent article (Berwick and Weinberg 1985), an argument is presented concerning the computational inefficiency of a backtracking approach to certain structural ambiguities. But what is of interest is that the argument is made, not against backtracking (i.e. reanalysis) as formulated as part of a psychological theory, but against a particular *implementation* of the theory. Thus Berwick and Weinberg (1985) argue that when an initial parse fails to correctly structure ambiguous input, in "a pure backtracking parser, we would have to unwind to all intermediate choice points." But this is not true of the selective reanalysis outlined in Frazier and Rayner (1982) or any other psycholinguistic approaches.

Although theories of reanalysis are often quite vague in the psycholinguistic literature, studies such as Frazier and Rayner (1982) demonstrate that backtracking in the computational sense (working blindly backward from the point the parse fails) is inconsistent with the experimental data. Given this, Berwick and Weinberg's (1985) argument can only be taken to demonstrate that a particular form of backtracking is inconsistent with the facts.

The more general argument, that serial parsing without backtracking is to be preferred over serial parsing with backtracking as an initial hypothesis, still holds. But of course what must be demonstrated is that (i) a deterministic parser can be descriptively adequate, and (ii) that the elimination of a reanalysis component can be accomplished without enriching the initial structure-building component of the parser.

As mentioned, the prime motivation for reanalysis is as a device for recovering from misanalyses of ambiguous input. I will first discuss the original proposal for a deterministic, psychologically plausible, parser in Marcus (1980) before turning to the more recent d-theory approach. The Marcus (1980) parser solves the problem of local indeterminacy by allowing the parser to delay the analysis of ambiguous material until a limited amount of additional input has been processed.[21] This "look-ahead" buffer operates in the following way. Consider the sentences in (27) and (28).

(27a)   Have the students take the exam today
(27b)   Have the students taken the exam today

(28a)   Have the students who missed class yesterday take the exam today
(28b)   Have the students who missed class yesterday taken the exam today

When the parser inputs the initial item in (27), *have*, the analysis of this item is indeterminate. This ambiguity is resolved by the form of the verb *take*. Marcus argued that the buffer consisted of three cells.[22] Thus the parser could place the verb *have* in the first cell of the buffer, analyze the NP *the students* and place it in the second cell. The verb *take/taken* can now be placed in the third cell and this information used to correctly analyze *have*. The sentences in (28) illustrate that the length of the constituents is not a factor in the parser's operation.

But despite the fact that the buffer allows the parser to correctly process a number of ambiguities, it fails to account for the fact that many ambiguities fail to produce conscious processing difficulties when disambiguating information is unavailable, i.e. outside the limits of the lookahead buffer. It also fails to account for the fact that many ambiguities do produce conscious difficulty even when disambiguating information is available. Consider the sentences in (29)–(31).

(29a)   Have the students put their books away.
(29b)   Have the students put their books away?

(30a)   The horse raced past the barn fell.
(30b)   While Mary was mending the sock fell off her lap.

(31)   I drove my aunt from Peoria's car.

The structure of the sentences in (29) is identical to the sentences in (27). None of these sentences appear to pose any processing difficulty. Yet, in (29), unlike (27), disambiguating information is not available, i.e. the information is not available to affect the parse before the capacity of the

---

[21] A full description of the Marcus parser is not necessary for the following discussion. See Marcus (1980) and Berwick and Weinberg (1984).

[22] But see Marcus (1980, Chapter 8) where the possibility of variation in buffer size is discussed.

buffer is exhausted. This, of course, is due to the fact that *put*, unlike *take*, is morphologically ambiguous with respect to the relevant readings.

In (30a), the parser will process the ambiguous *raced* and place it in the first cell of the buffer. The PP *past the barn* will then be placed in the second cell, leaving the third cell available for the disambiguating *fell*. But it is clear that this account cannot be correct. The disambiguating information is not consulted before the parser analyzes *raced*. In (30b), even a one-cell buffer would predict that the parser would use the disambiguating information (*fell*) before attaching *the sock* as the object of *mend*.

The problem that (31) poses for the Marcus parser is not related to properties of the buffer, but rather it stems from the particular way in which the parser schedules the attachment of nodes as it analyzes NPs. Given a post-verbal NP the parser will attach it to the VP as soon as the head noun is processed. The timing of this attachment is related to how the Marcus parser attempts to determine the attachment site of PPs occurring after post-verbal NPs.[23] The problem is that if the parser attaches *my aunt* in (31) as a direct object of *drive*, then a garden path should result when subsequent input (the genitive marker on *Peoria*) is processed. In effect, then, for the processing of such ambiguities, the parser has no lookahead buffer.

It is, in part, to account for the processing of sentences such as (31) that Marcus *et al.* (1983) modify the Marcus parser so that, instead of computing a structural representation as the parse proceeds, the parser computes a *description* of a structural representation that is then interpreted by other processors. The aspect of descriptions which has become a significant part of subsequent research is given in (32).[24]

(32)   The predicate for hierarchical structure is *dominates* rather than *directly dominates*.

The move from directly dominates to dominates as the "predicate of attachment" allows the parser to lower constituents in the structural description as the parse proceeds. For example, compare how a d-theory parser compares with the operation of MA in the Sausage Machine.

---

[23] See Shipman and Marcus (1979) and Marcus *et al.* (1983) for discussion.

[24] A description also differs from a representation in that it makes use of names rather than unique node labels. Thus, if two statements make reference to an NP, it is indeterminate whether or not the reference is to a single NP or to distinct NPs unless conflicting information renders the single NP interpretation impossible. In Marcus *et al.* (1983) the names are used to account for certain coordination phenomena.

Also, a description differs from a tree in that precedence relations are not computed for nonterminals.

Consider, once more, the grammar in (33) and the resulting trees/
descriptions in (31).

(33)   A ----→ B C
         B ----→ a
         C ----→ D E
         D ----→ b
         E ----→ c
         E ----→ F G
         F ----→ c
         G ----→ d

(34a)

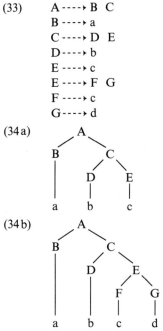

(34b)

The parser will initially encounter "a" and assert that d (B, a) and d (A,
B).[25] Next "b" is processed and the assertions d (D, b), d (C, D), and d (A,
C) are added to the description.[26] Despite the structural ambiguity, when
"c" is encountered, the parser does not need to choose between the
grammatical possibilities as, in either case, the assertion d (E, c) is true.
This is the only assertion concerning "c" that is justified by the input and
the only new assertion made at this point.

If the terminal string is the one in (34a), then the parse stops at this point.
Although the parser has not constructed a tree, but rather a description,
this description is interpreted by subsequent processors as a fully specified
tree, i.e. in the absence of conflicting information, the assertion d (E, c) is
interpreted as: E *directly dominates* c. In d-theory terms, the *standard
referent* of "dominates" is "directly dominates."

[25] I will put aside questions of whether the parse is top-down or bottom-up, or some
combination. I will give an arbitrary parse for the computation of nonterminals unrelated
to the issue at hand.

[26] I will omit precedence statements here as the d-theory parser does not compute precedence
relations for nonterminals. We return to the issue of the role of precedence in the next
chapter.

If the terminal string is, however, the one in (34b), the parser next encounters "d," then a grammatical description of this input requires the additional assertions: d (G, d), d (E, G), d (F, c), and d (E, F). Recall the structure-addition hypothesis of Frazier (1978), where the parser will initially compute "all and only as much structure as it had evidence for." If subsequent input forces reanalysis, the parser will reanalyze by either adding or altering structure, with structure-addition thought to be less costly. Frazier and Fodor (1978) argued that MA allowed for a uniform theory of reanalysis, i.e. that reanalysis would always involve adding nodes to the structure. Given this, we can think of d-theory as a particular instantiation of this approach, although numerous other assumptions vary. The descriptions in (34a) and (34b) can also be depicted as in (35a) and (35b) respectively.

(35a) d (B, a)   (35b) d (B, a)
       d (A, B)   d (A, B)
       d (D, b)   d (D, b)
       d (C, D)   d (C, D)
       d (A, C)   d (A, C)
       d (E, c)   d (E, c)
                           d (G, d)
                           d (E, G)
                           d (F, c)
                           d (E, F)

If we view descriptions as sets of dominance statements, then one description may be the subset of another. The description in (35a) is a subset of the one in (35b). Thus the "reanalysis" of the description of the string "abc" to a description of the string "abcd" does not violate determinism as all structure created by the parser (i.e. nodes and assertions of dominance relations) are part of the final output.[27]

For the processing of a sentence such as (31) the parser will initially assert that the NP *my aunt* is dominated by the VP. As additional input is received, additional assertions are made structuring this NP as part of a specifier of a larger NP *my aunt from Peoria's car*. This lowering of the NP does not require the parser to retract any dominance assertions as the NP *my aunt* remains dominated by the VP in the final output of the parse.

---

[27] There is a superficial similarity to the monotonicity claim (the Subset Principle) for the development of syntactic knowledge (Berwick 1985). But the motivations are quite distinct.

The d-theory parser is not as unconstrained as it might appear. This is because the parser makes attachment decisions based on a grammar consisting of explicit phrase-structure rules. Thus, the parser might employ a rule, e.g. A → B C, which encodes information concerning direct domination, but will construct a description that asserts only dominance relations (d (A, B)), The parser cannot make the assertion d (A, B) unless the grammar contains either (i) a rule stating that A directly dominates B in some environment, or (ii) a set of rules which would generate a structure in which A dominates B. Within d-theory, direct dominance is the "standard referent" for dominance, i.e. in the absence of conflicting information dominance is interpreted as direct dominance.[28]

A point to which we return in the next chapter is that this move from "directly dominates" to "dominates" has been mirrored by independent developments in GB theory. Recall from Chapter 2 that phrase-structure rules (assumed to be part of the grammar for a d-theory parser) encode information concerning direct dominance. But, as described in Chapter 2, the elimination of phrase-structure rules, in favor of wellformedness principles for phrase structure, also eliminates the necessity to refer to the direct domination of one maximal projection by another.

For example, consider the notion of direct object. In a phrase-structure grammar this position is generated by the rule VP → V NP, where the VP directly dominates the NP. But what is required within current GB theory is not that the object be immediately dominated by the VP, but that it be governed by the verb. This, in turn, requires (among other things) that all maximal projections dominating the object NP also dominate the verb. But the concept of direct dominance is never specifically required. We will see in the next chapter that this will allow us to dispense with the move from representations to descriptions (or, more generally, under-specification).

3.4   Minimal commitment theory

Barton and Berwick (1985) propose an "assertion set" approach to deterministic parsing. Just as the underspecification of descriptions in d-theory allows a deterministic parse of certain ambiguities problematic for the Marcus parser, the computation of (initially) underspecified assertion

---

[28] An important question is: Interpreted by what? Within d-theory this is done by the "semantic interpreter." But, as will become clear in Chapter 4, this begs the important question of the status of secondary syntactic relations (such as government) which refer to dominance and precedence relations.

sets permits the parser, at points of ambiguity, to "go ahead with the *common elements* of competing syntactic analyses [emphasis in original]." That is, if syntactic structures are viewed as sets of statements concerning node labels and structural relations, a generalization of the d-theory approach is possible.[29] Further, Barton and Berwick (1985) indicate that this approach may allow for an elimination of the lookahead device of the Marcus parser by "the implementation of a *wait-and-see* strategy [emphasis in original]."

Thus, as the parse proceeds, "information is monotonically preserved," and the only possible type of reanalysis is structure addition, i.e. either adding a new assertion or adding features to one that is underspecified. For example, a category labelled initially as [− N] might, at some later point in the parse, be specified as [− N, + V]. What is not permitted is to change a [− N] feature to [+ N]. Also, as in d-theory, dominates (and not directly dominates) is taken to be the predicate of hierarchical relations.

Weinberg (1988) refers to this type of device as a "minimal commitment" parser and argues that the lookahead buffer of Marcus (1980), and retained by Marcus *et al.* (1983), can be eliminated if initial underspecification is permitted. Consider the ambiguities (36) and (37).

(36a)   Mary expects Fred
(36b)   Mary expected Fred to leave

(37a)   Since Jay always jogs a mile it seems like a very short distance to him
(37b)   Since Jay always jogs a mile seems like a very short distance to him

As discussed above in the context of Frazier and Rayner's (1982) experimental work, the ambiguities involve the attachment of the post-verbal NPs as either objects of the preceding verbs or subjects of the following clauses. Weinberg (1988) points out that a minimal commitment parser can deterministically parse these sentences and also account for the Frazier and Rayner (1982) observation that the (b) sentences produce eye-movement patterns indicative of processing disruptions (see below). Weinberg (1988) argues that "At the ambiguous point, the parser will simply add as many statements to its assertion set as it can make with full confidence." If the sentences continue as in the (b) cases, then "the parser must add to its assertion set and so we would expect longer gaze duration

---

[29] Note that it cannot be the case that a structural representation for an input string is simply a set whose members constitute an unordered list of assertions concerning structural relations. Some internal organization of the set is required.

at this point." Therefore, in each case, the parse is deterministic in that information is monotonically preserved.

However, Pritchett (1987 and subsequent work) points out that the resolution of the ambiguity in (37b) leads to a conscious garden-path effect whereas the resolution in (36b) does not. He argues that the observed preference to structure the post-verbal NPs as direct objects follows from the parser computing an initial, maximally licensed, structure. Pritchett (1988) argues that "Every principle of the syntax attempts to be satisfied at every point during processing." Garden-path effects occur when the domain of reanalysis is exceeded. I will discuss Pritchett's model in detail in the next section, continuing to focus here on the minimal commitment approach.

The inability to distinguish the processing of (36b) and (37b) in Weinberg (1988) stems from the fact that the proposed parsing model did not have any property which forced a dominance assertion between *a mile* and the preceding VP in (37b). That is, the parser need only posit the structural relations "it can make with full confidence." Weinberg (1992) addresses this problem by incorporating Pritchett's incremental licensing approach. Given this, the contrast between (36b) and (37b) is due to the fact that, in each case, the post-verbal NP is analyzed as part of the preceding VP, but only in (36b) does this relation remain true as subsequent input is processed.

At this point it is necessary to consider in detail the implications of the elimination of lookahead in minimal commitment theory. An important question is this: Within d-theory, why was the lookahead device retained? The answer is actually quite simple, but no less surprising. It is impossible to maintain determinism of syntactic processing without a lookahead device. To understand why this is so, it is necessary to examine the use of the term *information* in the various models being considered.

In Marcus (1980) a parse was considered deterministic if and only if all information represented in the grammatical representation was preserved throughout the parse. Given the rule-based grammar that was assumed, this required that a node's final structural position (represented by direct dominance and precedence relations) also be its initial position. This also meant that the output of any interpretive processing dependent upon structural relations must remain constant throughout the parse.

Although the computational benefits of determinism are clear, there is a tremendous cost in terms of psychological plausibility. That is, if a node's initial attachment must be its final attachment, then attachment must be delayed until disambiguating information is processed. This delay is accomplished, of course, by the lookahead device. But sentence comprehension does not exhibit the types of pauses and delays that intermittent use of the lookahead buffer would predict. Therefore, in terms of psychological models of sentence processing, the elimination of lookahead is imperative.[30]

But now consider the implication if deterministic models must make incremental attachment decisions. Although the move is unstated, minimal commitment theory departs from the determinism hypothesis of Marcus (1980) in a radical way.[31] Consider some of the structural relations of GB theory discussed in Chapter 2, listed in (38). Consider also the incremental parse of (39).

(38a)   dominance
(38b)   precedence
(38c)   government
(38d)   c-command
(38e)   theta assignment
(38f)   case assignment
(38g)   binding

(39)   Ian knows Thomas is a train

In the Marcus parser, when *Thomas* is encountered, the lookahead device is used before an attachment is made. In addition to the attachment being delayed, i.e. relations (38a) and (38b) being posited, the realization of all other relations (38c–g) are delayed as well. This is what causes the problematic delay in interpretation that is absent from natural language processing.

[30] Van de Koot (1990) argues that a lookahead device is able to account for the contrast between (36b) and (37b) if it is assumed that for (36) the parser accesses the multiple subcategorization possibilities of *expect*, finds that the following NP fails to disambiguate, and thus uses lookahead for disambiguation.

For (37), on the other hand, *jog* occurs either with or without an NP and the appearance of *a mile* falsely appears to be sufficient disambiguation and the parser fails to make use of its lookahead capability. This explanation hinges on the fact that the matrix clause attachment is not considered. But the point is valid. However, the more general argument against lookahead, that it is inconsistent with incremental interpretation, still holds.

[31] This is clearly shown by the concept of *indelibility* inherent in the determinism hypothesis. Consider the definition given in (i), from McDonald (1979), cited in Church (1982). Although stated in terms of a production model, it captures the generality of Marcus' (1980) Determinism Hypothesis.

(i)   *Indelibility*: "Once a linguistic decision has been made, it cannot be retracted – it has been written with 'indelible ink'... It requires *every* choice made during the production process, at whatever level, cannot be changed once it has been made – choices must be made correctly the first time [emphasis in original]."

A minimal commitment parser, on the other hand, will immediately attach *Thomas* as dominated by the matrix VP (relation [38a]). This follows from Pritchett's principle of maximal licensing. In this position, the immediate realization of relations (35c–g) follows.[32] Thus the NP is governed by the verb and assigned a theta role and case. This permits incremental interpretation and avoids the problems inherent in lookahead. But when the embedded verb is encountered, all the relations (35c–g) must be reanalyzed. Within minimal commitment theory, it is not clear how this is done. Weinberg (1993) states that minimal commitment "architecture has no substantive theory of reanalysis." In fact, it is a standard argument for minimal commitment theory that it retains the computational advantages of deterministic models, without the additional complexity of either a lookahead device or a reanalysis component.

But it is clear that a minimal commitment parser is not a deterministic mechanism. The elimination of lookahead is only plausible insofar as secondary relations (see Chapter 2) are somehow immune to the mono-tonicity criterion.[33] Further, there must be a reanalysis component for these relations. This is no small matter as these relations (38c–g) are, in an important respect, the defining characteristics of principle-based grammars such as GB. Put more simply, a GB-based parser cannot be defined as deterministic if relations such as government and binding are not subject to determinism. Given this, an accurate characterization of a minimal commitment parser is as a serial parser which requires a backtracking component. This does not diminish the interest of this type of parser, but it does alter the criteria of evaluation. That is, the discussion shifts from the unsound conceptual argument concerning the existence of a reanalysis component to the unaddressed empirical argument concerning the nature of reanalysis in a GB-based parser. In the next section I discuss the principle-based parser of Pritchett (1992). This issue of reanalysis is one of Pritchett's main concerns. Pritchett's early work (1987, 1988) was the first to investigate the role of the grammar, not only in determining initial attachment decisions, but also in delimiting the operations of the reanalysis component.

---

[32] The precedence relation (38b) has an uncertain status in minimal commitment theory. See Chapter 4 for discussion.

[33] This issue of what is and is not subject to determinism was first raised, to my knowledge, by Stuart Shieber (quoted in Marcus 1987). Shieber, commenting on a talk on d-theory given by Marcus, asked, "The kind of stuff that some of the older systems used to do deterministically is now being split between something, one part of which is deterministic and one part of which isn't. Now that sort of leads you down a slippery slope where you start dumping stuff off to other things which don't have to be deterministic. Where does that stop?" I take up this issue in Chapter 4.

3.5   Generalized Theta Attachment and reanalysis

In Chapter 2 we saw that phrase-structure results from the interactions of various components of the grammar: X-bar theory, theta theory, case theory, etc. Pritchett (1987, 1992) is one of the first researchers to fully explore the implications of this conception of the grammar for parsing theory. That is, if the particular phrase structure for a terminal string is the interaction of X-bar theory and of modules of the grammar such as case theory and theta theory, then a reasonable hypothesis is that the computation of phrase structure in perception is driven by the on-line application of these grammatical principles. But, in a theory such as GB, in which wellformedness filters (e.g. ECP, Case Filter, Theta Criterion, Projection Principle, etc.) constrain the output of the overgenerating "structure generators," e.g. X-bar theory and Move alpha, it is not clear how to constrain overgeneration on-line (Berwick 1991). One approach to parsing design within a GB framework would be to reformulate the filters as constraints on structure formation. This is not trivial as structure must often be computed before it is possible to meet the conditions imposed by the filter. For example, a string-initial NP cannot receive case until a case assigner has been processed and the appropriate structure projected.

Pritchett (1992) investigates the implications of the manner in which phrase structure is generated within GB for theories of sentence comprehension. In particular, he focuses on the processing of structurally ambiguous strings. He also addresses a fundamental concern of serial parsing models: why do some structural ambiguities lead to garden-path effects whereas others appear to be unproblematic? As Pritchett (1992) elaborates and improves upon the proposal in Pritchett (1987, 1988), I will restrict the discussion to the more recent work.

Concerning the parser's initial structuring of the input, Pritchett assumes the properties in (40).

(40a)   Parsing is serial[34]

(40b)   Each lexical item is attached as it is encountered

(40c)   Attachment is motivated by principles of grammar (e.g. Case Filter, Theta Criterion, binding principles)

Pritchett formulates the motivation for initial attachment as a principle of Generalized Theta Attachment (GTA), given in (41).

---

[34] Pritchett (1992) notes that his approach is consistent with a version of ranked-parallelism in which the ranking is determined by properties of theta-attachment and the OLLC (to be discussed below). I will discuss Pritchett's model in terms of serial processing as he does not pursue the ranked-parallel approach.

(41) *GTA*: Every principle of the syntax attempts to be maximally satisfied at every point during processing.

There is an implied conditional in this formulation of the GTA: if there is a choice between a structure which satisfies a principle of syntax and a structure which does not, then choose the structure in which the principle can be satisfied. This addresses the fact that local satisfaction of principles such as the Case Filter is not always possible, e.g. a string-initial NP cannot be assigned grammatical features until subsequent material is processed.

In general, (41) predicts a preference for argument attachment over adjunct attachment. This is because argument attachment allows satisfaction of grammatical principles such as the Case Filter and the Theta Criterion. This follows from a central aspect of GB theory, i.e. principles of the various subtheories of grammar invariably focus on arguments rather than adjuncts. Thus the parser's satisfaction of these principles will favor an analysis of incoming items as arguments rather than adjuncts. We will see in subsequent discussion that this preference is predicted in different ways in different parsing models. For example, Frazier (1990) notes that it follows from the postulation of a separate thematic processor which operates in parallel with the structure building mechanism (Rayner *et al.* 1983). That is, argument attachments can be evaluated by the thematic processor and either confirmed or automatically reanalyzed. But adjunct attachments cannot benefit from the immediate evaluation of the thematic processor as adjuncts are nonthematic elements.

Returning to Pritchett's proposal, let us look at the familiar ambiguity of the sentence in (42) in terms of Pritchett's approach.

(42) Ian knows Thomas...

When the initial item *Ian* is encountered, lexical information, in conjunction with X-bar theory, will cause the parser to project a NP. Although the grammar requires that a NP receive case and a theta role, the parse does not fail at this point because there are no available case or theta-role assigners. Next, the parser inputs *knows* and an IP and VP are projected for the inflected verb. When *Thomas* is encountered, it is analyzed as an NP. Although this NP may be either a direct object of the verb or the subject of an embedded clause, the Case Filter and Theta Criterion attempt to be satisfied before any additional input is processed (i.e. the parser does not have a lookahead capacity).

The only available case and theta-role assigner is the verb *know*. Because case and theta roles are assigned under government, the parser will compute a structure in which the verb governs the NP *Thomas* and not one in which government is blocked by intervening maximal projections. This predicts that the parser will not compute the structure in which the post-verbal NP is the subject of an embedded clause, even though this analysis is compatible with the lexical specifications of the verb.

Pritchett also addresses the question of the parser's response when subsequent lexical material forces a reanalysis of this initial structure. Pritchett formulates a condition on automatic reanalysis, the On-Line Locality Constraint (OLLC), given in (43).

(43)   *On-Line Locality Constraint*: Upon reanalysis, the target position (if any) assumed by a constituent must be governed or dominated by its source position.

Put this way, reanalysis is thought of as moving a constituent from one position in a tree to a second position in a revised tree. We need to be careful in our understanding of the term *position*. If we consider (44), it is clear that the NP *Thomas* must now be analyzed as the specifier of the embedded IP, as (45) illustrates.

(44)   Ian knows Thomas is

(45)

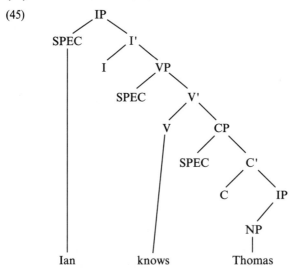

The source position of the NP *Thomas* before reanalysis (i.e. before the appearance of the verb *is*) was sister of the matrix V. That position is now occupied by the CP node. The prediction is that if that CP node either dominates or governs the NP in its new position (specifier of IP) then reanalysis is automatic. As (45) shows, the CP node does dominate the NP in its new position. Thus Pritchett's approach is consistent with Frazier and Rayner's (1982) experimental evidence for the parser initially attaching the post-verbal NP in (44) as a direct object. Further, it offers an explanation for why the subsequent reanalysis of this structure does not yield a garden-path effect.

Consider now another familiar ambiguity, one that produces a garden-path effect.

(46)   While Mary was mending the sock fell off her lap

As in (44) the parser will initially analyze the post-verbal NP as being governed by the verb (the motivation is identical). But consider now the structure required by the appearance of the verb *fall*.

(47)

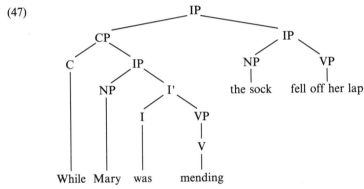

Here it is clear that the source position (sister of V) neither dominates nor governs the target position (specifier of the matrix IP). Here we must refer to the position "sister of V" even though, in the reanalyzed structure, there is no constituent occupying that position.

Consider now the contrast between the unproblematic ambiguity in (48) and the garden-path sentence in (49).

(48a)   Ian gave her earrings today
(48b)   Ian gave her earrings away

(49)   Ian put the candy on the table in his mouth

In (48a) the parser will initially attach *her* as an NP argument of *give*. When the noun *earrings* is processed, it projects an NP that is attached as the second object of the verb. Pritchett (1992) argues that this attachment follows from the parser attempting to maximally satisfy the Theta Criterion. But it is not the case that the syntactic realization of the second object is obligatory, i.e. the Theta Criterion would be fully satisfied if there were only one object. For example, if the recipient of the action is clear from the discourse, a single object is acceptable. Consider the discourse in (50) and how it contrasts with (51), where the verb *put* requires a locative phrase.

(50)   A: What does Mary give to the Red Cross?
        B: She usually gives some money.
(51)   A: What does Mary put in this closet?
        B: * She usually puts her coat.

Thus it appears that the principles of syntax are satisfied with an analysis of (48a) in which *her earrings* is analyzed as a single NP with *her* as specifier.[35] One way of forcing the double object analysis would be to say that if a verb has two potential theta-roles to assign, the parser will prefer an analysis which permits both roles to be assigned. This was exactly what Pritchett stated in a preliminary version of Theta-Attachment. Compare this version, given in (52), with (41).

(52)   *Theta-Attachment*: The Theta Criterion attempts to be satisfied at
        every point during processing, given the maximal theta-grid.

The maximal theta-grid of *give* contains two internal theta-roles. Given (52), or (41) with the understanding that maximal satisfaction of the Theta Criterion requires (if possible) a syntactic realization of the maximal theta grid, the parser will analyze the string *her earrings* as two NPs, each receiving a theta-role. We will return to this issue of the parser's initial response to strings such as (48a), but let us continue to assume Pritchett's analysis and see how (48b), where the initial analysis is disconfirmed, is parsed. It will be useful to look at the phrase-structure for the VPs in (48a) and (48b), given in (53a) and (53b), in order to understand the applicability of the OLLC to these structures.[36]

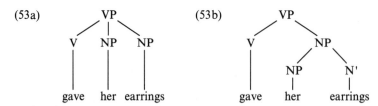

Recall that the OLLC refers to the source and target positions of reanalyzed constituents. In (48a) we must consider two constituents, the

---

[35] Note that Late Closure predicts that *her earrings* will be processed as a constituent. See the discussion of the parse of *Without her contributions* ... in (9b), Section 3.1.
[36] Following Pritchett (1992), I will assume a trinary branching structure for the double object construction. The present discussion, as well as subsequent analyses of the parsing of these constructions, can be carried over to a binary-branching analysis (Kayne 1984).

NP *her* and the NP *earrings*. If (53a) is the parser's initial analysis, then the source position is sister of V. The target position (shown in [53b]) is dominated by this position. Thus this reanalysis is unproblematic. The OLLC is trivially satisfied with respect to the NP *earrings* as the source and target positions are identical. That is, before reanalysis this NP is a sister of V and it remains so after reanalysis.[37]

Consider now the garden-path sentence (49), with the tree in (54) showing the structure of the VP after reanalysis.

(54)

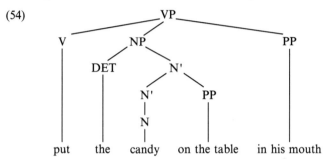

Initially, the parser will have analyzed the PP *on the table* as the locative argument of the verb (and not as an adjunct within the NP). Thus the source position for this phrase is the current position of the PP *in his mouth*. The OLLC correctly predicts the difficulty of this sentence because the source position fails to dominate or govern the target position.[38]

We turn next to sentences such as (55a), which produce a garden-path effect. The structure of the VP before the appearance of the embedded verb is given in (55b). The VP after reanalysis is given in (55c).

(55a)   Susan convinced her friends were unreliable

(55b)

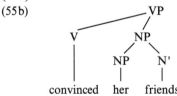

---

[37] Note that implicit in this analysis is the unproblematic reanalysis of theta-role labels. I return to this issue in Chapter 4.

[38] Similar remarks apply to sentences such as (i) and (ii).

(i)   John gave the boy the dog bit a bandage
(ii)   John gave the man the report criticized a demotion

Here the parser will initially attach the second post-verbal NP as the second object of the verb. Subsequent lowering into the relative clause creates a structure in which the target position is neither dominated by nor governed by the source position.

(55c)

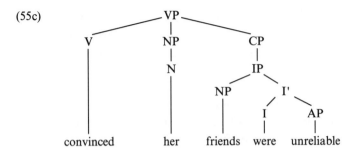

convinced   her   friends were unreliable

Sentence (55a) produces a garden-path effect because the parser initially builds an NP *her friends* whereas the correct analysis requires two NPs: one, the internal argument of *convince* and a second, the subject of the CP complement. Automatic reanalysis fails because the source position of *friends* fails to either dominate the target position (as it does in [44]) or govern this position (as it does in [48b]).

Let us now see how GTA and the OLLC predict the garden-path status of sentences such as (56). The initial analysis of the parser is given in (57a), with (57b) the tree resulting from reanalysis.

(56)   The boat floated down the river sank

(57a)

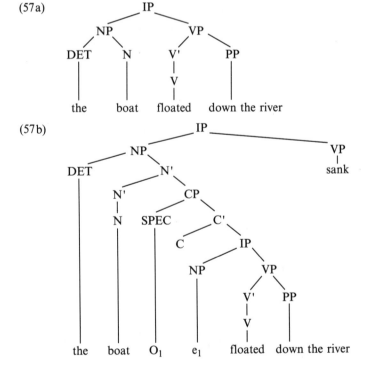

(57b)

The parser initially analyzes the NP *the boat* as the specifier of the IP, as (57a) indicates. The appearance of the verb *sink* disconfirms this analysis. The OLLC is violated as the source position of the N *boat* neither dominates nor governs the target position (as shown in [57b]).

Thus the GTA and the OLLC succeed in accounting for a variety of contrasts between problematic and unproblematic reanalyses. Pritchett's approach is of interest because it characterizes the role of abstract structural relations such as *government* and *dominance* in the operations of the parser. In doing so, Pritchett has addressed an important aspect of serial parsing models: the reanalysis component.

Recall that the OLLC is stated in terms of dominance and government. It's useful to think of the OLLC as a characterization of how close two elements must be in order for backtracking to be successful. Here "two elements" must refer to the target and source *positions* mentioned in the OLLC definition, NOT two constituents of the tree. As the discussion of sentence (46) made clear, the OLLC must apply even if there is no constituent occupying the source position. So, the OLLC is not a locality condition on the relation between two phrases in a structure, as is the case for syntactic relations such as government and binding.[39] Thus the OLLC is not of the form: if phrase XP bears some relation to phrase YP before reanalysis, this relation must still hold after reanalysis.

Thus, although the OLLC refers to the syntactic predicates dominance and government, these predicates do not define syntactic relations (as they do in the competence grammar). Thus we could not define either dominance or government in terms of the formal characterization of a phrase-structure tree, as discussed in Chapter 2. There, syntactic relations are, necessarily, relations between nodes in a tree. Given this, the OLLC is best viewed as a characterization of the type of structure alteration that can be performed by the reanalysis device.

But it is clear that the parser's initial structure-building operations are not restricted to a locality domain defined in terms of either predicate. Consider the sentences in (58).

(58a)   What did Ian eat last night
(58b)   Did Ian eat last night

Berwick and Weinberg (1984) argue that the parser will postulate a trace after an ambiguous verb such as *eat* only if there is an antecedent in [SPEC,

---

[39] Many definitions of government not only refer to structural conditions on the relation of government but also refer to properties of the governor. If the definition of government makes crucial reference to a governor (as in Chomsky 1981; Rizzi 1990) then this definition may have to be amended for inclusion in the OLLC.

CP], as in (58a). When the parser is processing the VP it must have access to a position that neither dominates nor governs the parser's current position (which we might think of as the "source position" for the operation). This means that the OLLC cannot function as a locality constraint on the parser's first-pass capabilities, but rather is a particular property of the reanalysis component.

Thus, an interesting question for a parser incorporating an initial structure-building component and a separate reanalysis device is why the operation of structure alteration should exhibit properties distinct from, and more limited than, the properties of structure building. As we have seen, this was a question initially posed in Frazier (1978). Pritchett's contribution to this line of research has been to change the focus of the discussion from agrammatical parsing strategies to the role that the incremental application of subtheories of syntax plays in explaining garden-path phenomena.

In Chapter 4 I will adopt a, somewhat simplified, version of Generalized Theta Attachment. Indeed, some version of GTA must be a core property of any principle-based parser which builds structure incrementally. But I will argue that the OLLC can be dispensed with in favor of a more natural constraint on reanalysis, one making crucial reference to the distinction between primary and secondary structural relations.

3.6   Parallel processing and constraints on processing load

Gibson (1991) details an interesting computational approach to distinguishing ambiguities which produce garden-path effects from those that do not. In general, he proposes that the parser computes multiple analyses in parallel when confronted with ambiguous input. Certain ambiguities produce garden-path effects because the parser fails to pursue (i.e. abandons) alternative analyses for these ambiguities. Gibson introduces the concept of a *processing load unit* (PLU) for evaluating structures associated with a given input string. This unit is used to define a *preference constant* P that the parser uses to determine if alternative analyses should be preserved or only a unique analysis pursued. That is, the parser will respond to all ambiguities by computing multiple structures. In certain cases these structures will be pursued in parallel, in others only a single analysis will be maintained. This can be thought of as a form of ranked parallelism in which the ranking has only two values: *pursue* or *abandon*.[40]

---

[40] The discussion of Gibson's parser will focus on how the pursue/abandon decision is made for the structures computed by the parser rather than the initial structure-building operations. See Gibson (1991, Chapter 4) for details.

Parallel processing is maintained if there is not a sufficiently strong preference for one analysis over its competitors, where preference is determined by the constant P. Preference is evaluated after each operation of the parser. PLUs are associated with certain properties of the parse state defined in terms of concepts within GB theory. For example, Gibson refers to the *Property of Thematic Reception* (59) as the dynamically applied Theta Criterion and the *Property of Lexical Requirement* (60) as the dynamically applied Projection Principle. Note that, unlike Pritchett (1992), Gibson's parser is a specifically *theta*-driven parser. In this regard it is similar in spirit to the proposal of Pritchett (1987) in which structure building was motivated by the Theta Criterion in particular, not grammatical principles in general.

(59)   *Property of Thematic Reception* (PTR): Associate a load of X(tr) PLUs to each constituent that is in a position to receive a theta role in some coexisting structure, but whose theta assigner is not unambiguously identifiable in the structure in question.

(60)   *Property of Lexical Requirement* (PLR): Associate a load of X(lr) PLUs to each lexical requirement that is obligatory in some coexisting structure, but is satisfied by an H-node[41] constituent containing no thematic elements in the structure in question.

In English the theta assigner for a subject NP is not identified when the subject is processed. Thus at that point in the parse the PTR states that the structure would be associated with 1(tr).[42] That is, there is a structure with one constituent that lacks a theta role but is in a theta position. We will see that the PTR is also applicable to certain argument–adjunct ambiguities.

The phrase "coexisting structure" refers to an alternative structure in which an identical copy of a constituent appears. For two constituents to be considered identical, Gibson (1991) states that they must "represent the same segment of the input string and they must have exactly the same X-bar structure, including the same lexical items as structural heads."

The PLR associates a processing load with representations in which the structure that would satisfy the lexical requirements of a particular head has been hypothesized, but as yet contains no thematic elements. Given (59) and (60), we can apply them to the parse of a simple sentence such as (61).

---

[41] An *H-node* is a hypothesized node, that is, part of a structure that is computed in advance of the appearance of lexical items.
[42] Gibson assumes that there will be a structure computed in which the initial NP of a string is structured as subject of a matrix clause, a theta position.

(61)   Fred likes Sue

When *Fred* is processed, the parser will build a structure with this NP as the subject of a clause.[43] This is a theta position but there is no identified theta assigner, so a PLU of 1(tr) is associated with the structure. When *likes* is processed it is identified as a theta assigner for the subject NP so that the PLU of 1(tr) is no longer associated with the structure. But now *likes* requires a nominal complement which has yet to appear. Thus the structure is associated with 1(lr) until *Sue* is processed. The PTR and the PLR predict that the parser will prefer argument attachment over adjunct attachment, as the former, but not the latter, satisfies thematic and lexical requirements (cf. Pritchett's Theta-Attachment Principle [1987]).

Certain nonthematic elements such as semantically-null complementizers (e.g. *that*) and prepositions (e.g. *of*) are subject to the Property of Thematic Transmission (62).

(62)   *Property of Thematic Transmission*: Associate a load of X(tt) PLUs to each semantically null category in a position that can receive a thematic role, but whose lexical requirement is currently satisfied by a hypothesized constituent containing no thematic elements.

Gibson's parser will compute hypothesized (H-) nodes in advance of their lexical realization. Unlike the operation of precomputation discussed in Section 3.2, Gibson allows optional as well as obligatory H-nodes. Consider a string such as *Ian realizes that* where the verb assigns a thematic role to its CP complement. Gibson's analysis is that this role is received by the CP and then must be transmitted to the IP complement of the complementizer (i.e. to the semantic object of the verb). The PTT associates a load of X(tt) with the complementizer *that* until a thematic element of the IP is processed (e.g. the subject NP). The reasoning is that the complementizer, in addition to satisfying its own lexical requirements, must also play the role of intermediary in the assignment of a theta-role from the verb to the IP.

Before applying these properties to the processing of ambiguous structures, it should be noted that Gibson's work reveals that the PLUs associated with the three properties cannot be equated. The PTR and the PLR do appear to be associated with equivalent PLUs and Gibson refers

---

[43] This assumes that NPs are attached to clausal nodes prior to the (possible) appearance of clausal elements such as verbs.

to this as X(int), where *int* is an abbreviation for *interpretation*, a reference to the Principle of Full Interpretation (Chomsky 1986b) from which it is hoped that both the Theta Criterion and the Projection Principle can be derived. Thus Gibson refers to the load associated with either the PTR or the PLR as X(int), while the term X(tt) is reserved for the load associated with the PTT.

Consider how Gibson's parallel approach, constrained by the preference constant, accounts for which ambiguities produce garden-path effects and which do not. Consider the contrast between (63) and (64).

(63)   Ian knew Mary (was ill)

(63a)   [$_{IP}$ [$_{NP}$ Ian] [$_{VP}$ knew [$_{NP}$ Mary]]]

(63b)   [$_{IP}$ [$_{NP}$ Ian] [$_{VP}$ knew [$_{IP}$ [$_{NP}$ Mary]]]]

(64)   Ian put the candy on the table in his mouth

(64a)   [$_{VP}$ [$_{V'}$ [$_{V}$ put] [$_{NP}$ the candy] [$_{PP}$ [$_{P}$ on] [$_{NP}$]]]]]

(64b)   [$_{VP}$ [$_{V'}$ [$_{V}$ put] [$_{NP}$ the candy [$_{PP}$ [$_{P}$ on] [$_{NP}$]]]]]]

For (63) the parser will compute the two structures (63a) and (63b). Structure (63a) is associated with 0 PLUs as there are no NPs in theta positions without an identified theta assigner or unsatisfied lexical requirements. Nor are there any semantically null theta transmitters. (63a) is a grammatically complete clause. However, (63b) is associated with 1(int), i.e. 1(tr), as the NP *Mary* is in a theta position (subject of the embedded clause) but there is no identified theta assigner. Given that (i) the ambiguity in (63) does not produce a garden-path effect, and (ii) the difference, in X(int) PLUs, between the structures is 1, Gibson concludes that the ranking of a structure with a processing load 1(int) more than the preferred structure (i.e. the structure associated with the least PLUs) is not sufficient for the parser to abandon that structure, as shown in (65). Therefore the parser pursues both structures and is prepared for (i.e. has computed a structure compatible with) either resolution of the ambiguity.

(65)   1(int) < P

Thus 1(int) is less than the preference constant P, the critical value for abandoning a less preferred structure. The ambiguity in (64), unlike the one in (63), does produce a garden-path effect and Gibson's approach accounts for this as follows. The (a) reading of the ambiguity, where the PP is attached as an argument of the verb, is associated with 1(int), i.e. 1(lr), because the preposition *on* requires an object which has not yet been processed. There are no other PLUs associated with (64a). However, (64b), where the PP is attached as a modifier of the nominal, is associated with 3(int). It is associated with 1(lr) as the verb *put* has an unsatisfied lexical requirement for a locative phrase (satisfied by the argument PP in [64a]). It is associated with an additional 1(lr) as the preposition *on* (as in [64a]) has an unsatisfied lexical requirement. The structure in (64b) is associated with a third PLU, 1(tr), as the PP receives a theta role in a coexisting structure (64a) but has no identified theta assigner in (64b).

Thus the difference between the preferred structure, (64a) with 1(int), and the less-preferred structure, (64b) with 3(int), is 2(int). Given the garden path status of (64), Gibson concludes that this is sufficient for the parser to abandon (64b). This is stated in (66).

(66)   2(int) > P

The association of PLUs with the two structures for sentence (64) illustrates the strong preference for argument over adjunct attachment. For example, if a constituent is attached as an obligatory argument of a verb, then (i) the verb assigns a theta role to that constituent and (ii) the verb's lexical requirement is satisfied. On the other hand, if a constituent is attached as an adjunct then a theta role remains unassigned and the verb's lexical requirement is still unmet. This means that attaching a constituent as an adjunct when it can be attached as an obligatory argument is predicted to always lead to a garden-path effect as such an attachment is associated with 2(int).

This approach accounts for the garden-path status of (67) as well.

(67)   The horse raced past the barn (fell)
(67a) $[_{IP} [_{NP}$ the horse $] [_{VP}$ raced $]]$
(67b) $[_{IP} [_{NP}$ the $[_{N'} [_{N}$ horse$_1$ $[_{CP}$ O$_1$ $[_{IP} [_{VP}$ raced e $]]]]]]$

The structure (67a) is associated with 0 PLUs as there are no unassigned theta roles or unmet lexical expectations. As with (63a), it is grammatically complete. Structure (67b) is associated with 2(int). The first is due to the fact that the theta assigner of the subject NP has not been identified (1(tr)), the second an additional X(tr) due to the fact that the operator (O$_1$) is in a position that can receive a theta role, but has not yet. It has not because it has not yet been coindexed with the empty object of *raced*, *e*. Recall that we noted above that preference is evaluated after each operation of the parser. With respect to (67b), this means that preference is evaluated after the operator has been attached but before it is coindexed with the empty category in the object position (with which it forms a chain receiving a theta role). Thus, the difference between the preferred and less preferred structure is 2(int) which exceeds the preference constant. Therefore the parser abandons (67b) and a garden-path effect occurs if subsequent material is compatible only with this analysis.

An interesting prediction of Gibson's approach is that, if the preferred structure in (67a) were, in some sense, *less preferred* (by being associated with additional PLUs), then the parser might continue to pursue both the preferred structure and an alternative which would otherwise have been abandoned. Gibson discusses sentences such as (68) as confirmation of this prediction.

(68)   The bird found in the room was dead

(68a) $[_{IP} [_{NP}$ the bird $] [_{VP} [_{V'} [_{V}$ found $[_{NP}$]]]]]

(68b) $[_{IP} [_{NP}$ the $[_{N'} [_{N}$ bird$_1 [_{CP}$ O$_1 [_{IP} [_{VP}$ found e]]]]]]]]

As with (67b), structure (68b) is associated with 2(int) PLUs. The structures are identical. However, (68a), unlike (67a), is associated with 1(int) as the lexical requirement of *found*, which is obligatorily transitive, is not yet met. Thus the difference between (68a) and (68b) is 1(int), as was true of (63a) and (63b), and no garden-path effect is predicted for (68).

But this account cannot be extended to examples such as those in (69) and (70).

(69a)   The children painted with bright paint all morning

(69b)   The children painted with bright colors were delighted

(70a)   The children walked to the principal's office today

(70b)   The children walked to the principal's office were upset

The verbs *paint* and *walk* may occur either with or without an object, but *paint*, unlike *walk*, is preferentially transitive (Connine *et al.* 1984). This lexical difference appears to affect the acceptability of the (b) sentences in (69) and (70). Intuition suggests that (69b) is easier to process than (70b). Thus it appears that lexical information plays a role in how these strings are parsed. I return to this issue in Chapter 4.

In general, Gibson's approach accounts for certain garden-path effects as the result of the parser abandoning a particular analysis of an ambiguity before material confirming that analysis appears. Ambiguities that are resolved without conscious effort are done so because the parser has continued to pursue an analysis that is confirmed by, or consistent with, disambiguating information. Let us now examine some perceptual phenomena that demand two additional properties associating structures with PLUs, the Property of Recency Preference, which can be stated as in (71), and the Principle of Preference Closure (72). The intent of (72) is, in part, to limit the number of possible attachment sites that must be evaluated by the parser. The Property of Recency Preference merely states the output of such an evaluation, but does not limit the increasing number of structures a parallel parser must consider in, for example, right-branching constructions.

(71)   *Property of Recency Preference* (PRP): The load associated with the structure resulting from attachment involving either a thematic or arbitrary H-node is equal to the number of more recent words that are associated with a corresponding thematic or arbitrary H-node.

(72)   *Principle of Preference Closure* (PPC): Given a structure, prune off all optional attachment sites in that structure whose processing loads after attachment would differ from a closure-comparable optional attachment site in that structure by at least the preference factor P PLUs.

Thus the units of the recency metric are either matching *thematic* or *arbitrary* nodes. A thematic H-node is a node that participates in either theta role assignment, transmission or reception. An arbitrary H-node is any H-node (including thematic H-nodes). Recall that Gibson's parser computes optional as well as obligatory H-nodes. So the PRP (unlike the earlier properties) is not limited to operations of theta-role assignment and reception. The PRP does require the parser, when processing a category (e.g. a verb), to construct H-nodes for all possible adjunct modifiers. It is the recency relations of matching H-nodes that are evaluated by the PRP. Consider the sentences (73) and (74), which exhibit strong recency effects.

(73)   Ian said Bill left yesterday

(74)   Ian figured that Mary took the cat out

For (73) the adverb *yesterday* may be attached as a modifier of either clause, but a strong preference exists for the embedded-clause attachment. The PRP can account for this preference in the following way. Attaching the adverb to the embedded clause results in a structure with 0 PLUs since the association is with the most recent word *left*. The matrix attachment, however, is associated with 1(rp) as there is 1 more recent matching word, i.e. *left*. Since this is the only difference between the structures, and the preference is quite strong, Gibson concludes that 1(rp) > P.

Similar remarks apply to (74). Here the relevant matching H-nodes will be the particle node associated with *figure* and the particle node associated with *take*. Again, the preference is for the more recent attachment. But this approach to these attachment preferences incorrectly predicts that if the embedded verb cannot be associated with a particle, that matrix attachment is unproblematic. This is because recency is stated in terms of a stack of H-nodes of a particular type. This is necessary for Gibson as the discussion of Kimball's (1973) and Church's (1980) Closure principles make clear.[44] Thus (75) is incorrectly predicted to be readily parsed.

(75)   Ian figured that Mary fed the cat out

But the association of the particle with the matrix verb in (75) is quite difficult, on a par with (74). Empirical problems with the PRP are important because this principle is instrumental in accounting for the garden-path status of familiar sentences such as (76).

(76)   While Mary was mending the sock fell off her lap
(76a)   while [$_{IP}$ [$_{NP}$ Mary [$_I$ was [$_{VP}$ mending [$_{NP}$ the sock]]]]] [$_{IP}$]
(76b)   while [$_{IP}$ [$_{NP}$ Mary [$_I$ was [$_{VP}$ mending]]] [$_{IP}$ [$_{NP}$ the sock]]]

With respect to the PTR, PLR and PTT, the structure in (76a) is associated with 0 PLUs as it is a complete clause. The structure in (76b) is associated with 1 PLU as the NP *the sock* does not have an identified theta assigner. Thus the difference between these two structures appears to be only 1(int), insufficient to account for the garden-path effect. But the PRP is applicable to (76) in the following way. As the structures in (76) indicate, each preposed clause is associated with a matrix IP. This H-node can be constructed when the initial clause is first processed. At the point in the parse after *mend* is processed, the structure (76a) will have two H-nodes, the matrix IP and the more recent NP object of *mend*. The structure (76b) will only have the IP H-node as here *mend* is analyzed as an intransitive verb. Thus the attachment of the NP *the sock* as an object in (76a) is an

---

[44] See the discussion in Gibson (1991, Section 7.1). The details are irrelevant here. But the issue can be illustrated with a sentence such as (i).

(i)   I convinced the woman who I think John loves very much that she should call him.

The sentence is a bit awkward but there appears to be little difficulty in associating the clause *that she should call him* with the verb *convince*, despite the presence of the more recent verb *think* (not to mention *loves*).

attachment to the most recent H-node constructed. But the alternative attachment of the NP as the subject of the matrix clause is an attachment to an H-node constructed prior to the attachment site in (76a). Thus the attachment in (76b) violates the recency restriction.

Note that what this means is that recency must be stated, not in terms of nodes in a particular structure, but in nodes constructed for all structures as the parse proceeds.[45] Thus it does not matter that, in (76b), the NP is being attached to the most recent H-node *in that structure*. What is forced then, is the attachment of a constituent in the structure with the most recently constructed appropriate H-node to that H-node.

In addition to the problem that structures such as (75) pose for Gibson's account of recency phenomena, consider also a sentence such as (77), from Pritchett (1992).

(77)   Ian knew the horse raced past the barn fell

Embedding the ambiguous string *the horse raced past the barn* under a matrix predicate does not alleviate the garden-path effect. Yet, as originally pointed out by Amy Weinberg, accounts which appeal to the fact that, in the less-preferred structure, the NP lacks a theta role (or identified theta-role assigner) incorrectly predict that such strings will be easily processed in contexts where a theta-role assigner has been processed. This is the case in (77). Recall that the account of (67) was that the less-preferred structure was abandoned because it was associated with 2(tr) PLUs, whereas the preferred structure was associated with 0 PLUs. Recall also that a difference of 1(tr) between structures will result in both structures being pursued and an avoidance of a garden-path effect.

Given this, recall also that 1(tr) for (67) is due to the lack of an identified theta assigner for the NP. Sentences such as (77) illustrate that, contrary to Gibson's account, this cannot be contributing to the garden-path effect. In (77) the verb *know* is identified as a theta assigner for the NP *the horse raced past the barn*. Sentences such as (77) are incorrectly predicted to be as easy to parse as (63b).

It is important to note that the PTR, PLR, PTT, and PRP are not properties of the structure-building component of the parser, but rather they assign a particular value (in terms of PLUs) to each (partial) representation the parser has constructed. This value determines whether or not the parser pursues or abandons a particular structure, i.e. it is

---

[45] Note that a different explanation is needed to account for the garden-path in (i).

(i)   Mary was drinking the water was still in the bucket and the plants were all dead.

evaluated with respect to the constant P. But these properties are particular requirements of Gibson's parallel parser. Similar to the way that serial parsers often require a separate reanalysis component, the design of Gibson's parser requires a separate evaluation component. Yet it is clear that the preference constant that emerges from Gibson's study makes correct predictions for a wide range of data. The question remains whether or not such empirical adequacy necessitates the additional machinery.

In the next chapter I detail a GB-based parser that incorporates many of the aspects of the theories discussed here, but addresses certain conceptual and empirical difficulties that each presents. As stated in Chapter 1, the intent is not to argue for GB on psycholinguistic grounds, but to assume the basic framework of GB, and demonstrate that grammatical relations and concepts, developed solely for the purpose of constructing a precise theory of grammatical knowledge, play an important role in our understanding of the process of sentence comprehension.

4 *Properties of the parser*

Unfortunately, there is as yet no standard terminology in this field, so the author has followed the usual practice ... namely to use words that are similar but not identical to the terms used in other books.

Donald E. Knuth

4.0   Introduction

The properties of the parser described in this chapter are motivated by the form of the grammar and the speed and efficiency with which interpretive processes are able to make use of the structural representation constructed by the parser. Before detailing the specific properties of the parser I will first consider some general issues. One important question concerns the role of primary structural relations in a principle-based parser and its grammatical database.

Following the work of Pritchett (1987, 1992), a number of proposals of the last few years have sought to move from form-based parsing strategies such as Minimal Attachment (Frazier 1978) to content-based strategies (e.g. Pritchett's 1992 Generalized Theta Attachment or Crocker's 1992 Argument Attachment).[1] There appear to be two motivations for this. The first is based on the intuition that the form of a phrase marker (however that is instantiated, e.g. as a tree or reduced phrase marker, etc.) is, in some

---

[1] I have taken these terms from Crocker (1992). The distinction is important and Crocker's discussion is enlightening. In fact, the distinction has a long, but largely unnoted, history in parsing theory. For example, one might consider Frazier (1978) as arguing for a move from content-based strategies to form-based strategies. As mentioned in Chapter 3, Frazier argues that a more general account of parsing preferences can be given if one simply refers to the number (Minimal Attachment) or proximity (Late Closure) of nodes in a structure rather than to the content (labelling) of the nodes, as in Bever's (1970) parsing strategies.

Also, there are a number of recent computational approaches to parsing which focus on content-based strategies, e.g. Abney (1987), Berwick (1991), Fong (1991), and Frank (1991). I will not discuss these approaches here, continuing to focus on psychological theories of sentence comprehension.

sense, derivative or secondary whereas the licensing relations (theta, case, etc.) are more central in current linguistic theory. That is, the role of a particular structural form is to allow certain licensing relations to hold between elements in the representation. Thus, content-based approaches are taken to be more "grammatically responsible" than form-based models.

Crocker states that

> Within the principles and parameters view of grammar, structures are licensed and ruled out by independent constraints, resulting in a less direct correspondence between structural descriptions and the principles which license them. Thus representations become mere "artefacts" of syntactic analysis rather than fundaments. Therefore to emphasise the role of the form of representations seems misguided with respect to views of syntax. (1992: 27)

Certainly the role of the formal nature of a syntactic structure is altered when one moves from a rule-based to a principle-based parsing model (Berwick 1991). Following Pritchett (1987, 1992) I assume a principle-based parser, i.e. one in which structure building is driven by grammatical principles (e.g. case, theta-role assignment, etc.) rather than phrase-structure rules. But I will argue that the most explanatory manner in which to state constraints on structure building and reanalysis is the formal vocabulary of structural relations, i.e. dominance and precedence relations. As is clear from the discussion in Chapter 2, a principle-based grammar is not one which abandons structural relations in favor of licensing relations, but one which defines the necessary conditions for licensing to hold (e.g. government) in terms of the primary structural relations.

Consider the Japanese sentences in (1), from Inoue (1991).

(1a)   Bob-ga   Mary-ni   ring-o   tabeta inu-o   ageta
       Bob-NOM Mary-DAT apple-ACC ate   dog-ACC gave
       "Bob gave the dog who ate an apple to Mary"

(1b)   Bob-ga   Mary-ni   ring-o   ageta
       Bob-NOM Mary-DAT apple-ACC gave
       "Bob gave an apple to Mary"

For (1a), there is a "surprise" effect at the verb *tabeta*. This is due to the fact that this verb does not take a dative argument. This surprise effect is attributed to the parser (minimally) structuring the three pre-verbal NPs into a single clause, i.e. as arguments of a single verb. Inoue (1991) states that the parser "analyses NPs into a clause structure by reference to case particle information (but in advance of argument structure information)."[2] This structuring creates an expectation for a verb compatible with three arguments. Sentence (1b) shows that this is a grammatical possibility. But the computed structure is incompatible with *tabeta* and reanalysis is required.

But a content-based approach which referred to maximal licensing rather than minimal structuring could not predict the parser's preference for the single-clause analysis. This is because both grammatical structures involve licensed argument positions for the three NPs. The only relevant difference appears to be structural complexity.[3] The point here is that, once the licensing of structure is allowed prior to the appearance of a licenser, some form of licensing-independent constraint on structure building is required.

The second motivation for content-based models concerns the role of the parser within a more general theory of language comprehension. That is, parsing strategies facilitate rapid interpretation. This is usually taken to indicate a bias toward argument versus adjunct attachment. For example, Weinberg (1993) argues that "the incremental satisfaction of licensing constraints, particularly the Theta Criterion, allows the parser to perform incremental semantic interpretation." Crocker (1992) argues along similar lines. Here, content-based approaches, in contrast to form-based approaches, are taken to be more in keeping with the general requirement of incremental comprehension. But theta-based (or argument-based) models are no more compatible with incremental interpretation than any parsing model in which structure is computed on-line. For example, it is unclear in what way particular types of grammatical attachments are more readily interpreted than other types of grammatical attachments.[4] For example, consider the sentence in (2).

(2)   Ian put the candy in his mouth ...

In (2), as discussed in the last chapter, there is a clear bias for the argument attachment of the PP. But what properties of the comprehension system

---

[2] Weinberg (1993) refers to this process as "internal licensing."

[3] Note that it does not appear possible to attribute the "surprise" effect at *tabeta* in (1a) to a complexity effect arising from the need to build the relative clause structure when the verb is encountered. This is because relative clause construction in Japanese is always "*post hoc*" in this manner. Thus it remains unclear, in the absence of pre-verbal structuring, how one might account for the effect Inoue notes. We return to this issue in the section on Japanese processing.

[4] I put aside here a consideration of the proposal for a Thematic Processor (Rayner *et al.* 1983; Frazier 1990) which predicts that thematic attachments are evaluated more efficiently than nonthematic attachments.

interpret arguments more efficiently than adjuncts? Certainly in (2) there is the benefit of a complete proposition. But I am unaware of any content-based proposal which demonstrates how, in general, an argument attachment can be more efficiently interpreted than an adjunct attachment. Therefore, it seems doubtful that the argument-attachment bias of content-based approaches could actually follow from the demands of incremental interpretation. Note that this issue is distinct from that of satisfying lexical preferences (Ford *et al.* 1982) or semantic/pragmatic expectations (Kurtzman 1985). It may be that the particular properties of verb-initial VPs appear to give argument attachments an interpretive advantage.

Given this, it is important to consider the potential interpretive effects of the processing of pre-verbal material in a verb-final clause.[5] Although a precise characterization is stated in different ways in different theories, it is clear that arguments are, in some sense, more closely tied to heads than are adjuncts (e.g. arguments are sisters to heads, theta-marked by heads, etc.).[6] This is clear in the Dutch clause (3a), discussed by Frazier (1987), where the argument reading of the *van* PP (3b) has an interpretation that is dependent on the verb (e.g. *het meisje van Holland houdt* means "the girl likes Holland"). On the other hand, the adjunct attachment of the PP within the NP (3c) allows this phrase to be interpreted independent of the verb, where *van Holland* means "from Holland."

(3a)   dat het meisje van   Holland
        that the girl   (from)
(3b)   [dat [het meisje] van Holland]
(3c)   [dat [het meisje] van Holland]

Therefore one might argue that the demands of incremental interpretation in head-final clauses actually favor adjunct attachment (assuming pre-verbal structuring). Consider the structure in (3c). When the parser processes *van Holland* in this way it can be interpreted as a locative adjunct without waiting for the appearance of the verb. But as an argument it cannot be correctly interpreted until the verb is processed.

---

[5] I will discuss the processing of verb-final clauses in detail when discussing Japanese and German syntactic processing later in this chapter. Here I will use the Dutch example to illustrate the specific point concerning interpretation and attachment preferences.

[6] For example, Marantz (1984) points out, as (i) and (ii) illustrate, that choice of (internal) argument often affects the interpretation given to a particular verb. But I am unaware of any comparable effect with adjuncts.

(i)   throw a baseball
(ii)   throw a party

Thus several problems arise if we attempt to motivate the preference for argument attachment as directly following from the need to efficiently interpret structured material. There is an implicit assumption that adjunct attachment (whether directly stated or as a consequence of a theta-driven approach) is less compatible with incremental interpretation than argument attachment. Although Weinberg (1993) states that "the incremental satisfaction of licensing constraints...allows the parser to perform incremental semantic interpretation," incremental interpretation is compatible with many forms of incremental structuring. It remains to be shown that the perceptual bias for argument attachment follows, in some particular fashion, from the demands of incremental interpretation. It seems, then, that content-based approaches cannot be motivated by either grammatical considerations (a desire to give licensing conditions a more salient role than structural relations) or interpretive concerns (rapid comprehension).

An important, but basic, issue that must be addressed is the use of the term *parser*. I will use it to refer to the processor responsible for constructing a syntactic representation of an input string. Given that I am assuming a GB grammar, the parser builds a representation which encodes (at least) the following information, given in (4).

(4a)   dominance
(4b)   precedence
(4c)   government
(4d)   c-command
(4e)   theta assignment
(4f)   case assignment
(4g)   binding

Thus the parser computes a structural representation, a tree, where nodes are connected via dominance and precedence relations (4a and 4b). Once these primary relations are computed, the realization of the secondary relations (4c–g) becomes possible. For example, whether or not a government relation holds between two nodes cannot be determined unless they are connected in a tree structure. Similar remarks apply to the other secondary relations.

The parser is principle-based in that, following Pritchett (1992), structure building is driven by principles of grammar (the Case Filter, the Theta Criterion, etc.). I will argue that other principles of grammar, most notably the Principle of Full Interpretation (Chomsky 1991), play an important role in the operations of the parser. In the next section I discuss these operations in detail. In Section 4.2 I relate this model of parsing to a number of experimental studies in the psycholinguistic literature. Section 4.3 examines the relationship between structure building by the parser and syntactically relevant lexical information. The processing of Wh-constructions is discussed in Section 4.4. Section 4.5 relates recent work investigating syntactic processing in a number of languages exhibiting properties not found in English to the proposed parsing model. As in the previous chapter, I will postpone discussion of semantic and discourse effects until Chapter 5.

4.1   Node creation and attachment

I will assume that the lexical processor outputs to the parser information concerning syntactically relevant lexical information for each item of the input string. For the moment I will put to the side some interesting issues concerning lexical ambiguity and the availability of subcategory information. The core operations of the parser are given in (5).

(5a)   node projection
(5b)   node creation
(5c)   node attachment

Node projection is motivated (i.e. licensed) by X-bar theory. For example, if the parser processes the N *cat* (where the N feature, or its address, is part of the output of lexical processing), it will project an NP in accord with the requirement that every X° project to an XP. Node creation (5b) is motivated by lexical requirements such as the argument structure of verbs. For example, if a verb (e.g. *buy*) obligatorily subcategorizes for an NP complement, then, when the VP is projected, an NP is created in argument position. Further, once this NP is created, an N is projected (downward) to fulfill the X-bar requirement that every XP be a projection of an X°. Thus "projection" as a parsing operation can either be from a lexical node to a maximal projection or from a maximal projection to a lexical node.

Node attachment (5c) is simply the structure-building operation of positing dominance and precedence relations between nodes. As discussed above, it is motivated by the principles of grammar governing the distribution of constituents in a syntactic structure.

Recall from Chapter 2 that the generation of structure within the grammar was constrained by the Principle of Full Interpretation (PFI),[7] repeated here as (6).

(6)   *PFI*: No vacuous structure

But the computation of structure by the parser, no less than the generation of structure by the grammar, must be constrained. Therefore the operations of the parser in (5) are governed by the incremental application of (6). I will refer to this principle as *Simplicity*, given in (7a). Simplicity is a constraint on the process of structure building whereas *Incremental Licensing* (7b) is what drives it.[8]

(7a)   *Simplicity*: No vacuous structure building
(7b)   *Incremental Licensing*: The parser attempts incrementally to satisfy principles of grammar

It should be clear that (7a) is but one particular way of instantiating Minimal Attachment (Frazier 1978, Frazier and Fodor 1978). There are two important differences between Simplicity and MA. The first is that I am assuming, in particular, that the parser is building a phrase-structure tree. Minimal Attachment, on the other hand, does not presuppose a particular type of structural representation. The second difference concerns the underlying grammatical assumptions. As discussed in Chapter 3, MA is not stated as a distinct parsing principle, but follows from the assumption of a rule-based grammar and the temporal advantages of minimal rule accessing. It will become clear below that the formulation in (7a) is not simply a move from minimal rule to minimal principle accessing.

In addition to being constrained, structure building must be driven by the grammar. This licensing of structure is stated in (7b). The similarity to Pritchett's (1992) GTA is clear. One important distinction is that, as we shall see below, Incremental Licensing does not refer to "maximal satisfaction" of grammatical principles. Recall from the discussion of Pritchett (1992) in the last chapter that the reference to maximal satisfaction served to constrain structure building by indirectly favoring minimal structures. In the model proposed here, this function is served by Simplicity. The formulation of Incremental Licensing in (7b) is the minimal statement necessary to drive structure building by a principle-based parser.

---

[7] To be more specific, the principle of economy of representation. Chomsky (1991) uses PFI to refer to economy of representation and derivation. In the representational framework adopted here, there are no derivations to constrain.

[8] As is clear from the discussion in Chapter 3, incremental structure-building is a common, if not universal, assumption in the psycholinguistics literature (cf. the Left-to-Right Principle of Frazier and Rayner [1987a]).

Similarly, Simplicity is the minimal statement required to constrain such computation. Structure building must be constrained for two reasons. The first is grammatical (the principle of economy of representation, Chomsky 1991). The second is perceptual (the preference for minimal structure at points of ambiguity). Simplicity unites both the grammatical and perceptual constraints on structure building.

Further, following earlier work (Gorrell 1992, 1993b) I will assume a limited, but well-motivated, form of determinism. As discussed above in the context of minimal commitment theory, the Determinism Hypothesis of Marcus (1980), although facilitating computational efficiency, is inconsistent with experimental and intuitive observations concerning incremental interpretation. Implicit in the move from representations to descriptions in d-theory is a limiting of the domain of determinism. The formulation of Structural Determinism (SD), given in (8), is consistent with this domain limitation but removes the ad hoc nature of the move by reference to a natural class of grammatical phenomena, primary structural relations.

(8)   *Structural Determinism*: The domain of determinism is limited to the primary structural relations, dominance and precedence.

Although it may appear that this domain, although stated in terms of a natural class, must be stipulated, I will argue that it follows from the parser's architecture. The argument will be similar in form to that originally given for MA (Frazier and Fodor 1978). Consider the division of labor depicted in (9).

(9)   ----▸ 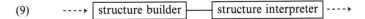 ----▸

The parser, then, consists of two components, a *structure builder* responsible for tree construction (dominance and precedence relations) and a *structure interpreter* which determines whether or not secondary relations (e.g. government) hold between nodes in the structure. The claim implicit in (8) is that the structure builder is simply that, a mechanism which can only perform the structure-building operations in (5). That is, it has no capacity for altering or deleting dominance and precedence relations. This is similar in spirit to aspects of d-theory and minimal commitment theory but does not require any form of underspecification, as will be shown below.

But a GB grammar is more than dominance and precedence relations and a GB-based parser must be more than a structure builder. The structure interpreter is concerned with interpreting the computed tree in terms of the secondary (or, licensing) relations. Recall that, in d-theory, dominance relations were interpreted by the "semantic" interpreter. But this type of direct semantic interpretation of a tree is not possible if one assumes a GB-type grammar. That is, relations such as government are *structural* relations, clearly within the domain of syntactic theory. Thus the parsing model in (9) reflects the form of the grammar in that the structure builder's domain is one type of structural relation and the structure interpreter's domain is another.

Given this, it is clear that (8) is a statement about the structure builder (not the structure interpreter) as it refers to primary relations. Thus the parsing model I am proposing is not a deterministic mechanism, but it does include a deterministic component. This division of the parser into two components mirrors the distinction of types of relations in the grammar, as discussed in Chapter 2. That is, the satisfaction of secondary (licensing) relations presupposes a structural representation in which these relations can be realized. From a grammatical perspective, the two components of the parser appear quite natural. In fact, it is difficult to see how a GB-based parser might otherwise be constructed.[9]

The initial, structure-building, component of the parser is governed by Simplicity (7a) and driven by Incremental Licensing (7b). Thus each component of the parser has access to the full grammar. Given that Simplicity is a particular instantiation of Minimal Attachment and is a general property of the deterministic component of the parser, it is important to explore the nature of reanalysis in prior models incorporating MA. Recall that, at the time that MA was initially proposed, the generation of phrase structure by PS rules was a common assumption. Therefore an empirically adequate parser needed to incorporate a reanalysis component that, in part, could retract assertions concerning immediate dominance and precedence. In addition, as discussed in Chapter 3, such a parser needed to access the appropriate PS rules for the new input. But such a "retraction component" to reanalysis is unnecessary if the need for such assertions is obviated by the move to a principle-based grammar in which immediate dominance and precedence are simply not part of the grammatical representation.

Although the reference to maximal satisfaction in Pritchett's (1992) GTA and the minimal structuring demanded by Simplicity may appear at odds, there is a clear relation between the parser's preference for simple

---

[9] See Berwick (1991) for a discussion of some of the computational issues involved in parsing with a "decentralized" grammar such as GB.

structures and the assignment of grammatical features. For example, consider the processing of an NP following a verb which permits either a nominal or sentential complement. The parser will simply compute an NP dominated by the VP. This is also the structure in which the verb governs the NP, i.e. a case and theta position. The more complex sentential complement structure would result in an NP that is not in a position to receive these grammatical features.

This relation is due to the nature of the grammar. Locality restrictions on relations such as government are stated in terms of how structurally *close* two elements must be in order for a relation to hold. That is, the grammars of natural language tend not to have relations which force elements to be "distant" in some way.[10] For example, government is not such that it holds *only if* there exists a maximal projection between the governor and the governed element. Thus comparatively simple structures will tend to be those in which the assignment of grammatical relations is not blocked by intervening structural barriers. Thus there are two coherent approaches to accounting for the parser's preference for simpler structures: either it is precisely that, a direct structural preference (e.g. MA, Simplicity), or it is a preference for assigning grammatical features which indirectly results in a particular structural preference (GTA). The motivation may be the same in either case; as discussed briefly above, the demands of efficient processing and the need to quickly structure input. But the question remains: what is the most explanatory vocabulary in which to state the preference? The GTA accounts for the general preference to analyze NPs as arguments (if possible) in terms of the assignment of secondary relations. Simplicity does not refer to these relations directly, but to the simplest structure (in terms of primary relations) justified by the input. Thus the preference for argument (versus adjunct) attachment follows in the current model from the fact that, at the onset of the ambiguity, the parser will not project the (potentially vacuous) intermediate nodes required for adjunct attachment. Argument attachment is structurally simpler and, therefore, preferred.

The discussion to follow will focus on the processing of ambiguous input and demonstrate the empirical adequacy of the claim that the theory of parsing does not need a distinct component of automatic reanalysis. The focus will be on the types of structural ambiguities discussed in the previous chapter. But before turning to a detailed discussion of these structures, it will be useful to begin with the processing of simple sentences

---

[10] Possible exceptions to this are the binding conditions for pronouns and names. But these are negative conditions, i.e. x must not be bound in a certain domain.

in order to understand the relation between properties of the grammar and properties of the parser. Consider the sentence in (10).

(10)   Ian buys books.

There is a tendency to think of simple sentences such as (10) as unambiguous. But it is important to realize that when the parser processes the initial item *Ian*, there are a number of possible ways of analyzing this word, as (11) illustrates.

(11a)   Ian and Mary buy books
(11b)   Ian and Mary's house is for sale
(11c)   Ian, I like
(11d)   Ian, I like him
(11e)   Ian and Mary
(11f)   Ian

The parser projects an NP structure for the noun *Ian*. It is the simplest structure justified by the input. Thus the parse state before processing the next item is (12). This structure is consistent with all the possibilities in (11). Also, the parser is not committed to a clausal analysis (i.e. the projection of CP, IP, and VP nodes). For example, *Ian* may appear in isolation or as part of a list.[11]

(12)

The next item to be analyzed is *buys*. This inflected verb causes the parser to build both an IP and VP structure, as indicated in (13).

(13)

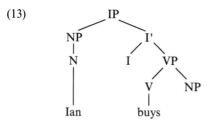

The post-verbal NP has been precomputed by the parser based on the subcategorization requirements of *buy*, which requires an NP object. When *books* is processed, it will be attached as this object.

---

[11] The parser is committed to a phrasal analysis (by X-bar theory).

But suppose that the input continued as in (14a). How would the parser "recover" from its initial misanalysis? The structure for conjoined NPs is given in (14b).[12] (14c) shows the structure of the VP after *books* is processed; (14d) shows its structure after *toys* is processed.

(14a)   Ian buys books and toys

(14b)   [NP [NP books] and [NPtoys]]

(14c)   (14d)

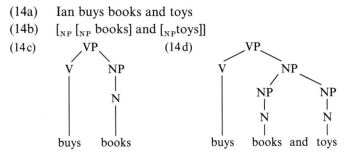

The tree in (14d) preserves all the primary relations in (14c). Therefore the change in structure required only operations within the capability of the structure builder. If such a change cannot be performed by the parser, then a garden-path effect will occur. However, due to the deterministic nature of structure building, if structure alteration or deletion were required, then a garden-path effect would be predicted.

At this point it is necessary to digress somewhat in order to examine more closely the meaning of the term *garden-path*. Recall from the previous chapter that there are two general ways in which it is used. One refers to the (conscious or unconscious) effect of needing to restructure input at the point of the resolution of an ambiguity (cf. Frazier and Rayner 1982). According to this view some types of restructuring are straightforward, that is, amenable to what Frazier and Rayner (1982) refer to as "the parser's normal (unconscious) reanalysis procedures." But other types of reanalysis are beyond the capacity of these procedures and require conscious problem solving. Thus, according to this view, initial structure-building operations, and some reanalysis procedures, are automatic and unconscious.

The other use of the term *garden-path* is based on the view that structure-building operations are automatic, but all structure-deleting and structure-altering operations are beyond the capacity of the reflexive operations of the parser. This is the Determinism Hypothesis. Recall that Marcus (1980) argued that a sentence that is understood "without conscious difficulty" could be parsed deterministically. Assume that the parser is a module in the

---

[12] I will assume a simple flat structure for conjuncts. The point holds if an asymmetric, binary-branching, structure is assumed (Munn 1992).

sense of J. A. Fodor (1983). We can start with the reasonable assumption that individuals do not have full access to the operations and intermediate outputs of the perceptual process. That is, individuals are able to report some aspects but not others. Consider the ambiguities in (15). These structures represent the types of reanalysis contrasted by Frazier and Rayner (1982) and discussed in Chapter 3.

(15a)   Ian knows Thomas is a train
(15b)   The horse raced past the barn fell

Frazier and Rayner sought to explain why (15a) was noticeably easier to process than (15b). According to a number of proposals, the preferential analysis of the ambiguities in each string is determined by a bias to pursue the minimal structure. Individuals are able to report the difficulty of processing strings such as (15b), whereas individuals fail to report such difficulties with (15a).

If the parser is a module which performs its operations in an automatic, reflexlike, manner, then it is not surprising that sentences should be processed without conscious attention. How do we then interpret the response to grammatical sentences such as (15b)?[13] The most straight-forward interpretation is that this type of sentence requires perceptual processes that are beyond the capacity of the automatic parsing mechanism. Specifically, input which cannot be assigned a grammatical structure by the (automatic, unconscious) operations of the parser produces perceptual difficulty that is available for report. If we assume, following Fodor, that access to the internal operations of modules is quite limited, then such availability for strings necessitating violations of monotonicity is support for the proposal that monotonicity is a necessary condition for the operations of the parser. As Pritchett (1992) observes, conscious reflection itself is unrevealing, but the *fact* that it occurs is a significant datum.

Given this discussion, we can characterize uses of the term *garden-path* as depending upon whether one assumes that the automatic processing mechanism includes (or does not include) a structure-altering and -deleting component. If one assumes that it does not, then *garden-path* is used to indicate structures requiring conscious restructuring. If one assumes that it does include such a component, then *garden-path* is used to indicate structures which involve either unconscious or conscious reanalysis. In this

---

[13] Note that individuals often have to be convinced of the grammatical status of (15b), an issue that does not arise with (15a).

chapter I will use the term *garden-path* to refer to processing difficulty which is available for conscious report.

If we assume that the structure builder is simply a tree-building mechanism, then it is somewhat misleading to use terms such as *reanalysis*, *recovery*, or *change in structure* because these terms appear to indicate that the operation is a specific response to ambiguity and its resolution. This is incorrect: the parser simply responds to input by building structure. For (14a), the parser does not have to reanalyze an initial assertion that *books* is the object of the verb *buys*. Terms such as *object* are not primitive but relational. After processing the noun *books*, the parser builds a structure in which it is true that the VP dominates the post-verbal NP. More structure will be built as more input is processed. This may or may not change certain grammatical relations as the parse proceeds, but the primitive relations between nodes in the tree, dominance and precedence, cannot be altered.

Examples such as (16a) illustrate the processing of relative clause structures within the proposed model. The tree is given in (16b).

(16a)   The boy who buys books

(16b)

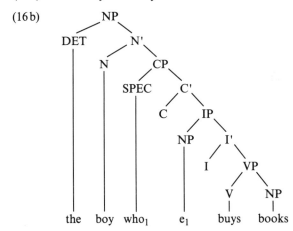

When the parser initially processes the string *the boy* it will build a structure in which the NP node dominates a DET and N node, which are in a precedence relation. When the relative operator *who* is processed, the parser builds the relevant CP structure and attaches it as an adjunct. Crucially, the original structural relations continue to be true as the change from the simple NP structure to a relative clause is a structure-building operation. Thus there is no GP effect.

Consider now the processing of a sentential complement structure, such as (17a), with the corresponding tree in (17b).

(17a)   Bill agrees (that) Ian buys books

(17b)

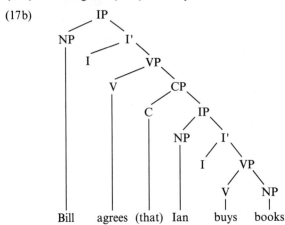

Bill   agrees   (that)   Ian   buys   books

For (17) the parse sequence is as before, except that the verb *agree* takes a CP complement. Thus the parser precomputes the predictable aspects of the CP structure. The complementizer *that* is the lexical head of CP. In the absence of this complementizer, an empty complementizer is placed in this position. The parse sequence for structures such as (17), in which the verb requires a clausal complement, differs from the sequence for strings in which the verb is ambiguous. Sentence (18a) contains the ambiguous verb *know*. The tree for (18a), after the processing of the post-verbal NP, is given in (18b).

(18a)   Bill knows Ian buys books

(18b)

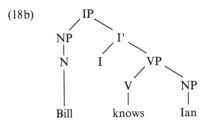

Bill   knows   Ian

The parser asserts that the post-verbal NP is dominated by the VP. In this position the NP is governed by the V. Also, the V precedes the NP; therefore the NP can receive a theta-role and case. When the verb *buys* is processed, additional structure is built, yielding a tree identical to (17b). As with other ambiguities that do not produce garden-path effects, no retraction of either precedence or dominance relations is required. For example, the matrix V node continues to precede the NP because it precedes the CP node which dominates this NP (this follows from the Nontangling Condition).

What does change is the status of relations between nodes which refer to dominance and precedence. Thus the matrix V no longer governs the NP, as there are now maximal projections which bar government by the V into the CP and IP. If government is blocked, so are case and theta-role assignment. Thus the structure interpreter, operating incrementally upon the output of the structure builder, will reinterpret this structure in the appropriate way. As structure building proceeds, structure interpretation keeps pace and secondary relations may be altered. It is clear from the lack of a garden-path effect in (18a) that incremental structuring is incompatible with determinism if the domain of determinism includes secondary structural relations. That is, a GB-based parser, if by GB is meant a theory of the relations in (4), cannot be a deterministic mechanism and maintain incremental interpretation. Thus, in contrast to minimal commitment models (Weinberg 1992, 1993), there is no claim that such ambiguities can be parsed deterministically.

It is also important to clarify the difference between the present approach and underspecification theories. In such approaches the theory of parsing is enriched to allow the computation of underspecified (i.e. ungrammatical) structures, e.g. the underspecified node labels in Barton and Berwick (1985). Consider again the processing of (18a) and the structure in (18b). This structure is identical to the one given for the unambiguous (17). There is no aspect of the structure that is particular to the ambiguity. Sentence (18a) is being processed as if it were unambiguous. This follows from the fact that there is no component of the parser that is specifically designed for processing ambiguous input. Rather there is a constraint on the operations of structure building, Simplicity. Thus there is a clear distinction between minimal structuring (MA, Simplicity) and underspecification.

This lack of a specific ambiguity response is close to the intent of Frazier (1978) and Frazier and Fodor (1978). There the parser would respond to input by constructing a grammatical representation. If there were multiple representations compatible with the input, the parser would attempt to construct these representations. The parser did not have the capacity for maintaining parallel structures so it only pursued the first one computed. Thus, the response to ambiguity was dictated by general properties of the

Sausage Machine, not by specific ambiguity resolution procedures. Many of the differences between the current approach and the Sausage Machine model follow from the changes in syntactic theory since the late 1970s, in particular the change from a rule-based to a principle-based grammar.

For example, consider a string such as (19) and assume that we have reliable evidence of an anomaly effect that occurs at the point of processing the post-verbal NP.

(19)   Ian knew the cow

It would be reasonable to conclude that such an anomaly effect is due either to the parser analyzing (or attempting to analyze) the post-verbal NP as the object of the verb and the detection that *the cow* is not an appropriate object for *know*. In a rule-based system, where the relevant rules are VP→V NP or VP→V S′, an anomaly effect for the string *knew the cow* would most straightforwardly be interpreted as evidence that the parser responded to the input by applying the rule VP→V NP, and not the rule VP→V S′. This would yield a structure in which the NP was immediately dominated by the VP.

In the GB-based parser outlined here, a V–NP anomaly effect would arise if the structural representation for the input was such that the verb governed the NP. This would permit theta-role assignment and syntax-external processes to interpret the structure. But government, unlike dominance and precedence, is not a primary relation in the grammar. If the government relation holds between two nodes at a particular point in the parse, it may not hold at a subsequent point (as shown in the parse of [18a]). Thus there is no inherent incompatibility between an independent structure-based processor and incremental interpretation.

But ambiguous input does affect when the parser creates and attaches nodes (see Weinberg's 1988 discussion of the Frazier and Rayner 1982 data). For example, compare the parsing of (17a) and (18a). In (17a) the parser is able to precompute aspects of the clausal complement when the matrix verb *agree* is processed. This is because the subcategorization information associated with *agree* is unambiguous. But in (18a) the matrix verb *know* is ambiguous. Therefore the parser does not compute any structure for the complement clause until the embedded verb is processed. We will see in the next section that this difference between the processing of ambiguous and unambiguous input is consistent with a number of experimental studies (e.g. Frazier and Rayner 1982; Rayner and Frazier 1987).

Consider now the processing of the complements of a verb such as *tell* which may occur either with an NP complement (20a) or with an NP CP complement (20b). The tree for the VP in (20b) is given in (21).

(20a) Ian told Bill
(20b) Ian told Bill that he buys books

(21)

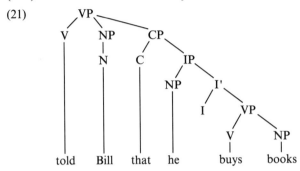

After the NP *Bill* has been attached (dominated by VP; preceded by V) the complementizer *that* is processed and the structure builder creates and attaches the CP node (dominated by VP, preceded by NP). The remainder of the clause is processed in the familiar way. But consider now an ambiguous string in which the CP may be attached either as a complement of the verb or as a relative clause within the post-verbal NP. Consider now the sentences in (22).

(22a) Ian told the man that he hired a story
(22b) Ian told the man that he hired to leave

The garden-path effect evident in (22), i.e. the preference for the complement attachment of the CP, follows from Simplicity. The attachment ambiguity in these sentences is between the two structures given in (23).

(23a)

```
        VP
       /  \
      V    NP    CP
          /  \
        DET   N
```

(23b)

```
        VP
       /  \
      V    NP
          /  \
        DET   N
             /  \
            N    CP
```

It is clear that the complement reading is the simpler analysis, not requiring the computation of potentially vacuous structure. This correctly predicts the initial preference, but what accounts for the garden-path effect is the fact that in (23a) the NP and CP nodes are in a precedence relation whereas in (23b) they are in a dominance relation. The structure builder cannot alter the initial precedence relation, nor can it posit a dominance relation as this would violate the Exclusivity Condition on well-formed trees discussed in Chapter 2. This condition forces two nodes to be (exclusively) in either a precedence or a dominance relation.

It is important to note that if precedence relations among complements were not expressed in the structure, then the trees in (24) would be equivalent, an unwelcome result as only the order expressed in (24a) is grammatical in English.

(24a)   (24b)

V   NP   CP   V   CP   NP

Further, if precedence relations among nonterminals were not expressed, as proposed by Marcus *et al.* (1983), then the trees in (25) would be equivalent.

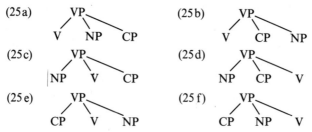

(25a)   VP   (25b)   VP
           V   NP   CP   V   CP   NP

(25c)   VP   (25d)   VP
          NP   V   CP   NP   CP   V

(25e)   VP   (25f)   VP
          CP   V   NP   CP   NP   V

The parser must be computing a structural representation of the input which includes precedence relations.[14]

The assignment of case and theta roles, important determinants of constituent order within GB, refer to precedence relations (Koopman 1983; Travis 1984). Thus the inclusion of these relations is required, not only for the computation of a well-formed tree, but for the assignment of grammatical features as well. These are syntactic requirements, not

---

[14] As mentioned in Chapter 2, precedence relations among nonterminals cannot be derived from the precedence relations among terminals, as the trees in (i) and (ii) illustrate.

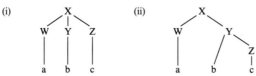

(i)   X   (ii)   X
        W   Y   Z   W   Y
        | | | | / \
        a   b   c   a   b   Z
                                            | |
                                            b   c

Assuming that both (i) and (ii) are well-formed trees, the precedence relations in the string *abc* cannot determine, even in conjunction with wellformedness conditions on trees, whether or not Y and Z are in a precedence relation (i) or a dominance relation (ii).

motivated by parsing concerns. Yet the inclusion of precedence relations allows us to account for the garden-path status of ambiguities such as (22b).

Consider now the processing of sentences such as (26a), discussed in Section 3.6, in which the ambiguity involving NP attachment is more revealing. The two possibilities for attaching the post-verbal NPs are given in (26b and c).

(26a)   Ian gave the man the report criticized a demotion

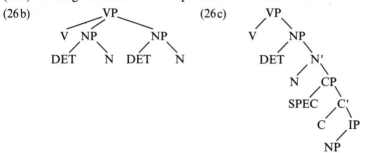

As with prior examples, there is little doubt concerning the preferred attachment. But the source of the garden-path effect is less evident. Note that, with respect to dominance relations, (26b) is consistent with (26c). Thus the garden-path effect is not the result of retracting dominance relations. The source of the processing difficulty in (26a) must be the retraction of the precedence relation between the NPs in (26b). This gives further support to the analysis of (22b) in terms of retraction of precedence relations.

The processing of (26a) contrasts in an interesting way with the processing of (27). In each case the structure builder must assign an analysis to the string *the man the report criticized*. Yet only in (26a) does this produce a garden-path effect.

(27)   The man the report criticized was demoted

In (27) we see the effects of an important distinction between Simplicity and Minimal Attachment. For the initial string in (27), MA would require that the parser commit to some structural relation between the two NPs (prior to the appearance of the verb). If we assume that the parser asserts a precedence relation, as in (26), then we cannot explain the lack of a garden-path effect in (27). This is because in each case a precedence relation must be retracted. However, if we assume that the parser is initially committed to a dominance relation between the two NPs, then we incorrectly predict that coordinate structures (e.g. *the man, the report, and the evidence*), in which the NPs are in a precedence relation, should produce processing difficulty. But neither Licensing nor Simplicity require (or allow) the parser to do more than process the internal structure of the two NPs. The situation is similar to the processing of a string-initial NP (as in [10] above). There is no justification for asserting any relation between the two NPs. I will return to this issue of pre-verbal structuring in examining the processing of verb-final clauses.

Consider now the processing of Bever's (1970) well-known garden-path sentence (28a). The relevant structures are given in (28b and c).

(28a)   The horse raced ...

(28b)   (28c)

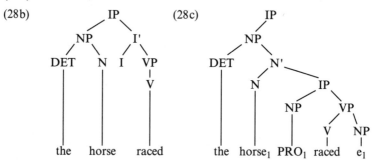

The garden-path effect stems from the fact that the VP projection of *raced* in (28b) is preceded by the NP projection of *horse*. This is not true in (28c) where the *raced* VP is dominated by the *horse* NP. Thus a garden-path effect is correctly predicted. But again we see that the retraction of a precedence statement is implicated in a garden-path effect.[15] Consider also the locus of the garden-path effect in a sentence such as (29a).

(29a)   The man told that the crowd was angry was upset
(29b)   The man told Bill that the crowd was upset

As with (28), when the ambiguous verb is processed it is analyzed as a simple past-tense form. But *tell* requires both a nominal and a sentential complement, as in (29b). What does not automatically occur in (29a) is that

---

[15] Assuming the correctness of the Internal Subject Hypothesis (ISH) discussed in Chapter 2, there is an alternative account for the garden-path effect in reduced relative ambiguities. That is, the preferred analysis of the initial NP as subject of the VP would require positing a trace of the raised subject within the VP. Clearly, reanalysis to the reduced relative reading would require deletion of this trace and the relevant nodes and structural relations. The important point for the present proposal is that, under either account, the locus of the effect is within the structure-building component of the grammar.

the lack of a post-verbal NP causes the parser to reanalyze the verb as a participle. This indicates the speed with which structural commitments are made by the parser. That is, the string *The man told that the* is unambiguous. There is only one grammatical analysis. Yet the parser is unable, due to prior assertions, to compute the correct structure.

Let us consider an additional garden-path that involves precedence relations. These ambiguities involve the attachment of PPs as either adjuncts (within an NP) or arguments of a verb. Consider (30a).

(30a)   Ian put the candy on the table in his mouth

(30b)   (30c)

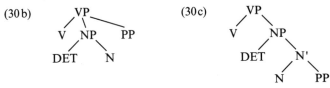

Again, if we restrict ourselves to dominance statements, the primary structural relations in (30c) are consistent with those in (30b). But in (30b) the PP is preceded by the NP whereas in (30c) the NP dominates the PP. Thus, the need to retract the precedence relation is the cause of the garden-path effect.

This analysis also applies to the much-discussed ambiguity in (31a), which may be analyzed as in (31b) or (31c) (see Taraban and McClelland 1988, Frazier 1990).

(31a)   Ian saw the man with the binoculars

(31b)   (31c)

As above, the complement reading (31b) is structurally simpler and therefore the preferred attachment. In (31b) the NP precedes the PP. This is not true in (31c) and the garden-path effect is predicted when this analysis is forced by subsequent material, as in (32). As with (30) the garden-path effect is not predicted if we exclude precedence assertions.

(32)   Ian saw the man with the binoculars with his telescope

Thus we have clear evidence that a number of different types of garden-path effects can be attributed to violations of Structural Determinism caused by the retraction of precedence relations. Thus, the previous discussion demonstrates that the characterization of a tree-building parser, as simply a mechanism which builds a tree, leads to a natural account of a wide range of garden-path phenomena. Crucial to this account is the assumption that a phrase-structure tree does not encode information concerning immediate dominance or precedence. This yields a very restrictive parsing theory: the parser can only build structure, and the only type of structure it can build is the type of structure generated by the competence grammar.

Let us compare this approach to Pritchett's (1992) On-line Locality Constraint (OLLC), a defining property of automatic reanalysis in his parser. The OLLC states that reanalysis can be performed only if the target position of the reanalyzed constituent is *dominated or governed* by the source position. In the last chapter we noted some problems with the inclusion of the concept of government in the OLLC, most importantly the fact that government is formally defined in the grammar as a relation between nodes in a structure. But the OLLC must refer to positions and not to nodes. This makes it difficult to formalize the relation and causes it to be distinct from the grammatical definition of government. Yet, despite the conceptual problems, its inclusion in the OLLC was motivated, in part, by the contrast between (33) and (34).

(33a)   Ian gave her earrings yesterday
(33b)   Ian gave her earrings to Mary

(34a)   Ian put the candy on the table last night
(34b)   Ian put the candy on the table in his mouth

Neither reading of the ambiguity in (33) produces a garden-path effect. Pritchett accounts for this because the source position (indicated by the rightmost NP position in [35]) governs the target position.[16] That is, the source position (the rightmost NP in [35a]) governs the NP, N′ and N projections of the reanalyzed constituent *earrings*. This is because the rightmost NP position governs the NP *her earrings*. If a maximal phrase is governed, so are all its projections. So reanalysis to (33b) is unproblematic. But (34b) does produce a garden-path effect. Here the source position fails to govern the target position, as shown in (35b). This is because the NP is a barrier to government (by the rightmost PP position) of the PP *on the table*. Thus the distinction appears to be due to an abstract property of the grammar, the definition of government, and its role in the OLLC.

---

[16] Note that, after reanalysis, there is no longer an NP in this position.

(35a)

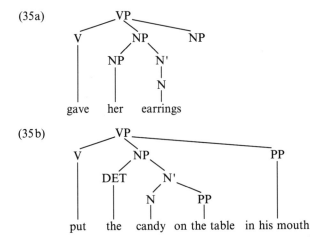

(35b)

Before analyzing this distinction within the framework of the present proposal, it is useful to note that there is a similarity between Structural Determinism and Pritchett's OLLC. For example, we could formulate a constraint on reanalysis as in (36).

(36)   Upon reanalysis, the reanalyzed constituent must participate in the same dominance and precedence relations as prior to reanalysis.

This, of course, is simply the constraint on retraction of dominance and precedence statements. Within the structure-building component, such a constraint does not have to be stated, as there is no operation to constrain. It is precisely this conceptual saving that is the aim of determinism (Marcus 1980) and underspecification (Barton and Berwick 1985). One difference between (36) and the OLLC is that the latter incorrectly predicts that there should be cases where automatic reanalysis involves the retraction of dominance statements. But I am unaware of any ambiguities for which this is true. Further, the garden-path effect in (34b) is accounted for within Structural Determinism if precedence relations are considered, as argued above.

Returning now to the contrast between (33) and (34), note that the "indelibility" of precedence relations predicts that, although lowering is generally allowed (as in d-theory), lowering into a predecessor (or successor) is beyond the capability of the structure builder. This is because such a lowering necessitates the retraction of a precedence relation. This appears to incorrectly predict that reanalysis to produce the correct structure for (33b) should produce a garden-path effect. But Weinberg (1993) points out that, if a DP analysis (Abney 1987) is assumed, Structural Determinism correctly predicts a deterministic reanalysis in (33). Consider the trees in (37).

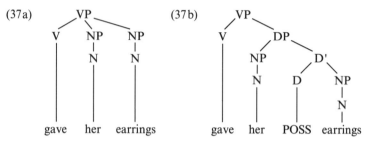

The tree in (37a) is the initial structure computed by the parser. Assume that POSS (the abstract possessive marker) projects to a DP and case-marks an NP in [SPEC, DP] position.[17] Given this, in (37b) the two NPs are still in a precedence relation. In this structure, the NP *her* is in [SPEC, DP] position and *earrings* is the complement of D°. Assuming the correctness of this analysis, the present proposal is able to account for the subtle contrast between (33) and (34) without recourse to the disjunction "*governs* or *dominates*" in the OLLC.

There is one other potential empirical distinction between Structural Determinism and the OLLC. Consider the sentences in (38).

(38a)   John warned the man cheated
(38b)   John warned the man
(38c)   John warned the man (that) Bill cheated
(38d)   John warned he cheated

Pritchett analyzes the processing difficulty evident in (38a) as a garden-path effect. That is, the parser initially structures the NP *the man* as the (goal) object of *warn* (consistent with [38b]). Under Pritchett's assumptions, the initial structuring of *the man* in (38a) puts it into a position preceding an optional proposition. This is illustrated in (38c) where both the goal NP and the proposition are realized. Thus the position of the goal NP neither governs nor dominates the position of subject of the proposition, occupied by *Bill* in (38c).

Thus the reanalysis from a structure such as (38b) to the correct structure for (38a) violates the OLLC as the initial (or source) position fails

---

[17] Just as the head of IP will case mark an NP in [SPEC,IP] position.

to either govern or dominate the final (or target) position. Of course this explanation is not available under the tree-building approach I've proposed. This is because the processing of (38a) is predicted to be identical to the processing of sentences such as (18a). The problematic garden-path analysis of (38a) presupposes the acceptability of (38d), where the case-marking on the preposition precludes the initial misanalysis. In my own judgment (38d) is quite marked, if not ungrammatical. Further, as Ted Gibson (personal communication) points out, verbs such as *bet* and *show* (identical to *warn* from the perspective of Pritchett's proposal) do not produce the processing difficulty evident with *warn*.

There is a well-known garden-path sentence which we have not yet discussed in terms of the current proposal. This is the sentence in (39a). Recall that the preferential attachment of the NP *the sock* as the object of the verb followed from Late Closure (Frazier 1978). Minimal Attachment was not applicable because a matrix IP would be precomputed regardless of the attachment site of the NP. Gibson's parser projected this structure as well. This precomputation was based on the obligatory nature of the main clause.

(39a)   While Mary was mending the sock

(39b)   Mary was mending the sock

But does the grammar require a main clause? In a grammar where phrase structure is projected from lexical categories, there doesn't appear to be any requirement for a syntactically-realized matrix clause that fails to dominate any lexical material. Consider the discourse in (40).

(40)   A: When did the baby wake up?

       B: While Mary was mending the sock.

We can analyze the syntactic structure of the response in (40) as either a simple adverbial clause (which can appear on its own because it is justified by the discourse), or a structure adjoined to a matrix IP node (which dominates a discourse-linked null element). There appears to be little motivation for the latter option.[18] Given the manner in which phrase structure is generated in GB, it would seem rather *ad hoc* to stipulate that "subordinate" clauses (or any syntactic category) must be connected to a structure dominated by a specified root node. Consider the discourse in (41).

---

[18] Note that this is distinct from Grimshaw's (1979) arguments for Null Complement Anaphora, where the phenomena in question concern selection and subcategorization.

(41)   A: Where did you go last night?
        B: To the movies.
        A: What did you eat?
        B: Some popcorn.

There appears to be no reason to require that the responses in (41) be connected to (empty) matrix clauses. On the contrary, it would be at odds with a basic property of X-bar theory: structure is projected from lexical items.[19] Given this, the processing of (39a) reduces to the processing of (39b). In each case, the post-verbal object is attached as part of the VP because it is the simplest structure justified by the input and grammar. Thus, in contrast to the analysis in Frazier (1978) and Gibson (1991), the attachment preference is due to a bias for simpler structures and not to a closure or recency effect. If this NP is followed by a verb (e.g. *fell*) a garden-path effect is evident. This is due to the fact that the reanalysis required of the structure builder would require the retraction of the assertion that the VP headed by *mend* dominates the following NP, as in Weinberg (1992).

In general, the proposed parsing model is quite well motivated. It is conceptually simple, performing only the structure-building operations in (5). Structure building is driven by Incremental Licensing (7b) and constrained by Simplicity (7a). Its empirical coverage is quite broad. It incorporates significant aspects of previous approaches (e.g. Frazier 1978; Frazier and Fodor 1978; Marcus *et al.* 1983; Pritchett 1992), and extends the descriptive adequacy of these parsing models by making crucial reference to the grammar's distinction between primary and secondary structural relations. Thus, the approach is well motivated, conceptually and empirically. In the next section we take a closer look at the current proposal in the light of experimental investigations.

4.2   Experimental studies of structural ambiguity

In the last chapter I briefly discussed Weinberg's (1988) claim that a deterministic parsing model is consistent with experimental results reported by Frazier and Rayner (1982).[20] Although I have argued that a deterministic parser is incompatible with incremental structure building and

---

[19] In a rule system where NP and PP are initially introduced on the right-hand side of a PS rule, such responses would have to be treated as exceptional, or analyzed as composed of the appropriate structure-dominating null elements.

[20] See also the discussion of Weinberg (1988) in Chapter 3.

interpretation, the parsing architecture proposed here does include a deterministic component, so it is important to explore this claim more closely here. Recall that Frazier and Rayner (1982) studied eye-movement patterns to investigate the parser's response to ambiguous sentences, such as (42). The discussion will focus on the attachment sentences because there is little controversy concerning the garden-path status of the closure sentences.

(42a)   The lawyers think his second wife will claim the inheritance
(42b)   The second wife will claim the inheritance belongs to her

As discussed in the last section, the parsing model proposed in Frazier and Rayner (1982) incorporates an initial structure-building component as well as "the parser's normal (unconscious) reanalysis procedures." The Determinism Hypothesis limits automatic reanalysis to the operation of structure building (node creation and attachment). This allows initial structure building and automatic reanalysis (continued structure building) to be performed by a single mechanism. But this appears to be inconsistent with the data reported by Frazier and Rayner (1982).

As mentioned in Chapter 3, for sentences such as (42a), reading times were significantly faster than for sentences such as (42b). In particular, there was a significant increase in fixation durations in the disambiguating region of the nonminimal sentences. For example, for sentences such as (42b), fixation durations increased from 226 milliseconds, just prior to the disambiguating word, to 292 milliseconds following the initial encounter with the disambiguating word. Frazier and Rayner (1982) interpret this increase in fixation durations as evidence that the parser has identified an initial misanalysis and must restructure previous input.

It is important to understand, as argued by Weinberg (1988), that evidence of an ambiguity effect for structures in which reanalysis is limited to structure addition does not disconfirm the hypothesis that structure building is deterministic. It will be useful to contrast the processing of (42b) with the processing of unambiguous strings such as (43). A similar contrast was briefly discussed in the last section.

(43)   The second wife will claim that the inheritance belongs to her

The presence of the complementizer *that* (in conjunction with the following determiner) unambiguously signals a clausal complement. This means that the parser can precompute structure prior to the appearance of clausal material. One way of characterizing the difference between (43) and (42b) is that in (43) disambiguating material occurs earlier than in (42b). Thus, when the embedded verb (the disambiguating material) is processed in unambiguous contexts such as (43), the predictable aspects of the CP, IP, and VP will have been constructed prior to the appearance of the verb. But in ambiguous contexts such as (42b), this structure will have to be computed *in response to* the appearance of the verb (i.e. when increased fixation durations are observed). Further, the fact that secondary structural relations (such as case and theta role assignment) are outside the limited domain of determinism in the present model does not entail that revision of these relations is without cost. It may well be that the ambiguity effect observed by Frazier and Rayner (1982) is due, not only to the timing of structure-building operations, but also to the changes in secondary relations such structure building will require.[21]

Thus, there are important distinctions between the deterministic processing of ambiguous and unambiguous structures, even in cases where structure building is deterministic. These differences are consistent with the results obtained by Rayner and Frazier (1987). They used an eye-movement study to investigate the processing of sentences such as those in (44).[22]

(44a)   The contestant imagined that the small tropical islands would be completely deserted

(44b)   The contestant imagined the small tropical islands would be completely deserted

(44c)   The contestant imagined the small tropical islands in the middle of the Pacific

The sentences in (44b) and (44c) were identical in structure to those tested in Frazier and Rayner's (1982) study. Rayner and Frazier (1987) report the results of an experiment which included unambiguous sentences such as (44a), similar to (43). They found that the (a) and (c) versions in (44) produced similar reading times whereas the reading times for the (b) version were significantly slower. Specifically, reading times increased in the disambiguating region of the (b) sentences. These results are consistent with Frazier and Rayner's (1982) account as well as the current proposal.[23]

---

[21] I am indebted to Matt Crocker for discussions of this issue.

[22] They also tested structures with embedded infinitival clauses, which are not germane to the current discussion.

[23] There is some controversy in the literature concerning these results. Kennedy, Murray, Jennings, and Reid (1989) report a different reading-time pattern. That is, sentences such

In Frazier and Rayner's (1982) study they also contrasted the effects of long and short ambiguous regions. The effect of the ambiguity on the processing of the nonminimal sentences was more marked in the sentences with long ambiguous regions. Note that this difference cannot be the effect of the type of restructuring as in each case it is the position of an NP that is affected. Frazier and Rayner (1982) hypothesize that semantic interpretation of a sentence "lags slightly behind its syntactic analysis ... in sentences with short ambiguous phrases, the erroneous analysis may have been revised before it affected the semantic interpretation of the sentence: whereas in sentences with long ambiguous phrases, the syntactic misanalysis of the ambiguous phrase may have had semantic consequences before the disambiguating material was encountered."

Given the speed with which interpretive processes yield perceptual effects, it is unlikely that the processing of a phrase such as *claim the inheritance* would fail to have semantic consequences before the appearance of the disambiguating word. However, there is some intuitive appeal to the notion that the longer that particular (primary) structural (and therefore, semantic and pragmatic) relations persist among constituents in a representation, the more marked will be the effect of changing those relations. But again, deterministic structure building is consistent with the experimental data.

Gorrell (1987) reported experimental results which were argued to disconfirm both a reanalysis approach to parsing and a minimal commitment approach. The argument was based, in part, on the results of a prior study by Wright and Garrett (1984).[24] Wright and Garrett conducted a series of experiments investigating the effect of syntactic context on lexical decision. Their results appeared to support the conclusion that lexical decision targets which represented optional, but grammatical, continuations of the context string produced similar reaction times to targets that represented ungrammatical continuations. Targets belonging to a syntactic category that was obligatory for a grammatical continuation of the context string produced significantly faster results.

---

as (44a) patterned with (44b) and not with (44c). They argue that what have been taken to be the effects of Minimal Attachment are actually complexity effects, i.e. the simpler structure is easier to process because it is less complex, not because it is preferred in ambiguous contexts.

It is unclear at this point how to resolve this discrepancy. But Ferreira and Henderson (1990) and Trueswell *et al.* (1993) also report experimental results consistent with Frazier and Rayner's data.

[24] See Section 3.2 for details.

Gorrell (1987) found that verb targets following ambiguous structures such as (42b) produced reaction times (RTs) which patterned with RTs for unambiguous structures such as (17a), where the matrix verb requires that a post-verbal NP be part of a clausal complement (i.e. a context requiring a verb). That is, verb targets following ambiguous contexts (for which verbs were a nonpreferred continuation) produced RTs statistically nondistinct from verb targets following unambiguous contexts (for which verbs were obligatory).

The conclusion drawn from these results was that parsing could not be serial or involve minimal commitment because these types of parser would predict longer RTs following the ambiguous context. This is due to the fact that neither a serial nor a minimal commitment parser would compute a structure that required a verb for a grammatical continuation of the context string. A parallel parser was proposed, as such a model would compute multiple structures for the ambiguous context, one of which requires a verb for a grammatical continuation.

But Gorrell (1988) reports that, contrary to the proposal of Wright and Garrett (1984), both optional and obligatory targets produce faster reaction times than ungrammatical targets.[25] This significantly weakens the argument in Gorrell (1987) for parallel processing, as the RTs for the verb targets following the ambiguous contexts may be due to the fact that they are optional continuations. Results reported by Blosfeld (1988) are relevant in this regard. As in Gorrell (1987), Blosfeld used a lexical decision task for targets following ambiguous contexts. Three experiments were conducted. In two, verb targets following ambiguous contexts failed to produce faster RTs (compared to an unambiguous context requiring a verb for a grammatical continuation). In the third experiment, which used a stimulus set similar to that of Gorrell (1987), ambiguous contexts did produce faster RTs than the obligatory contexts, but slower RTs than ungrammatical contexts. These latter results are consistent with the results of Gorrell (1988). The difference between Blosfeld's third experiment and those reported in Gorrell (1987) may be due to the fact that Gorrell's (Experiment 2) RTs averaged about 720 milliseconds whereas Blosfeld's (Experiment 3) averaged about 490 milliseconds. Given that Frazier and Rayner's (1982, Table 7) results show the effect of the disambiguating verb in the attachment sentences to be about 35–50 milliseconds/fixation, it

---

[25] See Wright (1982, Experiment 5), where there is a clear, but nonsignificant, trend in this direction. As Wright notes, the failure to obtain significance was probably due to irrelevant problems with the materials.

may be that Blosfeld's study was sensitive to processing distinctions that were masked by the comparatively slow RTs reported in Gorrell (1987).

The general conclusion to be drawn from the experimental results discussed in this section is that the parsing model proposed in Section 4.1 is compatible with the psycholinguistic evidence. The "ambiguity effect" within the context of a parser incorporating a deterministic structure builder is that (i) it alters when structure may be computed relative to the appearance of lexical material, and (ii) it permits the assignment of grammatical features (e.g. case, theta role) that may change as additional input is processed and additional structure computed. This view is consistent with the information-paced parsing model of Inoue (1991), which I discuss in Section 4.5.

Part of the explanation given here for the difference between the processing of ambiguous and unambiguous strings is that, in the absence of ambiguity, the parser may precompute structure based on either the need to satisfy general principles of the syntax or item-specific lexical information. In the next section we turn to an examination of the availability of this type of information in the parse sequence.

4.3   Lexical information

An important issue in parsing theory is the relationship between information associated with individual lexical items and general principles of syntactic wellformedness. For example, the fact that (in English) verbs precede their complements follows from general syntactic principles, whereas the presence or absence of a complement follows from idiosyncratic properties (e.g. the subcategorization frames of Chomsky 1965) of individual verbs.

Within the psycholinguistic literature, numerous studies have focused on the processing of verb-complement structures. For example, in one of the earliest investigations into the effects of verbal complexity on sentence processing, Fodor *et al.* (1968) concluded that the subcategory information associated with a verb was crucial for the rapid recovery of a sentence's deep structure. Further, they argued that processing complexity was a function, in part, of the number of distinct complement types a verb permits.

Fodor (1978) proposed a Lexical Expectation Model of Gap Detection which presupposed that subcategory information is available for use in determining the potential locations of Wh-traces in a sentence, and extends this concept to include not simply a list of the permissible complement structures, but also some representation of the relative likelihood of their occurrence. Clifton *et al.* (1984) have offered experimental support for this model.[26] Mitchell and Holmes (1985) offer evidence for a Verb Dominance Principle which extends the Lexical Expectation Model to the processing of complement structures in declaratives.

The well-known proposal of Ford *et al.* (1982) for the use of lexical preferences in parsing also depends upon the efficient use of subcategory information. Until quite recently there has been general agreement among researchers that syntactic processing involves the rapid use of subcategory information in computing a structural analysis for a given word string. For example, Clifton *et al.* (1984) argue that subcategory information is used at an early stage of processing, prior to any semantic or pragmatic influences. This is based on the observation that performance on a secondary task suffered when the lexical item following a verb conflicted with the verb's preferred complement structure.

However, recent investigations by Mitchell (1987), Frazier (1989), and Ferreira and Henderson (1990) argue that syntactic processing involves two distinct stages: one in which a preliminary structure is computed without the use of subcategory information; and a second stage in which this information serves to confirm or disconfirm the initial analysis.

For example, consider the sentence fragments in (45), where (45a) contains a transitive verb and (45b) an intransitive verb. The claim is that, for (45a) and (45b), the parser will initially compute the structures in (45c) and (45d); that is, with the following noun phrase analyzed as the direct object of the verb.

(45a)   The new owners bought NP
(45b)   The new owners slept NP
(45c)   The new owners [$_{VP}$ bought NP]
(45d)   The new owners [$_{VP}$ slept NP]

Thus the first-stage device makes use of category information (e.g. verb vs. noun) but ignores, or does not have access to, subcategory information. To test this hypothesis that the use of subcategory information is delayed, Mitchell (1987) used a phrase-by-phrase self-paced reading task and compared sentences in which a noun phrase followed either an intransitive

---

[26] We return to a discussion of the Lexical Expectation Model in the discussion of the processing of empty categories.

verb or an ambiguous verb (optionally transitive or intransitive). The phrase-by-phrase self-paced reading task proceeds in this way: there is an initial prompt on the screen of the monitor. The subject presses the space bar, which calls up the first display and starts a timer. The subject is instructed to read the display and press the space bar as soon as it's been read. This second key-press signals the end of the reading time for the first display, and starts the timer for the reading of the second display. The subject presses the space bar as soon as the second display has been read. For example, (46a) shows the two displays for a sentence containing an ambiguous verb, while (46b) contains an intransitive verb.

(46a)   After the child had visited the doctor [DISPLAY 1]
         prescribed a course of injections [DISPLAY 2]
(46b)   After the child had sneezed the doctor [DISPLAY 1]
         prescribed a course of injections [DISPLAY 2]

Reading times for the first display were significantly longer with phrases containing intransitive verbs, as compared to their transitive counterparts. But, for the second display, the effect was reversed, with reading times for the phrases containing transitive verbs significantly longer than the phrases with intransitive verbs.

Mitchell interpreted this pattern as follows. The DISPLAY 1 phrases with intransitive verbs (46b) produce longer reading times because the parser initially misanalyzes the intransitive verb–NP sequence as a VP. But this initial analysis is disconfirmed by the second-stage processor which makes use of subcategory information to check the output of the first stage. At this point, reanalysis is required, and it is the process of reanalysis which takes time, producing the longer reading times.

However, the additional time taken for reanalysis is offset by the fact that the string in the second display is consistent with this reanalyzed structure. Hence the comparatively fast reading times for this display with the intransitive examples. For the optionally transitive cases, as in (46a), the parser's initial reaction to the first display is the same as for the intransitive cases. That is, the verb–NP sequence is analyzed as a VP. This initial hypothesis is confirmed by the second-stage processor, which has access to the information that *visit* may take a noun phrase complement. Hence, there is no need for reanalysis, and reading times for the first display are fast compared to the intransitive cases. Unfortunately, the string presented as the second display is incompatible with the computed structure and reanalysis is required. This increases the reading time for the second display.

What is important to note here is that Mitchell's explanation for the pattern of reading times crucially relies on the fact that the availability of subcategory information is delayed, requiring the first stage device to build a structure which may be grammatically ill-formed. However, given the relative insensitivity of the phrase-by-phrase reading task, it is difficult to determine the locus of the processing difficulty resulting in the reading time asymmetries. For example, another plausible explanation is that, for the intransitive cases, reading times are long for DISPLAY 1 because subjects do make rapid use of subcategory information and are confused by the apparent oddity of strings such as *After the child sneezed the doctor.* An explanation along the lines suggested by Mitchell for the transitive cases may be correct. But here there appears to be little motivation for positing a processing stage prior to the use of subcategory information.

Gorrell (1991) used a lexical decision task to investigate the delay hypothesis, which predicts that the parser will initially treat all nouns following verbs as grammatical continuations. Thus we should observe comparable lexical decision times for nouns occurring after both transitive and intransitive verbs. If, however, the parser makes rapid use of subcategory information and this information is represented in the syntactic structure computed prior to the appearance of the lexical decision target, then RTs for noun targets should be significantly longer following intransitive verbs than transitive verbs.

The results reported in Gorrell (1991) are not consistent with the delay hypothesis. Nouns following contexts ending with intransitive verbs produced longer lexical decision times than nouns following transitive verbs. Subcategory information is apparently used quite early in the parse sequence. These results are consistent with those of previous studies, e.g. Clifton *et al.* (1984), as well as work using a cross-modal lexical decision task (Nicol 1988).

More recently, Trueswell *et al.* (1993) report experimental results consistent with the rapid use of subcategory information. Their first experiment used a cross-modal naming task to investigate whether or not context-target congruency was affected by subcategory information. They contrasted active contexts (e.g. *The old man*) with passive contexts (e.g. *The old man was*). Targets were either verbs which preferred nominal complements (e.g. *observe*) or verbs which did not (e.g. *insist*).[27] Passive

[27] Targets were categorized based on a preliminary normative study. See Trueswell *et al.* (1993, Appendix 1).

contexts were only congruent with the nominal-complement verbs. They used context-target quadruples such as (47).

(47a)   The old man INSISTED
(47b)   The old man OBSERVED
(47c)   The old man was INSISTED
(47d)   The old man was OBSERVED

After naming the target, subjects answered YES or NO to the query: "Good Continuation?" For the naming task there was a robust effect of subcategory information. That is, for the passive contexts, naming times were significantly longer for the verbs whose subcategorization frames did not permit nominal complements. Subjects' judgments as to the well-formedness of the continuation were consistent with the naming effect, i.e. 98 percent of the passive–intransitive trials were judged not to be good continuations. As with the studies discussed above, the results support the view that the availability of subcategory information is not delayed.

The second experiment reported by Trueswell *et al.* (1993) investigated whether there was a complexity effect due to analyzing a post-verbal NP as a complement rather than as a subject of an embedded clause. The concern which motivated this experiment was that if there were such an effect, it could be misinterpreted as resulting from the delayed availability of subcategory information. A cross-modal naming task was again used. Contexts ended in either NP-bias verbs (e.g. *accept*) or S-bias verbs (e.g. *insist*). Targets were either the nominative pronoun HE or the accusative HIM. The context-target pairs are illustrated in (48). The presence or absence of a complementizer was also contrasted. As with the first experiment, Trueswell *et al.* (1993) asked subjects whether or not the target was a "good continuation" of the context.

(48a)   The old man insisted HIM/HE
(48b)   The old man insisted that HIM/HE
(48c)   The old man accepted HIM/HE
(48d)   The old man accepted that HIM/HE

One uncontroversial prediction is that naming times for HIM in the complementizer condition (the 48b and 48d versions) should be elevated compared to the no-complementizer condition. This prediction was confirmed. Trueswell *et al.* (1993) also report that there was a significant interaction between the case of the pronoun and verb type. Specifically, the effect for verb type is significant for HIM. The results for HIM clearly indicate that subcategory information is already available when the target is presented (cf. Boland 1991).[28] Trueswell *et al.* (1993) also present the results of an eye-movement study which demonstrate the rapid availability of subcategory information. They argue persuasively that, once certain lexical preference effects and eye-fixation patterns are accounted for, the results of Ferreira and Henderson (1990) cannot be used to support the delay hypothesis.

Thus, there is considerable experimental support for the view that the parser makes rapid and efficient use of verb-specific information in computing an on-line structural representation.[29] The implications of this conclusion for the processing of empty categories (particularly the traces of Wh-movement) are explored in the next section.

4.4   Empty categories

Chomsky (1982) observes that "the properties of gaps are intrinsically significant in that the language learner can confront little direct evidence bearing on them." For purposes of the present inquiry, we can substitute "the parser" for "the language learner." That is, the presence of gaps, or empty categories, must be inferred either from properties of the lexical items in the input string or from general syntactic principles.[30]

Assuming the theory of empty categories discussed in Chapter 2, the parser must construct a tree which may contain various types of empty categories (e.g. PRO, NP-trace, Wh-trace). Consider the sentences in (49).

(49a)   Ian wants to leave the planet
(49b)   It is difficult to leave the planet
(49c)   This book was read by Ian last night
(49d)   Which book did Ian read last night

In (49a) the parser will be able to posit a PRO on the basis of the infinitive *to leave*. Here PRO is controlled (i.e. has its reference established) by the subject of the matrix clause. In (49b) PRO is not controlled (its reference is open). The task of the parser with respect to PRO is not difficult. PRO

---

[28] This interaction was not significant for HE. Trueswell *et al.* (1993) argue that this is due to a lexical co-occurrence effect, i.e. certain verbs permitting sentential complements display a stronger "*that* preference" than others. This preference appears to affect the processing of immediately following NPs. It was evident not only in the naming task but in an eye-movement study they also report.

[29] See Nicol (1988) and Boland *et al.* (1990) for evidence that verb-control information is used without delay.

[30] I put aside here the possible use of contraction phenomena.

is the subject of infinitival clauses unless there is a lexical NP in an Exceptional Case Marking (ECM) construction. Sentence (49c) contains the NP-trace of the movement of *this book* to subject position. Thus the trace occupies the argument position of the NP, adjacent to (and preceded by) the verb. Once the passive morphology of the verb is identified, the postulation of an NP-trace is straightforward. Furthermore, it is required by the grammar.[31]

But, as Fodor (1978) first pointed out, the effects of Wh-movement are quite different. First, unlike NP-movement, the effects of Wh-movement are not strictly local. The s-structure position of a Wh-phrase can be arbitrarily far from its d-structure position. Second, for a parser that makes structural commitments as each lexical item is processed, there can be considerable uncertainty as to the d-structure position of a preposed Wh-phrase. One source of this uncertainty is ambiguous verbs, i.e. verbs which may or may not take a nominal complement. Before considering the processing of wh-structures in which the trace position is uncertain, we first need to clarify the parse sequence for unambiguous examples. Consider (50a) and the tree in (50b).

(50a)   Which city did Ian visit

(50b)
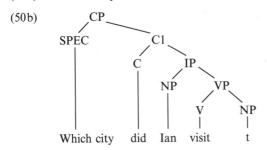

When the parser processes the Wh-phrase *which city*, it creates the relevant CP structure and attaches the phrase in the [SPEC, CP] position. As the IP is subcategorized by C, this structure is precomputed. Next the parser inputs *did* which is attached in the C position (I omit here the structure relevant to verb movement). After the subject of the clause is attached, the parser processes *visit*, a verb which requires a nominal complement.[32] Given this, an NP node is precomputed and attached within the VP.

---

[31] Of course, adjectival passives do not involve movement.
[32] At least in some dialects. Others allow sentences such as (i).

(i)   Ian visited last night

Further, as the parser has identified an antecedent and there is no other grammatical argument position for the preposed NP (compare * *Which book did Ian visit Paris after reading*), a trace is posited and attached to the post-verbal NP node. That is, the parser precomputes predictable aspects of obligatory structure.

Consider now the contrast in (51), from Berwick and Weinberg (1984).

(51a)   What did Ian say that Bill thought Fred would eat
(51b)   Did Ian say that Bill thought Fred would eat

The verb *eat* may be transitive or intransitive. Berwick and Weinberg argue that the parser must posit a trace only if there is an identifiable antecedent in the analyzed structure. Further, the parser cannot search for an antecedent through an arbitrarily long prior context, so there must be some locality restriction on "how far away" an antecedent can be from a potential trace site. Berwick and Weinberg propose that Subjacency would guarantee that the parser need only search the nearest [SPEC, CP] for an available antecedent.[33] Consider the structure in (52).

(52)

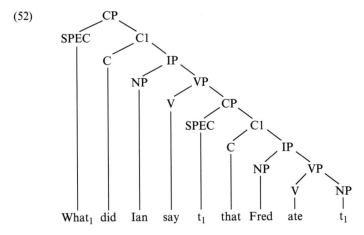

When the parser processes the verb *say* it has already identified the Wh-phrase. Despite the fact that *say* does not require an object, pre-computation of the NP node dominating a trace can proceed as this NP is obligatory (given the prohibition on vacuous quantification). Further, this

---

[33] The argument Berwick and Weinberg (1984) present is valid for any locality condition on Wh-traces. That is, the argument was not, strictly speaking, an argument for Subjacency, but an argument for some form of locality. The ECP would have served as well, but Subjacency was a more-established aspect of the grammar. It was also a prominent part of the Marcus parser. See Fodor (1985) for discussion.

NP must be dominated by the matrix VP, given the lexical properties of *say* and the general constraints on movement. The parser, then, processes the matrix verb and precomputes a trace-NP node that is dominated by the VP. If this is the final input, then the trace is in a case and theta position, governed by the verb. The output would be a question *What did Ian say?* with the trace in object position.

If the input is as in (51a), the parser next processes the complementizer *that* and projects a CP complement of the verb. As *say* does not permit a [NP, CP] complement structure, the trace-NP must be within the CP. Therefore the parser asserts that this NP is dominated by the CP. Following Berwick and Weinberg's (1984) Subjacency analysis, the trace is attached as (or, lowered into) the [SPEC, CP] of the embedded clause. This is the intermediate trace position indicated in (52). In order to insure that this lowering is deterministic, I will assume that the interpretation of a trace is "functionally determined" (see Chomsky 1982) by its antecedent and structural position. That is, the structure interpreter will determine the role an empty category has in the structure incrementally, just as secondary features might hold at one point in the parse but fail to hold at another (see Merlo 1992 for discussion of this issue).

The trace now in [SPEC, CP], the intermediate trace, functions as an antecedent in the same way as the initial Wh-phrase. When the verb *eat* is processed, there is an antecedent in the [SPEC, CP] position, and the parser creates a trace-NP node dominated by the VP and, in the absence of intervening structure, governed by the verb. Thus Subjacency guarantees that, in English, the processing of Wh-constructions is an operation confined to the local CP. That is, despite the fact that Wh-movement is unbounded at surface structure, the structure which the parser is building analyzes the antecedent-trace relation as a series of local relations.[34]

Consider now the ambiguity in the following sentences.

(53a)   Which book did Ian read to the children last night
(53b)   Which book did Ian read to the children from last night
(53c)   Which child did Ian walk to the office last night
(53d)   Which child did Ian walk to the office with last night

As Fodor (1978) notes, sentences such as (53b) are difficult compared to (53a). The intuition is that, in (53b), the parser has prematurely associated the Wh-phrase with the verb when the correct association is with the

---

[34] See Berwick and Weinberg (1985) for a discussion of the processing of parasitic gaps.

preposition. In terms of the present model, the parser has posited a trace of the Wh-phrase after the verb *read*. But this structure is incompatible with the appearance of the preposition *from*, which requires an object. But a different situation is evident in (53c) and (53d). Here it is (53c) which is awkward in comparison to its counterpart. The generalization appears to be that the parser is basing its decision concerning the location of a trace, in part, on the lexical preference of the verb. This intuition is supported by experimental work reported by Clifton *et al.* (1984). They found that performance on a lexical decision task was affected by whether or not ambiguous verbs such as *read* or *walk* prefer to be transitive or intransitive. Fodor's term for this was the Lexical Expectation Model.

Let us assume that the parser's operations of node creation and attachment can be affected by lexical preferences (see also Ford *et al.* 1982). For (53b) the parser will process the verb *read* and create the NP structure for a trace. This NP will be dominated by the VP and preceded by the V. When the PP *to the children* is processed, it too is dominated by the VP and preceded by the V. Also, it is preceded by the NP projection of the trace. The tree in (54a) illustrates the state of the parse after the PP is attached. When the preposition *from* appears, the parser must retract the assertion that the NP precedes the first PP, as (54b) shows.

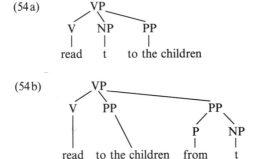

(54a)

(54b)

Notice that the dominance relations do not change as the parse proceeds (the NP is lowered into the new PP and continues to be dominated by the VP), so that the garden-path effect must be due to the retraction of a precedence relation. But this cannot explain the awkwardness of (53c). The effect here appears to follow from the difficulty of creating nodes which must precede already analyzed constituents (cf. the Left-to-Right Constraint of Marcus 1980).[35] The parse state after processing the adverbial phrase *last night* is given in (55a), with the correct tree in (55b).

(55a)

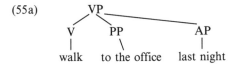

(55b)

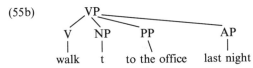

In general, despite the fact that they are not represented in the speech signal, empty categories do not appear to present perceptual difficulties which necessitate particular parsing mechanisms. This is largely due to the fact that the parser is building a structural representation according to general syntactic principles which govern the distribution of both lexical and empty categories.

There are a number of grammatical formalisms (e.g. Steedman 1987) which do not make reference to empty categories. The question arises as to whether or not there is psycholinguistic evidence for the existence of empty categories.[36] Some recent experimental evidence reported by Swinney *et al.* (1988) has been interpreted by many as support for an empty category analysis of Wh-constructions. Using a cross-modal lexical decision task, they observed associative priming effects for heads of preposed phrases (e.g. *boy* in [56]) at the site of the putative empty category, i.e. immediately after presentation of *accuse* in (56).

(56)   The policeman saw the boy that the crowd at the party accused of the crime

That is, lexical decision times for a semantic associate of *boy* were faster (compared to a control word) after, but not before, presentation of the

---

[35] Extraposition appears to produce a similar awkwardness, as (i) illustrates.

(i)   The boy entered the room who was handsome

But constructions such as (ii) are not as awkward as predicted by this account.

(ii)   They saw last night one of the most moving plays they had ever seen.

[36] See Fodor (1989) for an excellent discussion of these issues. Fodor discusses experimental findings with respect to the different types of empty categories posited by GB. I will focus here on Wh-trace.

verb *accuse*. This phenomenon is referred to as *reactivation*. It appears that a reasonable interpretation of these and other findings (e.g. Nicol 1988) is that the Wh-trace functions to "reactivate" the preposed phrase with which it is coindexed. Such an interpretation is consistent with the data. But as Pickering and Barry (1991) point out, the Swinney *et al.* data do not uniquely support an empty category analysis of Wh-constructions.[37]

Pickering and Barry point out that these and other studies investigating filler–gap dependencies used stimuli in which the putative trace site was always adjacent to the verb. The failure to investigate other putative trace sites allows for an alternative interpretation of these findings. That is, the effects usually attributed to traces (e.g. reactivation) may, in fact, be due to a direct filler–verb association. Within the framework of categorial grammar (Ades and Steedman 1982; Steedman 1987), a theory which posits no empty categories, they propose a "direct association hypothesis" (DAH) whereby fillers are associated with subcategorizers[38] without the intermediate filler–trace (and consequent subcategorizer–trace) dependency.

Consider sentences (57) and (58).

(57)   John put the cake in the box.

(58)   In which box did John put the cake
(58a)   [In which box]$_1$ did John put the cake t$_1$
(58b)   [In which box]$_1$ did John put$_1$ the cake

(58a) gives a structure which assumes an empty category analysis. Structure (58b) indicates a direct association between filler and verb. Although it may appear that the empty category analysis predicts that trace postulation (and consequent interpretation) will be delayed until all material prior to the trace site is processed, this is not the case. As with other structures discussed above, the parser precomputes the obligatory aspects of the tree in advance of the relevant lexical material, e.g. an NP node when an obligatorily transitive V is processed. Similarly, once a Wh-phrase has been processed, a trace is required and would be postulated when the processor encounters a verb.

There is some experimental evidence supporting this view of precomputation in Wh-constructions. For example, Boland (1991) reports experimental results which indicate that preposed arguments can be evaluated for plausibility prior to the appearance of the putative trace site,

---

[37] For a more detailed discussion of this issue, see Gorrell (1993a), Gibson and Hickok (1993), and Pickering (1993).   [38] PB's term for verbs and prepositions.

i.e. the gap. She tested sentence pairs such as those in (59). The preposed phrase was plausible in one version (e.g. [59a]) and implausible in the other version (e.g. [59b]). The task was a word-by-word self-paced reading task. That is, subjects pressed a key to present each new word of the sentence on a computer screen. If the sentence "stopped making sense," subjects pressed a different key which stopped the presentation of the sentence.

(59a) Which uneasy pupils did Harriet distribute the science exams to in class

(59b) Which car salesmen did Harriet distribute the science exams to in class

Boland found that plausibility effects (reflected in both the reading time and judgment scores) were evident before the gap after *to*. For example, there were significantly more "stopped making sense" judgments at the end of the post-verbal NP (e.g. at *exams*) in the implausible condition than in the plausible condition. This result is incompatible with a bottom-up approach to either filler–subcategorizer or filler–trace associations. This is because plausibility effects are evident not just before the appearance of the trace site, but also before the appearance of the subcategorizer (e.g. *to*).

As Boland observes, these results are consistent either with plausibility being evaluated without the mediation of syntactic structure, or with subcategorization information being used to project a syntactic structure in advance of bottom-up evidence. Presumably both of these options are available within the framework of the DAH, and it is clearly not the case, as PB implicitly assume, that pure bottom-up processing is a necessary property of the ec analysis.

Within the framework of the GB-based parser proposed here, the operation of the precomputation of structure accounts for the observation, and experimental results which demonstrate, that interpretive processes begin to evaluate aspects of preposed phrases when the verb is processed, i.e. prior to the appearance of bottom-up evidence for the trace. Further, this precomputation is consistent with a deterministic account as garden-path effects are only evident when assertions must be retracted, as when structural commitments are based on lexical expectations. These are independently motivated properties of the parser. Thus there is no reason to conclude that an empty category analysis of preposed constituents cannot form the basis for the process of comprehending such constructions. That is, the ec analysis, because it is compatible with the precomputation of obligatory structure, is consistent with the demands of incremental interpretation.

In the next section I discuss the issue of incremental structuring and interpretation in head-final clauses. The processing of these types of clause is of interest because argument-structure and licensing information is not available until comparatively late in the parse.

4.5   Head-final clauses

As discussed in Chapter 2, English is a head-initial language, e.g. verbs assign case and theta roles to the right. In contrast, in languages such as Japanese and German, complements tend to precede heads. For example, Japanese is a strictly head-final language. As Mazuka and Lust (1990) point out, this creates a number of left-branching constructions in Japanese that are not found in English. This difference presents immediate problems for parsing strategies based primarily on studies of English. Consider the following perceptual strategy (60), discussed by Chomsky and Lasnik (1977). This strategy explains, in part, the perceptual difficulty of strings such as (61a).

(60)   In analyzing construction C, given a structure that can stand as an independent clause, take it to be a main clause of C.

(61a)   * He left is a certainty
(61b)   That he left is a certainty

As Pritchett (1992) points out, this strategy is inapplicable to Japanese where, assuming incremental structuring, a string such as (62a) might be initially construed as a main clause. Yet, as Mazuka and Lust (1990) note, this string might actually be a subordinate clause, as in (62b).

(62a)   Hirosi-ga Masao-o mita
        Hirosi-N Masao-A saw
        "Hirosi saw Masao"

(62b)   Hirosi-ga Masao-o mita koto...
        Hirosi-N Masao-A saw that
        "that Hirosi saw Masao..."

Thus, it appears that (60) must be a parsing strategy particular to English (or languages in which complementizers precede clauses). But even this characterization runs into a number of problems. For example, consider the phrase *main clause* in (60). In the grammar discussed in Chapter 2, in which structure is "projected" from lexical information, it is unclear how we should interpret the term *main*. In Government-Binding theory, a "clause" is either a CP or IP, but I am unaware of any syntactic arguments for formally distinguishing "main" CPs (or IPs) from subordinate CPs (or IPs).[39]

Given that there is no general grammatical distinction, and assuming that the parser is constructing a grammatical representation, we then face the further difficulty that the perceptual model I am proposing (and d-theory as well) predicts that "lowering" an initial clause into a subordinate position is within the structure-building capability of the parser (recall the lowering of the NPs in [13] and [18]).[40] This works well for left-branching structures, e.g. string-initial subordinate clauses in Japanese. But it appears to leave us with no explanation for the difficulty of processing (61a). However, consider the grammatical string (63), which is quite easily parsed, yet is structurally identical (with respect to the strategy [60]) to (61a).

(63)   Who left is a mystery

The acceptability of (63), in contrast to (61a), demonstrates that the strategy (60) cannot be viewed as a general property of English sentence comprehension. The difficulty of parsing (61a) must follow from the fact that it is ungrammatical. Further, this ungrammaticality cannot be accounted for by appeal to a functional explanation involving strategies such as (60).

This is a welcome result as it allows us not only to maintain the generality of the current proposal, but also to extend the account to a typologically distinct language such as Japanese. Thus left-branching

---

[39] Syntactic differences between clauses (e.g. s-structure verb position in German) are argued to follow from the interaction of general syntactic principles and specific features of the clauses (e.g. properties of COMP).

[40] Inoue (1991) notes that, even if a main/subordinate (or root/nonroot) distinction were maintained in the grammar, it could readily be viewed, not as a structural distinction, but as a feature distinction with respect to the labelling of the clausal node. Within Inoue's processing model, changes in such feature assignments are not costly.

Inoue presents further arguments against a perceptual mechanism with language-particular properties, arguing persuasively that apparent parsing differences follow from grammatical distinctions yielding different word-order possibilities. That is, "there is no parameterization, but just a parser which postulates and labels nodes when they are predictable from the available context" (Inoue 1991: 163).

structures in Japanese should not, in general, present problems for the proposed parser.[41] That is, they do not force us to alter, or parameterize, our parsing model. Further, we should be able to define a natural class of constructions in Japanese which produce garden-path effects, i.e. structures which require the parser to alter prior primary structural commitments. This prediction presupposes another universal property of the parser: Simplicity. Consider sentences such as (64) and (65), adapted from Mazuka and Itoh (forthcoming). As with the English examples, we will see, as discussed by Weinberg (1992), the proposal of Marcus *et al.* (1983), in conjunction with some form of simplicity metric governing initial attachments, correctly predicts that input requiring alteration or deletion of primary structural relations leads to clear processing difficulty.

(64a)   Yamashita-ga yuuzin-o hoomonshita kaisya-de mikaketa
         Yamashita-N friend-A visited company-L saw
         "Yamashita saw his friend at the company he visited"

(64b)

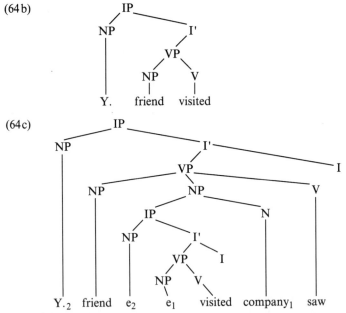

(64c)

For (64a), the parser will structure the initial string *Yamashita-ga yuuzin-o hoomonshita* with a clausal node dominating an NP (*Yamashita-ga*) and a VP (*yuuzin-o hoomonshita*), as shown in (64b). Thus the VP node will

---

[41] For discussion of this issue, see Mazuka and Lust (1990), Hasagawa (1990), and Inoue (1991).

dominate the NP *yuuzin-o*. But subsequent input is incompatible with this analysis, as this NP must be "raised" out of the VP headed by *hoomonshita* into the object position of the VP headed by the string-final verb *mikaketa*. This correctly predicts that strings such as (64a) will produce a garden-path effect. Consider also sentences such as (65a).

(65a)   Yamashita-ga yuuzin-o hoomonshita siriai-ni tegami-o kaita
       Yamashita-N friend-A visited   acquaintance-D letter-A wrote
       "Yamashita wrote a letter to an acquaintance who visited his
       friend"

(65b)

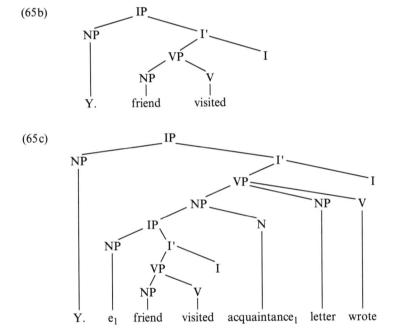

In contrast to (64), the restructuring in (65) requires only additional structure building and no garden-path effect is observed. As with (64), the parser initially computes an I′ and VP node dominating the NP *yuuzin-o* and *hoomonshita*, as shown in (65b). But here, these initial primary structural relations remain true throughout the parse (i.e. the entire I′ can be "lowered"). It is important to note that (64) and (65) are of comparable complexity. Thus we have a specific account for Mazuka and Itoh's (forthcoming) observation that processing difficulty occurs when "both the subject and the object need to be taken out of the lower clause." Under the present proposal, it is not the reanalysis of two constituents (subject and object), but rather the *type* of reanalysis, which accounts for the garden-path effect.[42]

Similar remarks apply to the garden-path sentence in (66a), where raising of a single constituent (a subject) produces a garden-path effect.[43] In (66a), the parser will initially structure the string *Yuuzin-ga moochoo de nyuuin siteita toki* as a clause containing the subject NP *yuuzin-ga* and the VP *moochoo de nyuuin siteita*, as in (66b). When the postposition *toki* is processed, this clause is structured as a complement of the preposition (66c). But subsequent input is incompatible with this analysis. As Mazuka *et al.* (1989) observe, when *kureru* is used as part of a compound verb (as in *kite kureta*), it indicates that something was done which benefits the speaker of the sentence. This forces the speaker to be interpreted (via the creation of an empty pronominal) as the subject of the temporal clause and requires that the NP *yuuzin-ga* be raised out of the PP to the position of matrix subject (66d). As we have seen, this results in a garden-path effect as primary structural commitments must be altered, e.g. the dominance relation between the PP and the *ga*-marked NP in (66c).

(66a)   Yuuzin-ga moochoo   de   nyuuin siteita   toki
         friend-N   appendicitis with was   hospitalized when
         mimai ni kite kureta
         came to visit
         "When I was hospitalized with appendicitis, a friend came to visit me"

(66b)

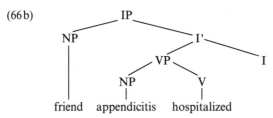

---

[42] Suh (1993) reports experimental support for this in the processing of ambiguous Korean sentences. Sentences in which Structural Determinism was violated (assuming that Simplicity governed initial attachments) produced marked processing difficulty, whereas sentences requiring comparable reanalysis (but limited to structure building) produced no such difficulty.

[43] Sentence (66a) is taken from Mazuka *et al.* (1989). They state that these types of sentences cause conscious reanalysis but are not difficult to understand. This observation is supported by their experimental results as well as the intuitions of numerous other Japanese speakers with whom I've consulted. It appears to have a status comparable to English garden-path sentences such as (i) in which there is an initial misanalysis that is easily "solved."

(i)   John put the candy in his mouth on the table

(66c)

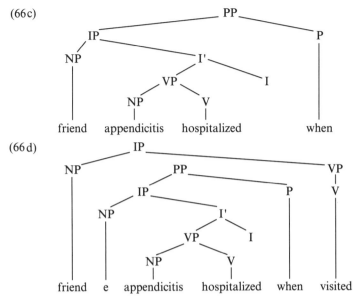

(66d)

Thus a theory of English and Japanese garden-path phenomena requires reference to a single, unparameterized, property of the parser: primary structural relations cannot be altered as the parse proceeds. Mazuka and Itoh (forthcoming) propose that, in Japanese, parsing decisions are "tentative." Within the analysis proposed here, English and Japanese parsers share the property that only secondary relations (e.g. government, abstract case assignment, theta-role assignment) are tentative, in that they may change as input is received and structure building proceeds. This parsing model is consistent with Inoue's (1991) proposal that the syntactic processor is an unparameterized perceptual mechanism.

Consider now some German examples which pose interesting problems for a parser incorporating Structural Determinism. In embedded clauses German is verb-final, with the exception that sentential complements of embedded verbs occur to the right of the verb (see Haegeman 1991). The problem this poses for the parser is that the trace of a Wh-phrase may occur either to the left of the verb (if a nominal object has been preposed) or to the right (if a phrase has been extracted from a sentential complement). If the parser initially posits a trace to the left of the verb and this analysis proves incorrect, a garden-path effect should result. Although there appears to be considerable evidence for early trace postulation (cf. the *Active Filler Hypothesis* of Frazier and Clifton 1989), Wh-constructions involving extraction from post-verbal sentential complements are not difficult to process. Consider (67), from Bayer (1992).

(67)   Welches Haschisch$_1$ hat Hans t$_2$ aufgehört [PRO t$_1$ zu rauchen]$_2$
        Which   pot   has Hans stopped   INF-smoke
        "Which kind of pot has Hans stopped smoking"

To preserve the generalization that German is a verb-final language, it is a common assumption that sentential complements of embedded verbs are base-generated in pre-verbal position and then "extraposed" to the right (Haegeman 1991).[44] Given the representational assumptions discussed in Chapter 2, this means that in pre-verbal position there is a trace (t$_2$) coindexed with the clause following the verb. The presence of this trace will allow us to straightforwardly account for the observation that structures such as (67) do not pose processing problems.

That is, given the presence of the Wh-phrase in the matrix [SPEC, CP] the parser will initially posit a trace preceding the verb *aufgehört*. When the extraposed clause is processed, the functional determination of the pre-verbal trace will cause the semantic interpreter to reinterpret it as coindexed with this clause. Finally, a trace for the Wh-phrase is created as object of *rauchen*. Note that this analysis of the processing of these constructions presupposes that indices are secondary relations which may change as the parse proceeds.[45] This is consistent with the discussion of Wh-constructions such as (52) above, repeated here as (68).

(68)   What did Ian say that Fred ate

In this type of structure, the parser will initially posit a trace as object of *say* (compare *What did Ian say?*). As additional input is processed, additional structure is built and this trace is "lowered" into the embedded [SPEC, CP] position. Thus the role of the trace in the structure changes from an argument governed by the matrix verb to an intermediate trace not in an argument position. Here, as well as in (67), although the status of the trace changes during the parse, what is not altered is the basic tree geometry, i.e. the dominance and precedence relations. Of course this is entirely in accord with Structural Determinism.

---

[44] This is not a universal assumption. One problem posed by this analysis is that extraposed phrases tend to be islands for extraction. See Bayer (1992) for an interesting discussion of this problem (as it relates to Bengali as well as German) and the competence/performance issues it raises.

[45] This analysis of indices as secondary relations is necessary to explain the interpretation of sentences such as (i), where *Bill* is initially interpreted as coindexed with *himself*. Subsequent processing alters this intuition, favoring the coindexation of *himself* with *Fred*.

(i)   Which picture of himself does Bill think Fred was embarrassed by?

Consider now an ambiguity studied by Bader and Lasser (forthcoming). In a reading-time study they tested ambiguities occurring in embedded clauses such as those in (69).

(69a)   dass sie   [nach dem Ergebnis zu fragen] tatsachlich erlaubt
         that she-N for   the   result   to ask   indeed   permitted
         hat
         has
         "that she indeed has given permission to ask for the result"
(69b)   dass [sie   nach dem Ergebnis zu fragen] tatsachlich erlaubt
         that she-A for   the   result   to ask   indeed   permitted
         worden ist
         been   is
         "that permission indeed has been given to ask her for the result"

The ambiguity concerns the case of *sie*, which functions as both the nominative and accusative form. In (69a), where *sie* is nominative, it is the subject of the higher clause. In (69b) *sie* is accusative and is the object within the lower clause. Disambiguation is given by the auxiliary verbs following *erlaubt*, as indicated in (69). The intent of Bader and Lasser's experiment is to investigate the parser's response to ambiguities which arise before the appearance of a verb.

They contrast a head-driven bottom-up parser (Pritchett 1991) with a top-down parser. A head-driven parser will not project nodes until a phrasal head is processed, whereas a top-down parser will make use of its grammatical knowledge to precompute structure. Furthermore, a content-based approach, whether head-driven or not, predicts that *sie* is initially attached as the object of *fragen* within the lower clause. This is because *fragen* is the first available licenser for the NP. In contrast to this, Bader and Lasser (forthcoming) report that "Native German speakers consistently report confusion upon hearing a sentence like [69b]." The results of Bader and Lasser's reading-time study support this intuition. Sentences such as (69b) produced significantly slower reading times (versus unambiguous controls using the masculine pronoun), whereas no such effect was evident for sentences such as (69a).

To understand why this effect obtains, consider the incremental structuring of embedded clauses. The complementizer *dass* signals an embedded clause and, following a proposal of Crocker (1992), we can assume that the parser precomputes the relevant CP and IP structure. The next item processed is the ambiguous *sie*. The only grammatical attachment sites for *sie* are within the embedded clause. The minimal attachment is to the IP. When the lower clause *nach dem Ergebnis zu fragen* is processed, *sie* may either be lowered into this clause as object of *fragen* or remain in its initial position, i.e. in subject position. Lowering is not forced as *fragen* is optionally transitive. Given Bader and Lasser's results, lowering is the less preferred option. But what accounts for the preference to keep *sie* in its initial position?

Fodor and Frazier (1980) formulated a *revision-as-last-resort* (RALR) principle which "requires that the partial phrase marker that has been constructed on the basis of the previous words in the sentence is not to be *changed* in response to subsequent words unless there is no other way of proceeding [emphasis in original]." Assuming RALR, the parser, having found a legitimate attachment site for *sie* in subject position (i.e. attached directly to IP), will not alter this attachment unless forced to do so. As noted, *fragen*, being optionally transitive, does not require an object and force lowering. Notice that we do not want to require the parser, having analyzed a case-ambiguous phrase in a particular way, to persist with this structure when reanalysis is required. Recall the discussion of (33) above, repeated here as (70).

(70a)   Ian gave her earrings yesterday
(70b)   Ian gave her earrings to Mary

Neither sentence in (70), as noted, produces processing difficulty. Yet, in (70a) *her* is assigned accusative case whereas in (70b) it is assigned possessive case. Assuming that there is an initial preference for the structure in (70a), reanalysis would require (abstract) case to be changed in order to yield the possessive reading in (70b). Again, this is consistent with Structural Determinism: the tree geometry (primary structural relations) remains constant but secondary relations, defined in terms of the tree, can be altered as input is processed.[46]

Thus the preference for the subject reading of *sie* in (69a) cannot follow from the parser's inability to reinterpret abstract case assignment. Of course any reinterpretation must be consistent with the morphological information, but that is not at issue here. Further, Fodor and Frazier (1980) note that RALR is a very natural principle as legitimate analyses are maintained unless conflicting information becomes available.

Bader and Lasser (forthcoming) argue that their results are more readily interpreted as due to the parser structuring material in advance of the

---

[46] As noted by Bader (1992), a similar effect is evident in German, where the case-marking is overt, but may be ambiguous.

argument structure information associated with the verb. Recall that this was an integral part of Inoue's (1991) information-paced parser. According to Inoue, case information is used to structure NPs within a clause before the verb appears. Sometimes this leads to processing difficulty if the pre-verbal structuring is inconsistent with a given verb's argument structure.

4.6   Summary

This chapter has demonstrated the psychological viability of a parsing model that (i) includes a deterministic component, and (ii) assumes a particular theory of grammar. Indeed, specific properties of the grammar (e.g. the distinction between primary and secondary relations) are crucial aspects of explanations for particular perceptual phenomena.

The proposed theory of parsing is responsive both to intuitive judgments and the results of experimental investigations. It is a very simple theory: the syntactic processor is a mechanism which builds phrase-structure trees as input is received. It makes rapid and efficient use of lexical information as well as the general principles of syntax. We have also seen that the postulation of empty categories is not problematic for the parser. What is clear is that an adequate theory of sentence comprehension must include a subtheory of syntactic processing. An adequate theory of syntactic processing requires a specific proposal for the form of the grammar. Without this it is impossible to distinguish, in any detailed way, properties of the parser from properties of the grammar.

Note that the distinction presented here between types of structural relations delimits not only the domain of application of determinism, but also the domain of reanalysis. As argued above, determinism is a property of the structure builder in particular, not of the parser in general. Similarly, reanalysis of secondary relations is the responsibility of the structure interpreter. This distinction ensures that reanalysis will always be in a local domain, e.g. a government domain, or a clausal domain. Thus reanalysis will never require the parser to reinterpret (or reinspect) the entire tree. This follows from the fact that grammatically defined concepts of locality are important properties of secondary relations such as government and binding. This local nature of reanalysis is only possible given the proposal that primary relations cannot be altered by the parser. That is, the grammar imposes no locality restrictions on dominance and precedence relations within a tree. For example, a root node dominates a terminal node, no matter how much intervening structure might exist. This view of reanalysis gives added support to the current proposal and its division of the parser into two components, a structure builder and a structure interpreter.

In the next chapter I will discuss the role of semantic and discourse factors in syntactic processing. But before turning to the issue of whether or not such factors can prevent initial syntactic misanalyses, it is important to also consider the implications of sentences such as those in (71), where the initial structural analysis is consistent with (or reinforced by) non-syntactic factors.

(71a)   Ian heard the noise was due to a design flaw
(71b)   Ian gave the man the book mentions an interview

In (71a) the NP *the noise* is clearly a plausible object for the verb *hear*. Despite this, a reanalysis of this structure to one in which *the noise* is no longer a matrix object is automatic and unconscious. In contrast, (71b) involves conscious processing difficulty. In this sentence, *the book* is a plausible second object for *give*. But here, reanalysis is quite conscious. It appears unlikely that there could be a semantic or pragmatic explanation for the contrast between the sentences in (71). In each case an inanimate NP is reanalyzed from object position to subject of a new clause. As argued above, there are clear structural differences which account for the observed distinction. Whether or not it is the case that semantic or discourse knowledge plays a role in the parser's initial attachment decisions, once these decisions have been made, structural factors play an important role in determining the ease of reanalysis.

As mentioned, in the next chapter I turn to another aspect of interpretation, i.e. the role of semantic and pragmatic factors in syntactic processing. I will assume in subsequent discussion the correctness of the parsing model discussed here and investigate the types of interaction or encapsulation required by Incremental Licensing and Structural Determinism.

5 Modularity and Structural Determinism

> Modularity is certainly a term whose time has come...What is considerably less clear is whether the term retains a constant meaning when it passes from one author to another.
>
> John C. Marshall

In this chapter I will be taking up the specific issue of the role of semantic and pragmatic factors in syntactic processing. I will not, however, be developing a theory of semantic and discourse processing. Rather, the focus here will be on incremental, deterministic, structure building and how this process is affected by nonsyntactic information. In order to draw out the main issues, I will contrast two views: (i) the modular theory (MT) of Rayner *et al.* (1983) and Clifton and Ferreira (1989), and (ii) the interactive theory (IT) of Crain and Steedman (1985) and Steedman and Altmann (1989). One reason to contrast these particular proposals is that they have each focused on the use of discourse information in the processing of a particular ambiguity – the reduced-relative ambiguity which has been a focus of research since Bever (1970).[1] Also, this ambiguity has been extensively studied with sensitive experimental techniques for the last few years. Thus, there is perhaps more data available for assessing the time course of information availability and use in ambiguous reduced-relative constructions than for any other type of processing phenomenon. Given this, it will serve as a useful probe into how Structural Determinism might be embedded in a more general language comprehension mechanism.

Although the versions of MT and IT which I will contrast here do not encompass the full range of models in the literature, the issues that arise in contrasting the forms of interaction that each theory permits are quite

---

[1] This is not to say that the intent of the two approaches is simply to account for particular ambiguities. Rather, the empirical argument in the last few years has come to focus on the details of the processing of these structures.

general.[2] I will argue that a parser which includes a deterministic structure builder, as proposed in the last chapter, is compatible only with an interactive comprehension model. However, in contrast to IT, which assumes at least some parallel syntactic processing, I will propose a serial, interactive, parser (SI). Further, I will argue that this incremental interaction does not obviate the need for a constraint on structure building such as Simplicity.

Before contrasting MT and IT and motivating a theory of SI parsing, it is necessary to first clarify the complex of issues that surround the use of the term "modularity." MT and IT are both modular theories in that they assume the existence of a distinct processor dedicated to the recovery of a structural analysis for a given sentence. Further, they are parsing models within the framework of J. A. Fodor's (1983) modularity thesis. It is a theory of "weak" interaction where, as Crain and Steedman (1985) observe, "syntactic processing independently 'proposes' alternatives... while semantics 'disposes' among these alternatives." It is the independent proposing of syntactic analyses that distinguishes weak from strongly interactive theories in which initial parsing decisions can be influenced by top-down processes.

Given that I will be contrasting different types of modular theories, it is important to clarify some of the properties attributed to modular parsers. As will become clear below, a major focus of experimental work investigating the relative merits of MT and IT is concerned with the speed of processing under different conditions and given varying types of structural and discourse factors. One reason for this focus is the simple fact that experimental work in parsing theory is almost solely concerned with detecting and interpreting temporal distinctions among comprehension processes. This is due, in part, to the popularity of, and reliance upon, the reaction time paradigm.[3] But it is also due to two distinct issues concerning speed of linguistic processing.

The first concerns the clausal hypothesis (Fodor *et al.* 1974) which, although it took various forms, appeared to necessitate at least some delay in semantic processing. Tyler (1981) observed that "any processing model which intends to maintain its links with [Transformational-Generative Grammar] must adhere to these two principles – autonomous syntax and

---

[2]   As will become clear below, these terms are misleading in that both theories are modular in many respects. I will continue to use these terms, as the distinctions I wish to draw between the two approaches are most often cast in these terms.

[3]   See Lachman *et al.* (1979) and Posner (1986) for discussion.

the delay of sentential semantic analysis..." Thus one motivation for demonstrating the rapidity of semantic interpretation is to test the hypothesis that the comprehension mechanism builds a syntactic representation prior to (and distinct from) a discourse representation. This issue will figure prominently in the discussion below concerning the independence of syntactic processing.

The second, related, issue concerns the discussion in Fodor (1983) of the temporal benefits which follow from a modular processing system. Fodor, in discussing the close-shadowing experiments of Marslen-Wilson (1973), observes "it may be that the phenomenon of fast shadowing shows that the efficiency of language processing comes very close to achieving theoretical limits."[4] This is based on the observation that the rate of normal speech is about four syllables per second. Close shadowers, who *understand* what they repeat, can shadow at a 250 millisecond latency. Given that the syllable appears to be the smallest reliably identifiable segment of the speech signal, Fodor notes "the following profoundly depressing possibility: the responses of fast shadowers lag a syllable behind the stimulus *not* because a quarter second is the upper bound on the speed of mental processes, but rather because, if the subject were to go any faster, he would overrun the ability of the speech stream to signal linguistic distinctions." That is, syntactic and semantic processing might actually be *as fast as they can be*, given the rate of speech.

But this point appears at odds with Fodor's view that such efficiency is one of the benefits of modular design. That is, Fodor assumes the output of the linguistic processor to be a "logical form," i.e. a linguistic representation that falls short of a full semantic representation (or discourse interpretation) of an utterance. But, as Marslen-Wilson and Tyler (1987) observe, "what is compelling about our real-time comprehension of language is not so much the immediacy with which linguistic form becomes available as the immediacy with which interpreted meaning becomes available." Thus the benefit which Fodor argues follows from modular design appears to be evident in what, for Fodor, is a nonmodular system.

It is important here to consider some points from Fodor (1989). One question Fodor poses is: "Why should perceptual inferences be carried out by specialized mechanisms?" Fodor notes that nonmodular problem-solving typically has two parts. Assuming the problem to be suitably identified, one must (i) determine how to solve it, and (ii) proceed to solve

---

[4] Shadowing is the repetition of speech as it is heard.

it. Fodor argues that part of the specialization of a module is to have the first part already in place so that the second part can simply be triggered by the appropriate input. Given this, a modular perceptual mechanism is one in which "the space of hypotheses that's available to be confirmed is determined *a priori.*" In linguistic processing this means that the space is limited to the well-formed structural descriptions that can be assigned to an utterance.

J. A. Fodor (1983, 1989) also argues that the informational encapsulation of a modular mechanism allows for a delimiting of the confirmation relations that must be computed in the process of stimulus identification. That is, encapsulation potentially yields two benefits: (i) it limits how much information there is to search through but, more importantly, (ii) it limits the amount of computation required to bring this information to bear on the process of stimulus identification and integration. Although it is possible that (pre-)specified search procedures could reduce the cost of searching a large domain, Fodor argues that no such reduction is possible for the second point because the variables involved in bringing information to bear on a particular stimulus in a particular situation cannot be delimited in advance.

There appears to be little doubt as to the validity of these arguments for the benefits of a modular system. But then what explains the rapidity of interpretation noted by Marslen-Wilson and Tyler (1987)? It must be that discourse processing, as much recent work suggests, is the responsibility of a dedicated mechanism whose operations are fast and efficient because, as with speech processing and parsing, the space of hypotheses is determined in advance. To put this simply, there are principles of discourse processing and these principles are brought to bear on the process of intergrating sentence-level information into a larger information structure.

All of this is familiar, but the specific point relevant to the present discussion is that theories which are "interactive" posit specific processors which interact. That is, it is not the case that interactive theories are simply nonmodular, but rather that they are modular in specific ways. This point has been emphasized by Steedman and Altmann (1989). Of course, this observation can be turned around and a similar point made from the perspective of modular approaches. That is, it is not the case that modular theories are simply noninteractive, but that they are interactive in specific ways (Rayner *et al.* 1983).

Returning to the point that Fodor's (1983) view of modular linguistic processing appears at odds with fast and efficient discourse processing, we can hold to the spirit of Fodor's proposal by continuing to posit a specialized syntactic processor, while at the same time incorporating an equally specialized discourse processor responsible (at least) for relating the output of the parser to a structured discourse representation. In addition to Fodor's arguments for modular input systems, Forster (1979) makes an important point concerning the independence of syntax and syntactic processing. Forster notes that "The whole point of a language having a syntax is to provide a clear and unmistakable indication of the correct interpretation of the sentence. Otherwise there would be no way to convey the meaning embodied in sentences such as [(1a) and (1b)]. Any move to allow the syntactic processor to be influenced by pragmatic factors works against the fundamental purpose of syntax."

(1a)   The patient cured the doctor
(1b)   The boy sold the man to the newspaper

The point here, of course, is that the extent to which semantic and discourse processes can influence the interpretation must be delimited by the solution space determined by the parser. The syntactic structure of (1a) delimits the possible interpretations to those consistent with *the patient* being the subject of *cure*, and with *the doctor* being its object. Both MT and IT agree on these points concerning structurally unambiguous sentences. Borrowing a term from Marslen-Wilson and Tyler (1987), we can refer to this property of the language comprehension system as "bottom-up priority."[5] What will be of interest here, as in the previous chapter, are sentences containing temporary structural ambiguities, in particular reduced-relative ambiguities.

This type of structure has become an important focus of study for a number of reasons. Following work by Crain (1980) and Crain and Steedman (1985), proponents of IT have questioned the use of experimental paradigms in which sentences are studied in isolation. In particular, they argue that the null context is not a "neutral" context with respect to NP modification. Roughly put, one of the primary discourse functions of modification is to select a particular object from a set of similar or identical objects. For example, if there is only one dog in a particular context, then the simple NP *the dog* is sufficient for successful reference. More complex NPs, e.g. *the brown dog* or *the dog the girl likes*, are referentially unnecessary and, unless they serve some other specific

---

[5]   Marslen-Wilson and Tyler (1987) abandon the use of this term as it presupposes a distinction of representational levels. As I hold to the presupposition, I will use the term.

function, violate the presupposition that additional structure or lexical material is not superfluous.[6]

From this perspective, the reduced-relative ambiguity is not only between syntactic representations of unequal structural complexity, but also between a reading that involves modification and one that does not. In the null context there is no established set of discourse objects and modification serves no referential function. Thus a discourse-based view of the preference for simpler structures is that they are preferred, not because of comparative structural simplicity, but because they are consistent with the presuppositions of the null context.

A useful starting point for the discussion to follow is the contrast studied by Ferreira and Clifton (1986), given in (2).

(2a)   The defendant examined by the lawyer turned out to be unreliable

(2b)   The evidence examined by the lawyer turned out to be unreliable

(2c)   The defendant that was examined by the lawyer turned out to be unreliable

(2d)   The evidence that was examined by the lawyer turned out to be unreliable

In an eye-movement study, Ferreira and Clifton found that ambiguous sentences with animate subjects such as (2a) produced longer first-pass reading times at the *by*-phrase than their unambiguous counterparts (2c). This was interpreted as due to an initial misanalysis of the NP *the defendant* as the subject of the matrix, past-tense, verb *examined* (the Minimal Attachment [MA] reading). Ferreira and Clifton also found that sentences such as (2b), with inanimate subjects, produced faster reading times at the initial verb (e.g. *examined*) than unambiguous sentences such as (2d). This latter finding was interpreted as a semantic anomaly effect, i.e. "readers were sensitive to the fact that the preferred analysis resulted in an anomaly." Thus, semantic interpretation is available with sufficient speed that it can affect eye-movment patterns *at the next word*. But also, Ferreira and Clifton argue, this information is unable to affect the initial structure computed by the parser. That is, it is not the case that the syntactic processor failed to compute the structurally simpler representation in order to avoid the semantic anomaly. Rather, it is argued that the structure is first computed and then the resulting anomaly detected.

Further, Ferreira and Clifton (1986) also studied the processing of reduced-relative ambiguities "in context." That is, sentences in which the

---

[6] Compare Grice's (1975) Maxim of Quantity: Be brief. It is interesting to note that "principles of economy" operate in the discourse as well as in the syntax.

reduced-relative ambiguity was resolved in favor of MA (the matrix reading) followed either a neutral context or a MA-biasing context. Sentences in which the relative clause reading proved correct followed either a context which favored this reading or one that was neutral.[7] The neutral contexts "contained information that *permits* both analyses, but does not strongly *select* for one or the other [emphasis in original]." For example, a neutral context for a string such as *The editor played the tape* referred to "one of the editors" whereas a biasing context for the reduced-relative reading specifically mentions two editors, one of whom had been played a tape.[8] Ferreira and Clifton (1986) report that context did not alter the parser's first-pass operations. The parser is initially sensitive to structural factors "but it is not sensitive to such nonsyntactic information as the semantic properties of nouns that make them appropriate for certain thematic roles associated with verbs, or the pragmatic information provided by a discourse context." These nonsyntactic factors, however, do facilitate reanalysis, as evidenced by the fact that there is often no conscious processing difficulty associated with reduced-relative structures in the proper context.

But this view of ambiguity resolution is incompatible with Structural Determinism. That is, if (i) primary structural relations cannot be automatically revised by the parser, and (ii) such relations, i.e. attachments, are made independent of semantic or discourse information, then there should be no possibility of automatic reanalysis when such information becomes available. Assuming the correctness of Structural Determinism, it must be the case that the automatic processing of reduced relative structures involves the intervention of nonsyntactic factors to prevent the parser positing the primary relations consistent with the structurally simpler reading.

Consider the results of some recent experiments by Trueswell *et al.* (1992) and Altmann *et al.* (1992). Trueswell *et al.* (1992) point out that in Ferreira and Clifton's (1986) first experiment, the animacy manipulation was less clear-cut than intended, i.e. "about half the sentences with inanimate nouns could have been plausibly continued as a main clause up through the verb." For example, strings such as *the car towed* and *the trash smelled* are both plausible simple active structures.

---

[7]   See Clifton and Ferreira (1989) and Steedman and Altmann (1989) for a discussion of the validity of a crossed-context design, that is, one in which biasing contexts are crossed with ambiguity resolution.

[8]   Note that the ambiguous verb from the test sentences, e.g. *played*, did not occur in the contexts.

Further, Trueswell *et al.* (1992) note that the mode of presentation used by Ferreira and Clifton could have played a role in producing the observed eye-movement patterns. The test sentences were displayed on two lines, with line-breaks occurring in the ambiguous region. In order to minimize the effect of this break, Ferreira and Clifton equated the position of the line-break for both reduced and unreduced sentences. But this produced a visual asymmetry between the two sentence types. The first line of a reduced relative (which averaged about nine characters less than its unreduced counterpart) ended well before the end of the screen. Trueswell *et al.* (1992) report pilot work which indicates that such early line-breaks increase reading times. If this effect were present in the Ferreira and Clifton (1986) experiments, it would have increased reading times for the reduced relatives, in the disambiguating region. This could give the appearance of difficulty with the structural analysis of the string when it is really a product of the mode of presentation. Trueswell *et al.* (1992) also point out that readers often do not fixate on short function words (e.g. *that*) and, in eye-movement studies, unreduced relatives might not be proper controls for reduced relatives. Thus eye-movement patterns might differ between construction types for reasons unrelated to the types of information (syntactic and nonsyntactic) being investigated.

Trueswell *et al.* (1992) addressed these concerns and conducted an eye-movement study designed to investigate the role of NP animacy on the parser's initial structuring of reduced-relative ambiguities. They used unambiguous verbs, e.g. *taken*, rather than unreduced relatives, to establish a baseline for investigating the processing of reduced-relative ambiguities. Also, there was no line-break, and "weak" manipulations (e.g. *the car towed*) were eliminated.

In contrast to Ferreira and Clifton (1986), who had found an ambiguity effect regardless of animacy specification, Trueswell *et al.* (1992) report that "reduced relative clauses with animate nouns had longer first and second pass reading times compared to their unreduced counterparts and compared to reduced relatives with inanimate nouns." In contrast, no such difference was observed with the inanimate-NP sentences. Thus the semantic constraint of animacy specification affected first-pass reading times.[9]

---

[9]   As noted in Chapter 1, such constraints are usually considered semantic because of the difficulty presented by such contexts as (i).

(i)   John is crazy and believes that rocks talk

That is, a syntactic theory should not be so formulated that it fails to generate structures such as *Rocks talk*. See McCawley (1971) and Jackendoff (1972) for discussion.

This finding is not consistent with the view that the ambiguity was initially resolved solely on the basis of structural criteria.

Experimental work by Altmann *et al.* (1992) also points to this conclusion. In an eye-movement study, they report the immediate effect of referential context on syntactic processing. In addition to presenting ambiguous sentences (e.g. [4]) in isolation (the null context), presentation also followed contexts such as those in (3).

(3a)   An off-duty fireman was talking to a man and a woman. He was telling them how serious the situation had been when their house had caught fire. The fireman had risked his life to rescue the woman while the man had waited outside.

(3b)   An off-duty fireman was talking to two women. He was telling them how serious the situation had been when their house had caught fire. The fireman had risked his life to rescue one of the women while the other had waited outside.

(4)   He told the woman he'd risked his life for ...

Context (3a) is *complement supporting* whereas the one in (3b) is *relative supporting*. Context (3b) is relative supporting because it refers to a set of firemen, and successful reference to one of them requires modification. Altmann *et al.* (1992) report that eye-movement patterns for reduced relatives presented in isolation exhibit a clear garden-path effect. This result is consistent with both the MT and IT approaches to ambiguity resolution. However, in a relative supporting context, first-pass reading times fail to reveal any garden-path effect, even a "momentary" effect. As Altmann *et al.* (1992) observe, "In accord with the predictions of the referential hypothesis, the provision of a felicitous context completely eliminated the reading time difference which had been observed in the null context between the ambiguous relative and the unambiguous control." This lack of even an unconscious, momentary, garden-path is incompatible with MT.[10]

But it does provide a way of relating Structural Determinism to the incremental effects of semantic and discourse information. The principle of Simplicity discussed in the last chapter states that computed structure must be justified. If a weak form of serial interaction is adopted, then this

[10] But see Mitchell *et al.* (1992) and Mitchell and Corley (forthcoming) where it is argued that, as in Ferreira and Clifton (1986), an unconscious garden-path exists even in disambiguating contexts. See below for the potential relevance of this to Structural Determinism.

concept of justification can be extended in a specific way. Assume that the parser's structure-building operations are governed by Simplicity. If, for example, a string such as (4) is being processed, then *the woman* will justify the building of an NP. In accord with incremental interpretation there is no delay in relating this phrase to the discourse model. If it fails to refer (see Crain and Steedman 1985; Steedman and Altmann 1989), an error signal will be sent from the discourse processor to the parser. This signal, which is minimal in content, will cause the parser to seek alternative analyses; given the timing of the signal, perhaps, specifically, alternative NP analyses. But little is known about the specifics of interaction, despite the fact that it is clear that there is interaction.

Note that this signal from the discourse processor to the parser is required by all approaches to syntactic processing. Given a structural ambiguity and an informative context, then, under any current parsing proposal, that context determines which analysis is pursued (whether initially or after a small delay). But for this to occur there must be some feedback to the parser telling it which analysis to continue computing. In IT this takes the form of "B, not A" if A and B are the syntactic analyses momentarily computed in parallel. In MT this takes the form (via the thematic processor) of "not A, try something that has the thematic properties of B." Consider another example: in Chapter 4 it was argued that a string-initial NP did not cause the parser to compute clausal structure as this was not justified by the input. But it is quite possible that certain intonational information (cf. Cooper and Paccia-Cooper 1980) might justify the building of a clause in advance of lexical justification. Similarly, semantic or discourse information may, in certain cases, justify the computation of structure not otherwise licensed.

The picture that emerges from this discussion is that the syntactic processor is dedicated and informationally encapsulated, in J. A. Fodor's (1983; 1989) sense, but it is not isolated. Returning to the examples discussed by Forster (1979), it is important to ensure that the solution space is delimited by the parser (bottom-up priority).[11] Thus the discourse

---

[11] But there remain phenomena which are quite puzzling, no matter how interaction is fashioned. For example, Trueswell and Tanenhaus (1991) demonstrated the rapid availability of discourse-based tense restrictions on the processing of reduced-relative ambiguities. But consider (i) and (ii), where the past-tense specification on the verb *do* fails to disambiguate.

(i)   Did the horse raced past the barn fall
(ii)   John bought the horse raced past the barn
(iii) The horse raced past the barn fell

processor cannot propose syntactic analyses, but it can signal a problem with computed structures. It is unclear whether or not such signals occur in unambiguous contexts, but, assuming serial interaction (SI), there is reason to think that they do. That is, if the discourse processor is encapsulated from syntactic information, it cannot determine whether or not the input is syntactically ambiguous. Thus the feedback from discourse processor to parser would be automatic, not determined by the syntactic context. Of course, in a structurally unambiguous context the parser can only compute the licensed analysis.

Assuming this sketch of how a parser incorporating a deterministic structure-building component might be embedded in an incremental-interactive comprehension mechanism, the question arises as to the necessity of retaining a structural principle such as Simplicity. Recall that the justification of Simplicity was twofold: (i) the principle of economy of representation, and (ii) structural ambiguity. In ambiguous contexts, a serial (weakly) interactive processor must initially propose an analysis to the discourse processor. There must be some principle or set of principles which determine this initial analysis. I have argued that Simplicity is that principle. Further, the principle of economy of representation demands that there be such a principle.

This principle of economy relates to the fact that an IT-type parallelism is not an option, given the grammatical assumptions motivated in Chapter 2. That is, the GB-based parser assumed here cannot compute all analyses in parallel, even momentarily. The most important reason is that the grammar is recursive and allows infinite embedding.[12] Further, as discussed in Chapter 2, the projection of a lexical node to a maximal phrase must be constrained by a principle such as Speas' (1990) "no vacuous projection" proposal.

Consider, then, the processing of (4) in both the null and the relative supporting context. When the parser computes the NP *the woman* in the null context, there is no error signal generated by the discourse processor.[13]

In experiments discussed in Gorrell (in preparation), there was clear evidence of garden-pathing in (i), (ii) and (iii). The question is, why doesn't the disambiguating information provided by *did* (in [i]) and *bought*, which does not permit a clausal complement, in [ii], appear to affect the parser's response to *raced*?

[12] Recall the discussion of Minimal Attachment in Frazier and Fodor (1978) concerning the impossibility of stating a principle of Maximal Attachment. Clifton and Ferreira (1989) make a similar remark with respect to IT, but Steedman and Altmann (1989) assume a distinct grammatical framework (Steedman 1987) in which this problem simply does not arise.

[13] It is, perhaps, no accident that the minimal presuppositional context is also the context for minimal syntactic structuring. Note that there is no interaction required if the structure

Therefore the parser continues to pursue the simplest structural analysis as there is neither internal justification (within the syntax) nor external justification (within the discourse) for additional structure. This simplest structure involves the positing of a precedence relation between the post-verbal NP *the woman* and the CP *he'd risked his life for*. When subsequent material forces the relative-clause reading, in which the CP must be dominated by the NP, a garden-path results. This is the analysis given in Chapter 4. In contrast, in the relative supporting context when the NP *the woman* is processed and related to the discourse model, an error signal is relayed to the parser, providing justification for the parser to pursue a nonminimal analysis of the ambiguous string.[14]

In some respects this model is similar to the constraint-based approach of Tanenhaus and colleagues (Spivey-Knowlton *et al.* forthcoming; Trueswell and Tanenhaus 1991; Trueswell *et al.* 1992; Trueswell *et al.* 1993; Tabossi *et al.* forthcoming; and MacDonald 1994). But it is also distinct in important ways. Trueswell *et al.* (1993) state that, "Structures are partially activated with the strength of activation dependent upon their likelihood given the input. The effects of a contextual constraint will depend upon its strength and the availability of alternative structures. To a first approximation, these are the same factors that are important for lexical ambiguity resolution."

The reference to lexical ambiguity is motivated by the fact that many garden-path sentences in English result from a morphological ambiguity (e.g. *raced*). But clearly such an approach cannot address the phenomenon of structural ambiguity in its full generality. This is particularly true of the processing of verb-final clauses where attachment preferences, as Sungki Suh (personal communication) points out, cannot follow from lexical factors. Further, the remarks above concerning the recursive nature of the grammar also apply to constraint-based approaches.

An important component of such approaches is the use of frequency information by the comprehension system. But if syntactic ambiguities cannot be reduced to lexical factors, then it is unclear how frequency effects are to be captured in the proposed model. One might attempt to account

---

justified by Simplicity is also justified by the context. This is a specific instance of Marslen-Wilson and Tyler's (1987) "bottom-up priority." That is, the system is operating in a modular fashion when there is concord among the "default" operations of the individual processors. When this concord breaks down, some specified forms of feedback occur.

[14] As Altmann *et al.* (1992) point out, a stronger test of the interactive model would involve *inducing* garden-paths that involve computation of the minimal structural analysis in contexts supporting a more complex representation.

for sentence-level frequency effects in terms of the relative frequency of particular constructions but, given that syntactic theory has abandoned construction-specific rules or principles, this way of conceptualizing the grammar–parser relation is less direct than is assumed in the present work. And, just as it is the responsibility of grammatical approaches such as Structural Determinism to address non-grammatical factors such as frequency in language comprehension, it is also important that constraint-based approaches clarify their grammatical assumptions.[15]

Also, constraint-based and discourse-based approaches must address the fact that certain types of syntactic anomalies are detected at a faster rate than pragmatic anomalies. Consider the following sentences, from Ni *et al.* (1993).

(5a)   It seems that the cat across the road won't eating ...
(5b)   It seems that the cat across the road won't bake ...
(5c)   It seems that the cat across the road won't baking ...
(5d)   It seems that the cat across the road won't eat ...

Sentence (5a) contains a syntactic anomaly (*won't eating*), (5b) a pragmatic anomaly (*cat ... bake*), and (5c) exhibits both anomalies. Sentence (5d) is a well-formed control sentence. Using a cross-modal lexical decision task, Ni *et al.* found that "sensitivity to pragmatic errors is significantly delayed relative to sensitivity to syntactic errors." Assuming a distinct syntactic processor, an account of this finding is straightforward. That is, as a distinct component, the syntactic processor may well yield an analysis more efficiently than a discourse component which must integrate distinct types of information.

Consider also the results reported in Gorrell (in preparation). Using a lexical decision paradigm, it was found that if the lexical decision target represented a structurally well-formed continuation of the context string, as in (6a), lexical decision times were faster than in (6b), where the target represented a syntactically ill-formed continuation.

(6a)   It is clear that sincerity will ADMIRE
(6b)   It is clear that people will ADMIRE
(6c)   It is clear that some very old ADMIRE

---

[15] For example, an extreme version of a constraint-based approach might analyze the processing difficulty associated with multiply center-embedded constructions as a direct result of their infrequency. But this type of analysis would raise a number of important questions. For example, frequency-based explanations must address the question of why a particular construction type might be infrequent. Also, at the level of the syntax, are the stored processes associated not only with active and passive constructions, but also right-branching, left-branching and center-embedded constructions?

At a "normal" presentation rate of 300 milliseconds per word, it was also found that selectional restriction violations, such as (6c), patterned with (6b).[16] However, at the faster presentation rate of 180 milliseconds per word, a distinct pattern was observed. That is, violations such as (6c) patterned with (6a), producing significantly faster lexical decision times than targets in (6b).

An explanation for this effect within the context of the proposed parsing model is that, at normal reading rates, the system can afford the "luxury" of interaction. That is, the syntactic processor can respond to error signals based on animacy information so long as its operations are not taxed by faster-than-normal input. When input occurs at increased rates the processor is forced to rely exclusively on internal justification and cannot take into account external signals.

Clearly more research is needed to sort out all the issues discussed here. For example, how might the present proposal account for the subtle, momentary and unconscious increases in fixation duration reported by Ferreira and Clifton (1986) and Mitchell *et al.* (1992)? One possibility is that the momentary disruptions revealed in these experiments are not the result of a disconfirmed misanalysis but rather the effect of the interaction between components. That is, this momentary slowdown in reading rate might reflect the fact that communication between processors is slightly less efficient than module-internal operations. This seems quite plausible and is consistent with the proposal that when there is concord between default operations of the processor there is no need for interaction. The experiments discussed here all report a lack of even the most subtle slowdown in these contexts.

---

[16] This is in contrast to pilot work reported in Gorrell (1990). The present results, unlike those reported in the pilot study, are consistent with the results of Boland (1991).

6   *Conclusion*

Again, one thinks of Don Quixote. He may see a windmill as a giant, but
he doesn't see a giant unless there is a windmill there.

W. H. Auden

In this book I have outlined a theory of syntactic knowledge and examined
its role in language comprehension. Although I have argued that syntax
plays a significant role in perception, it is clearly the case that numerous
other factors also play a role. For example, there are currently underway
a number of important studies within the general framework of constraint-
based comprehension systems. As briefly discussed in the last chapter, it is
important that theories of syntactic processing incorporate, in some way,
the effects of frequency of both individual lexical items as well as co-
occurrence probabilities (MacDonald 1994, Trueswell *et al.* 1993). I have
not attempted to do that here. Rather the focus has been to establish the
role of structural variables in sentence processing.

One of the most important aspects of the parsing model proposed here
is the grammatical distinction between primary and secondary structural
relations in a phrase-structure tree. This distinction is reflected in the
design of the processing model, given in (1). The types of syntactic relations
which a GB-based parser must encode in the structural representation it
builds are listed in (2).

(1)   ----▸ | structure builder |———| structure interpreter | ----▸

(2a)   dominance
(2b)   precedence
(2c)   government
(2d)   c-command
(2e)   theta assignment
(2f)   case assignment
(2g)   binding

The structure builder is responsible for node creation, projection, and attachment, as described in Chapter 4. The primary structural relations of dominance and precedence (2a and 2b) are the predicates of attachment and projection. Any two nodes in a well-formed tree are either in a precedence or a dominance relation. The structure builder is the deterministic component of the parser (Structural Determinism). This means that dominance and precedence relations, once posited, cannot be altered or deleted. It was shown in Chapter 4 that this restriction was able to account for a wide variety of garden-path phenomena. It was also argued that the structure builder is governed by Simplicity (3) and driven by (4). Incremental Licensing is, essentially, a simplified version of Pritchett's (1992) principle of Generalized Theta Attachment (see Section 3.5). That is, it does not require reference to *maximal* satisfaction of principles of grammar. This constraint on structure building is accomplished by Simplicity, which is independently motivated.

(3)   *Simplicity*: No vacuous structure building

(4)   *Incremental Licensing*: The parser attempts incrementally
                              to satisfy principles of grammar

The structure interpreter is responsible for the interpretation of the tree in terms of secondary relations (2c–2g). The structure interpreter requires the output of the structure builder in order to determine whether or not certain relations hold. This is due to the grammatical distinction of information types. For example, it cannot be determined if government obtains between two nodes unless dominance and precedence relations have been established. Given this, the design of the parser in (1) is quite natural from a grammatical perspective. The interpretation of structure is not deterministic. As demonstrated in Chapter 4, incremental structure building requires that secondary relations be allowed to change as the parse proceeds. For example, at one point in the parse, government may hold between two nodes – but it may be the case that additional structure building will result in a tree where government no longer holds between those nodes.

But the incremental reanalysis of secondary relations is constrained by the local nature of these relations. For example, government is quite local and the analysis of Wh-constructions, essentially, limits the domain to the current clause (or, perhaps, current maximal projection). As noted in Chapters 1 and 2, recent work in GB theory has sought to explain a number of distinct phenomena as either a particular type of government relation, or a series of government relations (Chomsky 1986a; Koster 1986; Manzini 1992). As noted, the representational approach of Koster (1986) is good news from the parsing perspective as the more locality built into secondary relations, the more limited is the potential domain for reanalysis. As argued in Chapter 4, the deterministic nature of primary relations prevents the parser from needing to reinspect (or reinterpret) the entire tree. This would not be the case if primary relations were not subject to the determinism constraint.

Given the representational form of GB proposed by Koster (1978, 1986), there is no need to determine how the parser computes a d-structure, an LF, or the derivational mapping between these levels. This is an important point as most work in GB-based parsing simply ignores the issue of distinct levels of representation and the derivational mapping between levels. But it must be emphasized that this move to a monostratal GB is justified only by the fact that there is a well-motivated, empirically adequate, alternative to the standard derivational approach of Chomsky (1981, 1986b). It is simply not sufficient to assume a theory of grammar that cannot account for the important phenomena which form the research base for syntactic theory.

It was also shown that Structural Determinism interacted in an interesting way with proposals for the parser's ability to make use of nonsyntactic information. I proposed a weakly interactive system that, in most contexts, obeyed the principle of bottom-up priority. But, in certain types of ambiguous contexts, the parser is able to respond to an error signal from the discourse processor. It is important to note that the form of the response is constrained both by the grammar (the computed representation must be syntactically well-formed) and the structure builder (computed structure cannot be altered or deleted). This form of interaction does not differ in any important respect from that posited in other parsing models such as the modular theory of Ferreira and Clifton (1986) or the interactive theory of Steedman and Altmann (1989).

It must be stressed that Structural Determinism is not a complete theory of language processing. For example, for a number of different sentence types, the comprehension mechanism is able to recover from misanalyses requiring the recomputation of primary relations. Consider the sentences in (5), where it is evident that, despite the clear disruption involved, recovery can be quite efficient.

(5a)   While Mary was mending the sock fell off her lap
(5b)   Ian put the candy on the table in his mouth

Detailing the mechanisms involved in this type of reanalysis has been an elusive goal for theories of sentence processing, which have focused on determining initial structural preferences (e.g. Frazier 1987) and distinguishing reanalyses which are automatic from those which are not (Pritchett 1992). This has also been the focus of the present work. As is the case of all current parsing models, an evaluation of Structural Determinism in terms of a specific proposal concerning garden-path recovery must await the development of such a proposal.

Of course there is an enormous amount of work still to be done to test the proposals outlined here. Perhaps most importantly, there needs to be an emphasis on typologically distinct languages. The situation is similar to work within generative grammar in the early 1970s. Many of the studies current at that time were primarily based upon studies of English syntax. But these proposals were soon forced to bear the additional empirical burden arising from the syntactic study of an increasing number of the world's languages. One result of this cross-linguistic work is what is now known as the principles-and-parameters framework (Chomsky 1986b).

Just as a theory-driven examination of a wide variety of languages brought fundamental changes to syntactic theory, it seems reasonable to expect that similar changes await theories of syntactic processing. The discussion of the parsing of head-final clauses in Chapter 4 reveals that Simplicity, Incremental Licensing, and Structural Determinism interact in interesting ways to account for a wide variety of phenomena across construction types. Thus the approach pursued here seems promising and gives support to the view that the perceptual mechanism responsible for the recovery of syntactic structure, as proposed by Inoue (1991), is an invariant cognitive module.

References

Abney, S. (1987) "Licensing and parsing," in Proceedings of NELS 17.

Abney, S. (1989) "A computational model of human parsing," *Journal of Psycholinguistic Research 18*, 129–144.

Ades, A. and Steedman, M. J. (1982) "On the order of words," *Linguistics and Philosophy*, *4*, 517–558.

Altmann, G., Garnham, A., and Dennis, Y. (1992) "Avoiding the garden path: Eye movements in reading," *Journal of Memory and Language 31*, 685–712.

Anderson, S. (1983) "Types of dependency in anaphors: Icelandic and other reflexives," *Journal of Linguistic Research 2*, 1–23.

Antonisse, M. (1990) "Length and structure in syntactic processing," Proceedings of ESCOL '90.

Aoun, J. and Sportiche, D. (1983) "On the formal theory of government," *The Linguistic Review 2*, 211–236.

Bader, M. (1992) "Attachment ambiguities," unpublished manuscript, University of Stuttgart.

Bader, M. and Lasser, I. (forthcoming) "In defense of top-down parsing: Evidence from German," in C. Clifton, L. Frazier and K. Rayner (eds.) *Perspectives on Sentence Processing.*

Baker, C. L. (1970) "Notes on the description of English questions: The role of an abstract question morpheme," *Foundations of Language 6*, 197–219.

Baltin, M. (1989) "Heads and projections," in M. R. Baltin and A. S. Kroch (eds.) *Alternative Conceptions of Phrase Structure.* Chicago, IL: University of Chicago Press, pp. 1–16.

Barton, E. and Berwick, R. (1985) "Parsing with assertion sets and information monotonicity," *Proceedings of the Ninth International Joint Conference on Artificial Intelligence*, 769–771.

Bayer, J. (1992) "On the origin of sentential arguments in German and Bengali," unpublished manuscript, Heinrich Heine University.

Berwick, R. (1985) *The Acquisition of Syntactic Knowledge.* Cambridge, MA: MIT Press.

Berwick, R. (1991) "Principle-based parsing," in P. Sells, S. Shieber and T. Wasow (eds.) *Foundational Issues in Natural Language Processing.* Cambridge, MA: MIT Press.

Berwick, R. and Weinberg, A. (1984) *The Grammatical Basis of Linguistic Performance.* Cambridge, MA: MIT Press.

167

Berwick, R. and Weinberg, A. (1985) "Deterministic parsing and linguistic explanation," *Language and Cognitive Processes 1*, 109–134.

Bever, T. (1970) "The cognitive basis for linguistic structures," in J. R. Hayes (ed.) *Cognition and the Development of Language*. New York: Wiley, pp. 279–352.

Blosfeld, M. (1988) "Parallel versus serial processing in the parsing of ambiguous sentences," paper presented at the Sixth Australian Language and Speech Conference, Sydney, Australia.

Boland, J. (1991) "The use of lexical knowledge in sentence processing, unpublished Ph.D. dissertation, University of Rochester.

Boland, J. E., Tanenhaus, M. K., and Garnsey, S. M. (1990) "Evidence for the immediate use of verb control information in sentence processing," *Journal of Memory and Language 29*, 413–432.

Borer, H. (1984) *Parametric Syntax*. Dordrecht: Foris Publishers.

Bresnan, J. (1978) "A realistic transformational grammar," in M. Halle, J. Bresnan and G. Miller (eds.) *Linguistic Theory and Psychological Reality*. Cambridge, MA: MIT Press, pp. 1–59.

Burzio, L. (1986) *Italian Syntax*. Dordrecht: D. Reidel Publishing Company.

Carello, C., Lukatela, G., and Turvey, M. (1988) "Rapid naming is affected by association but not by syntax," *Memory and Cognition 16*, 187–195.

Carlson, G. and Tanenhaus, M. (1982) "Some preliminaries to psycholinguistics," *Chicago Linguistic Society 18*, 48–59.

Chomsky, N. (1955) *Logical Structure of Linguistic Theory*. New York: Plenum Publishers, 1975.

Chomsky, N. (1965) *Aspects of the Theory of Syntax*. Cambridge, MA: MIT Press.

Chomsky, N. (1970) "Remarks on nominalization," in R. Jacobs and P. Rosenbaum (eds.) *Readings in English Transformational Grammar*. Waltham, MA: Ginn, pp. 184–221.

Chomsky, N. (1973) "Conditions on transformations," in S. Anderson and P. Kiparsky (eds.) *A Festschrift for Morris Halle*. New York: Holt, Reinhart and Winston, pp. 232–286.

Chomsky, N. (1975) *Questions of Form and Interpretation*. Ghent: Peter de Ridder Press.

Chomsky, N. (1977) "On wh-movement," in P. Culicover, T. Wasow and A. Akmajian (eds.) *Formal Syntax*. New York: Academic Press, 71–132.

Chomsky, N. (1981) *Lectures on Government and Binding*. Dordrecht: Foris Publishers.

Chomsky, N. (1982) *Some Concepts and Consequences of the Theory of Government and Binding*. Cambridge, MA: MIT Press.

Chomsky, N. (1986a) *Barriers*. Cambridge, MA: MIT Press.

Chomsky, N. (1986b) *Knowledge of Language: Its Nature, Origin and Use*. New York: Praeger.

Chomsky, N. (1988) *The Generative Enterprise*. Dordrecht: Foris Publishers.

Chomsky, N. (1991) "Some notes on economy of derivation and representation," in R. Freidin (ed.) *Principles and Parameters in Comparative Grammar*. Cambridge, MA: MIT Press, pp. 417–454.

Chomsky, N. (1992) "A minimalist program for linguistic theory," MIT Occasional Papers in Linguistics, No. 1. Department of Linguistics and Philosophy, Massachusetts Institute of Technology.

Chomsky, N. and Lasnik, H. (1977) "Filters and control," *Linguistic Inquiry 8*, 425–504.

Church, K. (1982) *On Memory Limitations in Natural Language Processing*. Distributed by the Indiana University Linguistics Club.

Clifton, C. and Ferreira, F. (1989). "Ambiguity in context," *Language and Cognitive Processes 4*, 77–104.

Clifton, C., Frazier, L., and Connine, C. (1984) "Lexical expectations in sentence comprehension," *Journal of Verbal Learning and Verbal Behavior 23*, 696–708.

Connine, C., Ferreira, F., Jones, C., Clifton, C., and Frazier, L. (1984) "Verb frame preferences: descriptive norms," *Journal of Psycholinguistic Research 13*, 307–319.

Cooper, W. and Paccia-Cooper, J. (1980) *Syntax and Speech*. Cambridge, MA: MIT Press.

Crain, S. (1980) "Contextual constraints on sentence comprehension," unpublished Ph.D. dissertation, University of California, Irvine.

Crain, S. and Steedman, M. (1985) "On not being led up the garden path: the use of context by the psychological parser," in D. Dowty, L. Karttunen, and A. Zwicky (eds.) *Natural Language Processing: Psychological, Computational, and Theoretical Perspectives*. Cambridge: Cambridge University Press, pp. 320–358.

Crocker, M. (1992) "A logical model of competence and performance in the human sentence processor," unpublished Ph.D. dissertation, University of Edinburgh.

Emonds, J. (1970). "Root and structure preserving transformations," unpublished Ph.D. dissertation, Massachusetts Institute of Technology.

Ferreira, F. and Clifton, C. (1986) "The independence of syntactic processing," *Journal of Memory and Language 25*, 348–368.

Ferreira, F. and Henderson, J. (1990) "The use of verb information in syntactic parsing: a comparison of evidence from eye movements and word-by-word self-paced reading," *Journal of Experimental Psychology: Learning, Memory and Cognition 16*, 555–568.

Fodor, J. A. (1983) *The Modularity of Mind*. Cambridge, MA: MIT Press.

Fodor, J. A. (1989) "Why should the mind be modular?" in A. George (ed.) *Reflections on Chomsky*. London: Basil Blackwell, pp. 1–22.

Fodor, J. A., Bever, T. G., and Garrett, M. (1974) *The Psychology of Language*. New York: McGraw Hill.

Fodor, J. A., Garrett, M., and Bever, T. (1968) "Some syntactic determinants of sentential complexity II, verb structure," *Perception and Psychophysics 3*, 453–461.

Fodor, J. D. (1978) "Parsing strategies and constraints on transformations," *Linguistic Inquiry 9*, 427–473.

Fodor, J. D. (1983) "Phrase structure parsing and the island constraints," *Linguistics and Philosophy 6*, 163–223.

Fodor, J. D. (1985). "Deterministic parsing and subjacency," *Language and Cognitive Processes 1*, 3–42.

Fodor, J. D. and Frazier, L. (1980) "Is the human sentence processing mechanism an ATN?" *Cognition 8*, 417–459.

Fong, S. (1991) "Computational properties of principle-based grammatical theories," unpublished Ph.D. dissertation, Massachusetts Institute of Technology.

Ford, M., Bresnan J., and Kaplan, R. (1982) "A competence-based theory of syntactic closure," in J. Bresnan (ed.), *The Mental Representation of Grammatical Relations*. Cambridge, MA: MIT Press, pp. 727–851.

Forster, K. (1979) "Levels of processing and the structure of the language processor," in W. Cooper and E. Walker (eds.) *Sentence Processing: Studies Presented to Merrill Garrett*. Hillsdale, NJ: Lawrence Erlbaum Associates, pp. 27–86.

Frank, R. (1991) "Two types of locality in government and binding parsing," unpublished manuscript, University of Pennsylvania.

Frazier, L. (1978) "On comprehending sentences: syntactic parsing strategies" unpublished Ph.D. dissertation, University of Connecticut. Distributed by the Indiana University Linguistics Club.

Frazier, L. (1987) "Sentence processing: a tutorial review," in M. Coltheart (ed.) *Attention and Performance XII, The Psychology of Reading*. Hillsdale, NJ: Lawrence Erlbaum Publishers, pp. 559–586.

Frazier, L. (1989) "Against lexical generation of syntax," in W. Marslen-Wilson (ed.) *Lexical Representation and Process*. Cambridge, MA: MIT Press, pp. 505–528.

Frazier, L. (1990) "Parsing modifiers: Special purpose routines in the human sentence processing mechanism?" in D. A. Balota, G. B. Flores d'Arcais, and K. Rayner (eds.) *Comprehension Processes in Reading*. Hillsdale, NJ: Lawrence Erlbaum Associates, pp. 303–330.

Frazier, L. and Clifton, C. (1989) "Successive cyclicity in the grammar and the parser," *Language and Cognitive Processes 4*, 93–126.

Frazier, L. and Fodor, J. D. (1978) "The sausage machine: a new two-stage parsing model," *Cognition 6*, 291–325.

Frazier, L. and Rayner, K. (1982) "Making and correcting errors during sentence comprehension: eye movements in the analysis of structurally ambiguous sentences," *Cognitive Psychology 14*, 178–210.

Frazier, L. and Rayner, K. (1987a) "Parameterizing the language processing system: left- versus right-branching within and across languages," in J. Hawkins (ed.) *Explaining Language Universals*. Oxford: Basil Blackwell, pp. 247–279.

Frazier, L. and Rayner, K. (1987b) "Resolution of syntactic category ambiguities: Eye movements in parsing lexically ambiguous sentences," *Journal of Memory and Language 26*, 505–526.

Freidin, R. (1978) "Cyclicity and the theory of grammar," *Linguistic Inquiry 9*, 519–549.

Garman, M. (1990) *Psycholinguistics*. Cambridge: Cambridge University Press.

Garrett, M. (1990) "Sentence processing," in D. Osherson and H. Lasnik (eds.) *Language: An Invitation to Cognitive Science, Vol. 1.* Cambridge, MA: MIT Press, pp. 133–176.

Gazdar, G., Klein, E., Pullum, G., and Sag, I. (1985) *Generalized Phrase-Structure Grammar.* Cambridge, MA: Harvard University Press.

Gibson, E. (1991) "A computational theory of human linguistic processing: memory limitations and processing breakdown," unpublished Ph.D. dissertation, Carnegie Mellon University.

Gibson, E. and Hickok, G. (1993) "Sentence processing with empty categories," *Language and Cognitive Processes 8*, 147–162.

Gibson, E. and Wexler, K. (forthcoming) "Triggers," *Linguistic Inquiry.*

Goodall, G. (1987) *Parallel Structures in Syntax.* Cambridge: Cambridge University Press.

Goodman, G., McClelland, J., and Gibbs, R. (1981) "The role of syntactic context in word recognition," *Memory and Cognition 9*, 580–586.

Gorrell, P. (1987) "Studies in human syntactic processing: ranked-parallel versus serial models," unpublished Ph.D. dissertation, University of Connecticut.

Gorrell, P. (1988) "Evaluating the heads-of-phrases hypothesis," unpublished manuscript, University of Maryland.

Gorrell, P. (1989) "Establishing the loci of serial and parallel effects in syntactic processing," *Journal of Psycholinguistic Research 18*, 61–74.

Gorrell, P. (1990) "Informational encapsulation and syntactic processing," Proceedings of NELS 21.

Gorrell, P. (1991) "Subcategorization and sentence processing", in R. C. Berwick, S. P. Abney and C. Tenny (eds.) *Principle-Based Parsing: Computation and Psycholinguistics.* Dordrecht: Kluwer Academic Publishers, pp. 279–300.

Gorrell, P. (1992) "The parser as tree builder," unpublished manuscript, University of Maryland.

Gorrell, P. (1993a) "Evaluating the direct association hypothesis: a reply to Pickering & Barry (1991)," *Language and Cognitive Processes 8*, 129–146.

Gorrell, P. (1993b) "Incremental structure building and the determinism hypothesis," talk given at the CUNY Sentence Processing Conference, University of Massachusetts, Amherst.

Gorrell, P. (in preparation) "Syntactic processing and lexical decision," unpublished manuscript, University of Maryland.

Grice, P. (1975) "Logic and conversation," in P. Cole and J. Morgan (eds.) *Syntax and Semantics, Vol. III: Speech Acts.* New York: Seminar Press, pp. 41–58.

Grimshaw, J. (1979) "Complement selection and the lexicon," *Linguistic Inquiry 10*, 279–236.

Grimshaw, J. (1981) "Form, function, and the language acquisition device," in C. Baker and J. McCarthy (eds.) *The Logical Problem of Language Acquisition.* Cambridge: MIT Press, pp. 165–182.

Grimshaw, J. (1991) "Extended projections," unpublished manuscript, Brandeis University.

Haegeman, L. (1991) *Introduction to Government Binding Theory.* London: Basil Blackwell.

Haik, I. (1984) "Indirect binding," *Linguistic Inquiry 15*, 185–223.

Hasagawa, N. (1990) "Comments on Mazuka and Lust's paper," in L. Frazier and J. de Villiers (eds.) *Language Processing and Language Acquisition*. Dordrecht: Kluwer Academic Publishers, pp. 207–223.

Heny, F. (1979) "Review of Chomsky (1975)," *Synthese 40*, 317–342.

Higginbotham, J. (1985) "On semantics," *Linguistic Inquiry 16*, 547–594.

Huang, J. (1982). "Logical relations in Chinese and the theory of grammar," unpublished Ph.D. dissertation, Massachusetts Institute of Technology.

Huang, J. (1993) "Reconstruction and the structure of VP: Some theoretical consequences," *Linguistic Inquiry 24*, 103–138.

Huang, J. and Tang, C. (1991) "The local nature of the long-distance reflexive in Chinese," in J. Koster and E. Reuland (eds.) *Long-distance Anaphora*. Cambridge: Cambridge University Press, pp. 263–282.

Huck, G. and Ojeda, A. (1987) *Syntax and Semantics 20: Discontinuous Constituency*. New York: Academic Press.

Inoue, A. (1991) "A comparative study of parsing in English and Japanese," unpublished Ph.D. dissertation, University of Connecticut.

Inoue, A. and Fodor, J. D. (to appear) "Information-paced parsing of Japanese," in R. Mazuka and N. Nagai (eds.) *Japanese Syntactic Processing*. Hillsdale, NJ: Lawrence Erlbaum Associates.

Jackendoff, R. (1972) *Semantic Interpretation in Generative Grammar*. Cambridge, MA: MIT Press.

Kaplan, R. and Bresnan, J. (1982) "Lexical-Functional Grammar: a formal system for grammatical representation," in J. Bresnan (ed.) *The Mental Representation of Grammatical Relations*. Cambridge, MA: MIT Press, pp. 173–281.

Kayne, R. (1984) *Connectedness and Binary Branching*. Dordrecht.

Kayne, R. (1993) "The antisymmetry of syntax," unpublished manuscript, City University of New York.

Kennedy, A., Murray, W. S., Jennings, F., and Reid, C. (1989) "Parsing complements: Comments on the generality of the principle of minimal attachment," *Language and Cognitive Processes 4*, 51–76.

Kimball, J. (1973) "Seven principles of surface structure parsing in natural language," *Cognition 2*, 15–47.

Koopman, H. (1983) *The Syntax of Verbs*. Dordrecht: Foris Publishers.

Koopman, H., and Sportiche, D. (1985) "Theta theory and extraction," *GLOW Newsletter 14*, 57–58.

Koster, J. (1978) *Locality Principles in Syntax*. Dordrecht: Foris Publishers.

Koster, J. (1986) *Domains and Dynasties*. Dordrecht: Foris Publishers.

Kuroda, S-Y. (1988) "Whether we agree or not," *Linguisticae Investigationes 12*, 1–47.

Kurtzman, H. (1985) "Studies in syntactic ambiguity resolution," unpublished doctoral dissertation, Massachusetts Institute of Technology. Distributed by Indiana University Linguistics Club.

Kurtzman, H. and MacDonald, M (1990). "Resolving quantifier scope ambiguities," talk presented at the CUNY Sentence Processing Conference, City University of New York.

Lachman, R., Lachman, J., and Butterfield, E. (1979) *Cognitive Psychology and Information Processing: An Introduction.* Hillsdale, NJ: Lawrence Erlbaum Associates.

Lackner, J. and Garrett, M. (1973) "Resolving ambiguity: effects of biasing context in the unattended ear," *Cognition 1*, 359–372.

Lasnik, H. and Kupin, J. (1977) "A restrictive theory of transformational grammar," *Theoretical Linguistics 4*, 173–196.

Lasnik, H. and Uriagereka, J. (1988) *A Course in GB Syntax.* Cambridge, MA: MIT Press.

Lukatela, G., Kostic, A., Feldman, L., and Turvey, M. (1983) "Grammatical priming of inflected nouns," *Memory and Cognition 11*, 59–63.

Lyons, J. (1968). *Introduction to Theoretical Linguistics.* Cambridge: Cambridge University Press.

McCawley, J. (1971) "Where do noun phrases come from?" in D. Steinberg and L. Jakobovits (eds.) *Semantics: An Interdisciplinary Reader in Philosophy, Linguistics & Psychology.* Cambridge: Cambridge University Press, pp. 166–183.

McCawley, J. (1982) "Parentheticals and discontinuous constituent structure," *Linguistic Inquiry 13*, 91–106.

McDonald, D. (1979) "Steps toward a psycholinguistic model of language production," AI Memo No. 500, Massachusetts Institute of Technology.

MacDonald, M. (1994) "Probabilistic constraints and syntactic ambiguity resolution," *Language and Cognitive Processes 9*, 157–201.

Maling, J. (1981) "Non-clause-bounded reflexives in Icelandic," in T. Fretheim and L. Hellan (eds.) *Papers from the Sixth Scandinavian Conference on Linguistics.* Tapir, Trondheim.

Manzini, R. (1983) "On control and control theory," *Linguistic Inquiry 14*, 421–446.

Manzini, R. (1992) *Locality: A Theory and Some of Its Empirical Consequences.* Cambridge, MA: MIT Press.

Manzini, R. and Wexler, K. (1987) "Binding theory, parameters, and learnability," *Linguistic Inquiry 18*, 413–444.

Marantz, A. (1984) *On the Nature of Grammatical Relations.* Cambridge, MA: MIT Press.

Marcus, M. (1980) *A Theory of Syntactic Recognition for Natural Language.* Cambridge, MA: MIT Press.

Marcus, M. (1987) "Deterministic parsing and description theory," in P. Whitelock, M. Wood, H. Somers, R. Johnson and P. Bennett (eds.) *Linguistic Theory and Computer Applications.* New York: Academic Press, pp. 69–112.

Marcus, M., Hindle, D., and Fleck, M. (1983) "D-theory: Talking about talking about trees," *Association for Computational Linguistics 21*, 129–136.

Marslen-Wilson, W. (1973) "Speech shadowing and speech perception," unpublished Ph.D. dissertation, Massachusetts Institute of Technology.

Marslen-Wilson, W. (1975) "The limited compatibility of linguistic and perceptual explanations," *Proceedings of Chicago Linguistic Society 11, Papers from the Parasession on Functionalism.*

Marslen-Wilson, W. and Tyler, L. (1980) "The temporal structure of spoken language understanding," *Cognition 25*, 71–102.

Marslen-Wilson, W. and Tyler, L. (1987) "Against modularity," in J. Garfield (ed.) *Modularity in Knowledge Representation and Natural-Language Processing*. Cambridge, MA: MIT Press, pp. 37–62.

May, R. (1977) "The grammar of quantification," unpublished Ph.D. dissertation, Massachusetts Institute of Technology.

May, R. (1985) *Logical Form*. Cambridge, MA: MIT Press.

Mazuka, R. and Lust, B. (1990) "On parameter setting and parsing: predictions for cross-linguistic differences in adult and child processing," in L. Frazier and J. de Villiers (eds.) *Language Processing and Language Acquisition*. Dordrecht: Kluwer Academic Publishers, pp. 163–205.

Mazuka, R. and Itoh, K. (forthcoming) "Can Japanese be led down the garden path?" in R. Mazuka and N. Nagai (eds.) *Japanese Syntactic Processing*. Hillsdale, NJ: Lawrence Erlbaum Associates.

Mazuka, R., Itoh, K., Kiritani, S., Niwa, S., Ikejiri, K., and Naitoh, K. (1989) "Processing of Japanese garden-path, center-embedded, and multiply-left-embedded sentences: reading time data from an eye movement study," *Annual Bulletin of the Research Institute of Logopedics and Phoniatrics 23*, 187–212.

Merlo, P. (1992) "On modularity and compilation in a Government-Binding parser," unpublished Ph.D. dissertation, University of Maryland.

Milsark, G. (1983) "On length and structure in sentence parsing", *Cognition 13*, 129–134.

Mitchell, D. (1987) "Lexical guidance in human parsing: Locus and processing characteristics," in M. Coltheart (ed.) *Attention and Performance XII: The Psychology of Reading*. Hillsdale: LEA Publishers, pp. 601–618.

Mitchell, D., and Corley, M. (to appear) "Immediate bias in parsing: discourse effects or experimental artefacts?" *Journal of Experimental Psychology: Learning, Memory and Cognition*.

Mitchell, D. and Holmes, V. (1985) "The role of specific information about the verb in parsing sentences with local structural ambiguity," *Journal of Memory and Language 24*, 542–559.

Mitchell, D., Corley, M., and Garnham, A. (1992) "Effects of context in human sentence parsing: evidence against a discourse-based proposal mechanism," *Journal of Experimental Psychology: Learning, Memory and Cognition 18*, 69–88.

Munn, A. (1992) "A null operator analysis of ATB gaps," *The Linguistic Review 9*, 1–26.

Newmeyer, F. (1980) *Linguistic Theory in America*. New York: Academic Press.

Ni, W. and Crain, S. (1990) "How to resolve structural ambiguities," *Proceedings of NELS 20*.

Ni, W., Fodor, J. D., Crain, S., and Shankweiler, D. (1993) "Evidence for the autonomy of syntax and pragmatics," talk given at the CUNY Sentence Processing Conference, University of Massachusetts, Amherst.

Nicol, J. (1988) "What the parser knows about the grammar: psycholinguistic evidence," *Proceedings of WCCFL VIII*.

Partee, B., ter Meulen, A., and Wall, R. E. (1993) *Mathematical Methods in Linguistics*. Dordrecht: Kluwer Academic Publishers.

Pesetsky, D. (1982) "Paths and categories," unpublished Ph.D. dissertation, Massachusetts Institute of Technology.

Pickering, M. (1991) "Processing dependencies," unpublished Ph.D. dissertation, University of Edinburgh.

Pickering, M. (1993) "Direct association and sentence processing: a reply to Gorrell and to Gibson and Hickok," *Language and Cognitive Processes 8*, 163–196.

Pickering, M. and Barry, G. (1991) "Sentence processing without empty categories," *Language and Cognitive Processes 6*, 169–264.

Posner, M. (1986) *Chronometric Explorations of Mind*. Oxford: Oxford University Press.

Pritchett, B. (1987) "Garden path phenomena and the grammatical basis of language processing," unpublished Ph.D. dissertation, Harvard University.

Pritchett, B. (1988) "Garden path phenomena and the grammatical basis of language processing," *Language 64*, 539–576.

Pritchett, B. (1991) "Head position and parsing ambiguity," *Journal of Psycholinguistic Research 20*, 251–270.

Pritchett, B. (1992) *Grammatical Competence and Parsing Performance*. Chicago, IL: University of Chicago Press.

Rayner, K. and Frazier, L. (1987) "Parsing temporarily ambiguous complements," *The Quarterly Journal of Experimental Psychology 39*, 657–673.

Rayner, K., Carlson, M., and Frazier, L. (1983) "The interaction of syntax and semantics during sentence processing: eye movements in the analysis of semantically biased sentences," *Journal of Verbal Learning and Verbal Behavior 22*, 358–374.

Reese, R. (1989) "Effects of syntactic context on lexical decision," unpublished M.A. thesis, University of Maryland.

Rizzi, L. (1990) *Relativized Minimality*. Cambridge, MA: MIT Press.

Sells, P. (1985) *Lectures on Contemporary Syntactic Theory*. Center for the Study of Language and Information, Stanford, CA.

Shipman, D. and Marcus, M. (1979) "Towards minimal data structures for deterministic parsing," *Proceedings of the International Joint Conference on Artificial Intelligence*.

Solan, L. and Roeper, T. (1978) "Children's use of syntactic structure in interpreting relative clauses," in H. Goodluck and L. Solan (eds.) *Papers in the Structure and Development of Child Language*. University of Massachusetts Occasional Papers in Linguistics, No. 4: Amherst, MA, pp. 105–126.

Speas, M. (1990) *Phrase Structure in Natural Language*. Dordrecht: Kluwer Academic Publishers.

Spivey-Knowlton, M., Trueswell, J., and Tanenhaus, M. (forthcoming) "Context effects in syntactic ambiguity resolution: discourse and semantic influences in parsing reduced relative clauses," *Canadian Journal of Experimental Psychology: special issue*.

Sportiche, D. (1988) "A theory of quantifiers and its corollaries for constituent structure," *Linguistic Inquiry 19*, 425–450.

Steedman, M. (1987) "Combinatory grammars and parasitic gaps," *Natural Language and Linguistic Theory 5*, 403–439.

Steedman, M. and Altmann, G. (1989) "Ambiguity in context: a reply," *Language and Cognitive Processes 4*, 105–122.

Stowell, T. (1981) "Origins of phrase structure," unpublished Ph.D. dissertation, Massachusetts Institute of Technology.

Suh, S. (1993) "How to process constituent structure in head-final languages: The case of Korean," talk presented to the twenty-ninth Meeting of the Chicago Linguistic Society.

Swinney, D., Ford, M., Frauenfelder, U., and Bresnan, J. (1988) "On the temporal course of gap-filling and antecedent assignment during sentence comprehension," unpublished manuscript, Stanford University and the Center for the Study of Language and Information.

Tabossi, P., Spivey-Knowlton, M., McRae, K., and Tanenhaus, M. (forthcoming) "Semantic effects on syntactic ambiguity resolution: evidence for a constraint-based resolution process," *Attention and Performance XV*. Hillsdale, NJ: Lawrence Erlbaum Associates.

Taraban, R. and McClelland, J. (1988) "Constituent attachment and thematic role assignment in sentence processing: influences of content-based expectations," *Journal of Memory and Language 27*, 231–263.

Thiersch, C. (1985) "VP and scrambling in the German Mittelfeld," unpublished manuscript, University of Cologne and University of Connecticut.

Thrainsson, H. (1976) "Reflexives and subjunctives in Icelandic," Proceedings of NELS 6, 225–239.

Travis, L. (1984) "Parameters and effects of word-order variation," unpublished Ph.D. dissertation, Massachusetts Institute of Technology.

Trueswell, J. and Tanenhaus, M. (1991) "Tense, temporal context and syntactic ambiguity resolution," *Language and Cognitive Processes 6*, 303–338.

Trueswell, J., Tanenhaus, M., and Garnsey, S. (1992) "Semantic influences on parsing: use of thematic role information in syntactic ambiguity resolution," unpublished manuscript, University of Rochester and University of Illinois.

Trueswell, J., Tanenhaus, M., and Kello, C. (1993) "Verb-specific constraints in sentence processing: separating effects of lexical preference from garden-paths," *Journal of Experimental Psychology: Learning, Memory and Cognition 19*, 528–553.

Tyler, L. (1981) "Serial and interactive-parallel theories of sentence processing," *Theoretical Linguistics 8*, 29–65.

van de Koot, J. (1990) *An Essay on Grammar–Parser Relations*. Dordrecht: Foris Publishers.

Wanner, E. (1980) "The ATN and the sausage machine: which one is baloney?" *Cognition 8*, 209–225.

Weinberg, A. (1988) "Locality principles in syntax and in parsing," unpublished Ph.D. dissertation, Massachusetts Institute of Technology.

Weinberg, A. (1992) "Parameterizing the parser: A grammar-based theory of garden-paths," talk given at the CUNY Sentence Processing Conference, City University of New York.

Weinberg, A. (1993) "Parameters in the theory of sentence processing: minimal commitment theory goes east," *Journal of Psycholinguistic Research 22*, 339–364.

Williams, E. (1984) "Grammatical relations," *Linguistic Inquiry 15*, 639–673.

Winograd, T. (1972) *Understanding Natural Language*. New York: Academic Press.

Wright, B. (1982) "Syntactic effects from lexical decisions in sentences," unpublished Ph.D. dissertation, Massachusetts Institute of Technology.

Wright, B. and Garrett, M. (1984) "Lexical decision in sentences: Effects of syntactic structure," *Memory and Cognition 12*, 31–45.

Wu, A. (1993) "A minimalist universal parser," unpublished manuscript, University of California at Los Angeles.

Index

Abney, S., 16, 49n., 94n., 188
Active Filler Hypothesis, 143
Ades, M., 4, 136
adjunct attachment, 77, 88, 103
adjuncts, 15, 16
Altmann, G., 149, 152, 155, 157, 159n.,
    160n., 165
Anderson, S., 38
Antonisse, M., 8n.
Aoun, J., 21
argument attachment, 77, 88, 103

Bader, M., 145, 146n.
Baltin, M., 17
barrier (to government), 14, 21, 34
Barry, G., 136
Barton, E., 5, 71, 72, 109, 117
Bayer, J., 144
Berwick, R., 5, 66, 67n., 71, 72, 76, 83,
    94n., 95, 102n., 109, 117, 132, 133
Bever, T., 2, 47, 114, 149
binding conditions, 23–4, 33
binding theory, 21, 23, 31, 74, 98, 163
Blosfeld, M., 124
Boland, J., 130, 136, 137, 162n.
Borer, H., 38
bounding theory, 20, 23, 31, 74; see also
    Subjacency
branches (in a phrase-structure tree), 11
Bresnan, J., 7n., 22n.

Carlson, G., 7
Case Filter, 22–3, 26; and parsing, 76–7, 98
case theory, 11, 20, 74, 98, 163
c-command, 74, 98, 163
Church, K., 74n., 91
Clifton, C., 126, 128, 134, 143, 149, 154–6,
    159n., 162, 165
complement, 14, 16
content-based parsing strategies, 94–8
control theory, 21
Cooper, W., 158
Corley, M., 157n.

Crain, S., 149–50, 153, 158
Crocker, M., 94–6, 122n., 145

derivational GB, 25
Derivational Theory of Complexity
    (DTC), 2
description theory, see d-theory
determinism, 64–71, 73, 105, 109, 117, 164
Determinism Hypothesis, 64–5, 74n., 105
direct association hypothesis (DAH), 136–7
dominance relation, 4, 10–13, 21n., 22; and
    parsing, 68–70, 73–4, 78, 98, 163–4
DP Hypothesis, 16; and Structural
    Determinism, 118
d-structure, 25–6, 28, 30, 33, 42
d-theory, 64–71, 73, 101

economy of representation, 5, 15, 42
Emonds, J., 26
empty categories and parsing theory, 130–8
Exclusivity Condition, 12, 21n.

Ferreira, F., 126, 130, 149, 154–6, 159n.,
    162, 165
Fodor, J. A., 2–3, 6, 44, 48, 106, 125,
    150–2, 158
Fodor, J. D., 1, 3, 6, 46–8, 50–2, 61, 109,
    120, 125–6, 131, 132n., 134, 146
Fong, S., 94n.
Ford, M., 97, 126
form-based parsing strategies, 94
Forster, K., 153, 158
Frank, R., 94n.
Frazier, L., 1, 3, 6, 46–57, 61, 64, 66, 72,
    79, 84, 94, 97, 100n., 105–6, 109–10,
    120–5, 143, 146, 166

garden-path, 46, 73, 76, 105–7
Garman, M., 47n.
Garrett, M., 44n., 57n., 59–63, 123
Gazdar, G., 4
Generalized Theta Attachment (GTA),
    76–84, 100, 102–3, 164

Gibson, E., 10, 84–93, 119–20, 136n.
Goodall, G., 59
Goodman, G., 59
Gorrell, P., 59–62, 64, 123–4, 128, 136n., 161, 162n.
governing category, 24
government, 11, 21–2, 74, 78, 83, 98, 101, 109, 163, 164
Government-Binding (GB) theory, 1, 4–5, 9, 11, 18, 20, 44, 77, 101
Grice, P., 154n.
Grimshaw, J., 16n., 119n.
GTA, *see* Generalized Theta Attachment

Haegman, L., 143–4
Haik, I., 40–1
Hasagawa, N., 140n.
heads-of-phrases hypothesis, 60
head-final clauses, 138–47
Henderson, J., 126, 130
Heny, F., 18
Hickok, G., 136n.
Higginbotham, J., 9n., 14n.
Holmes, V., 126
Huang, J., 17, 29, 35n., 37, 39–40

Incremental Licensing, 100, 102, 120, 148, 164
incremental structure building, 2, 74, 109, 164
Inoue, A., 5, 95, 125, 139n., 143, 147, 166
Internal Subject Hypothesis (ISH), 17, 35n., 36, 114n.
Itoh, K., 140–1

Jackendoff, R., 8, 156n.

Kaplan, R., 22n.
Kayne, R., 10n., 80n.
Kimball, J., 2, 47, 91
Koopman, H., 17, 19n., 112
Koster, J., 4, 9, 25, 30–2, 35–7, 39–40, 41n., 165
Kupin, J., 5, 9n., 14, 15n.
Kuroda, S.-Y., 17
Kurtzman, H., 41, 57–9, 97

Lachman, R., 150n.
Lackner, J., 57n.
Lasnik, H., 5, 9n., 14, 15n., 18, 22–4, 138
Lasser, I., 145, 147
Late Closure (LC), 47–51, 53, 55, 57, 119
Left-to-Right Constraint, 134–5
Left-to-Right Principle, 100n.
lexical categories, 14

lexical decision and syntactic context, 59–64
Lexical Expectation Model, 125–6, 134
lexical information in parsing, 125–30, 134
Lexical Parameterization Hypothesis, 38
LF, 25, 28–9, 39–42
locality, 5, 31, 38
lookahead device, 66–8, 73; elimination of, 72–5; *see also* Marcus parser
Lukatela, G., 59
Lust, B., 138, 140n.

McCawlwy, J., 8, 9n., 156n.
McDonald, D., 74n.
MacDonald, M., 41, 160, 163
MA, *see* Minimal Attachment
Manzini, R., 4, 23n., 25, 38, 39, 165
Marantz, A., 97n.
Marcus, M., 46, 52, 64–8, 105, 117, 120
Marcus parser, 64–73
Marslen-Wilson, W., 2, 43, 46, 151–2, 153n.
May, R., 28–30, 34, 39–41
Mazuka, R., 138, 140–2
Merlo, P., 11n., 133
Milsark, G., 8n.
Minimal Attachment (MA), 1, 5, 47–53, 55, 57, 68, 100–3, 119, 154–5, 159n.
minimal commitment theory, 71–5, 109
minimalist program, 41n.
Mitchell, D., 126–7, 157n., 162
modularity, 149–62
monostratal grammar, 6
monotonicity, 65n., 72
Move alpha, 7, 23n., 26
Munn, A., 105n.

Newmeyer, F., 3
Ni, W., 161
Nicol, J., 128, 130n.
node attachment, 99, 134, 164
node creation, 99, 134, 164
node projection, 99, 104, 164
node (in a phrase-structure tree), 11
Nontangling Condition, 12–13
NP movement, 26

On-Line Locality Constraint (OLLC), 76n., 78–84, 116–18

parallel parsing, 44–46, 61–4, 84–93; *see also* ranked-parallel parsing
parameters, *see* syntactic parameters
Partee, B., 11, 12
phrase-structure tree, 5, 9, 11, 17; and parsing, 100

Pickering, M., 4, 136
Posner, M., 150n.
precedence relation, 4, 10–13, 18, 21n., 22;
    and parsing, 73, 98, 112–17, 163–4
precomputation of structure, 61, 132
Preliminary Phrase Packager (PPP), 47,
    49n., 51, 61; *see also* Sausage Machine
pre-verbal structuring, 95–8, 138–47
phrase-structure rules, 17, 18; and Minimal
    Attachment, 102
phrase-structure trees, 11–20; generation
    of, 17–20
primary structural relations, 4, 11, 101,
    147–8; *see also* dominance relations,
    precedence relations
principle-based parsing, 5, 76, 100
Principle of Full Interpretation (PFI), 15,
    87, 98, 100
principles of grammar, 10
Principle of Preference Closure (PPC), 90–2
Pritchett, B., 22, 49, 73, 76–84, 94–5, 98,
    102, 116–17, 119–20, 138, 166
processing load unit (plu), 84–93
Projection Principle, 27–8, 87
Property of Lexical Requirement (PLR),
    85–92
Property of Recency Preference (PRP),
    90–2
Property of Thematic Reception (PTR),
    86–92

Quantifier Raising (QR), 28, 39–40

RALR, *see* revision-as-last-resort
ranked-parallel parsing, 57–64, 76n.
reanalysis of computed structure, 53–9,
    63–4, 78, 107, 147–8; domain of, 147;
    and minimal committment theory, 75;
    see also determinism, On-Line Locality
    Constraint, Structure-addition
    hypothesis, Structural Determinism
representational GB, 30
revision-as-last-resort (RALR), 146–7
Rayner, K., 46–7, 55–7, 64, 66, 72, 79,
    96n., 100n., 105–6, 110, 121–5, 149,
    152
Rizzi, L., 1
Roeper, T., 13n.

Sausage Machine, 3, 47, 68, 110
scope indexing rule, 40
secondary structural relations, 4, 23, 98,
    101, 109, 147–8
selectional restrictions, 7
Sentence Structure Supervisor (SSS), 47,
    51, 54–5, 61; *see also* Sausage machine
serial-interactive parsing (SI), 150

serial parsing, 44–6, 61–4
Shieber, S., 75n.
Simplicity, 5–6, 100–2, 120, 157–9, 164
Solan, L., 13n.
Speas, M., 1, 15–16, 159
specifier, 14
Spivey-Knowlton, M., 160
Sportiche, D., 17, 21
s-structure, 6, 25–6, 28, 33, 40
Steedman, M., 4, 135–6, 149–50, 152–3,
    158, 159n., 165
Stowell, T., 18
structural ambiguity, 43
Structural Determinism, 101, 115, 117–18,
    143, 148, 155, 157, 161, 165
Structure-addition hypothesis, 54, 70
Suh, S., 142n., 160
subcategorization, 16–17; use of in parsing,
    126–8
Subjacency, 23, 26, 28, 30, 132–3; *see also*
    bounding theory
syntactic parameters, 10

Tang, C., 37
Tanenhaus, M., 7, 158, 160
thematic processor, 96n.
Theta Criterion, 22–3; and parsing, 76–7,
    79–80, 87, 96, 98
theta theory, 11, 20, 74, 98, 163
Thiersch, C., 14
Thrainsson, H., 38
trace theory, 6, 27
Travis, L., 19n., 112
tree, *see* phrase-structure tree
Trueswell, J., 128–30, 155–6, 158, 160, 163
Tyler, L., 46, 150–2, 153n., 159n.

underspecification in parsing, 46, 71, 117
Uriagereka, J., 18, 22–4

van de Koot, J., 74n.
verb-final clauses, 6; and parsing, 95–8,
    138–47

'wait-and-see' strategy, 72
Wanner, E., 50n.
Weinberg, A., 5, 66, 67n., 72–3, 75, 83, 92,
    96, 98, 109, 118, 120–1, 132–3, 140
Wexler, K., 10, 38
Wh-criterion, 39
Wh-movement, 26, 29, 32; and parsing,
    131–3
Williams, E., 22n.
Winograd, T., 54
Wright, B., 59–63, 123, 124n.
Wu, A., 7